The Road to Somewhere

A Creative Writing Companion

Second Edition

Edited by
ROBERT GRAHAM, HEATHER LEACH
AND HELEN NEWALL

Conceived by
Julie Armstrong
Robert Graham
Heather Leach
Helen Newall
John Singleton

palgrave
macmillan

First edition published 2005
Second edition published 2014 by
PALGRAVE MACMILLAN

Palgrave Macmillan in the UK is an imprint of Macmillan Publishers Limited, registered in England, company number 785998, of Houndmills, Basingstoke, Hampshire RG21 6XS.

Palgrave Macmillan in the US is a division of St Martin's Press LLC, 175 Fifth Avenue, New York, NY 10010.

Palgrave Macmillan is the global academic imprint of the above companies and has companies and representatives throughout the world.

Palgrave® and Macmillan® are registered trademarks in the United States, the United Kingdom, Europe and other countries

ISBN: 978–1–137–26357–5 hardback
ISBN: 978–1–137–26356–8 paperback

This book is printed on paper suitable for recycling and made from fully managed and sustained forest sources. Logging, pulping and manufacturing processes are expected to conform to the environmental regulations of the country of origin.

A catalogue record for this book is available from the British Library.

A catalog record for this book is available from the Library of Congress.

Printed in China

Contents

'As a writer y⬚ ⬚ ⬚ ⬚ ⬚ ⬚ ⬚ ⬚ ⬚ ⬚ .ing ... If you are starting out and are feeling a little lost and lonely, here is an excellent companion.' – **Richard Bell**, *Writing Magazine*

This revised, updated and expanded new edition of *The Road to Somewhere* will help you to acquire the craft and disciplines needed to develop as a writer in today's world. It is ideal for anyone – student writers, writing teachers and seasoned authors – seeking practical guidance, new ideas and creative inspiration.

The Road to Somewhere: A Creative Writing Companion, second edition offers:

- new chapters on writing for digital media, flash fiction, memoir, style and taking your writing out into the world
- updated chapters on fiction, scripts, poetry, and experimental forms
- an examination of creative processes and advice on how to read as a writer
- many practical exercises and useable course materials
- extensive references and suggestions for further reading
- information on how to get work published or produced, in real and virtual worlds
- tips on how to set up and run writing workshops and groups
- a complete *Agony Aunt* section to help with blocks and barriers
- guidance on the more technical aspects of writing such as layout and grammar.

And, to lighten your writing journey a little, we've tried to make this second edition even wittier and smarter than the first. So whether you see yourself as a published professional or a dedicated dabbler, this is the book to take along for the ride.

Robert Graham is Programme Leader of Creative Writing at Manchester Metropolitan University (MMU), Cheshire.

Heather Leach is a now a full time writer and was formerly Senior Lecturer in Creative Writing at MMU, Cheshire.

Helen Newall is Reader in Performing Arts at Edge Hill University.

www.palgrave.com

Related titles from Palgrave Macmillan:

Craig Batty and Zara Waldeback, *Writing for the Screen*
Amanda Boulter, *Writing Fiction*
Catherine Brady, *Story Logic and the Craft of Fiction*
Julia Casterton, *Creative Writing: A Practical Guide*, 3rd edition
Chad Davidson and Gregory Fraser, *Writing Poetry*
Robert Graham, *How To Write Fiction (And Think About It)*
Celia Hunt and Fiona Sampson, *Writing: Self and Reflexivity*
John Singleton, *The Creative Writing Workbook*
John Singleton and Mary Luckhurst (eds), *The Creative Writing Handbook*, 2nd edition
Jayne Steel (ed.), *Wordsmithery: The Writer's Craft and Practice*
Karen Stevens (ed.), *Writing a First Novel*

John Singleton

This second edition is dedicated to the memory of our co-writer and editor John Singleton, who died, far too soon, in 2007. John was one of the first people to establish Creative Writing as a legitimate subject within the university curriculum, so giving generations of aspiring students that crucial leg-up onto the first rung of the creative ladder. He was a generous and professional colleague, an inspirational and erudite teacher, a passionate lover of words and language, as well as an accomplished poet and novelist. With the kind agreement of John's wife, we are proud to include his chapters from the first edition. We miss him.

Acknowledgements

Robert Graham: Thank you to David, Robert, Scott, Angi, Elizabeth and James for their generous contributions; to my students in general (and particularly those who allowed us to quote their thoughts about writing); to Calum Kerr for helpful memoir-writing suggestions; to Jo Selley for excellent suggested improvements to the first edition (including the what-it-says-on-the-tin approach to the chapter titles on the Contents pages); to Jane Boyd for Mrs Joe's bread and butter; and to Heather and Helen, who were formidable, fab and fun throughout.

Helen Newall: Brian, Laurie and Alastair; Tony Lindsay for help with the Scriptwriting chapter; Russ Tunney at the Nuffield Theatre, Southampton; Jenny Newman and Jim Friel at Liverpool John Moores University.

Heather Leach: Grateful thanks to all those students who let me practise on them, to my colleagues at MMU Cheshire who helped me find time to write, and to my dear husband, Roger, for his love and support.

Helen Newall wrote the *Agony Aunt* sections.

Heather Leach wrote the Writers' and Readers' Festivals section.

The editors and publisher wish to thank the following for the use of copyright material:

Taylor & Francis Books Ltd, for the figure on p. 138 from Sharples: *How We Write*, p. 73, © 1999, Routledge

Salt Publishing, for 'Happy Place' from Gaffney: *Sawn Off Tales*, © 2006, Salt Publishing

Every effort has been made to trace the copyright holders but, if any have been inadvertently overlooked, the publishers will be pleased to make the necessary arrangements at the first opportunity.

Notes on Contributors

Julie Armstrong is the author of *Mirror Cities* (Troubador, 2010) and *Dream Space* (Troubador, 2012). She is currently at work on *Experimental Writing for Readers and Writers of Fiction* for Bloomsbury. She teaches Creative Writing and Practice as Research at Manchester Metropolitan University's Cheshire faculty. Her most recent paper, 'Paths To Knowing & Knowledge: Memory Mindfulness, Neuroscience & The Stories We Tell Ourselves', delivered at the Roehampton University, London conference, 'Practice, Process and Paradox: Creativity and the Academy' (2013), explored how research evolved into her creative text: *Special Things*: www.juliearmstrongwriting.com.

David Gaffney is the author of three critically acclaimed micro-fiction collections – *Sawn-off Tales* (Salt, 2006), *Aromabingo* (Salt, 2007) and *The Half-life of Songs* (Salt, 2010), which was long-listed for the Edge Hill Prize. Tindal Street Press published his novel *Never Never* (2008) and in May 2013, his new collection of short stories, *More Sawn-off Tales*, was published by Salt.

Robert Graham is the author of *How to Write Fiction (And Think About It)* (Palgrave Macmillan, 2006); *Holy Joe* (Troubadour, 2006); *The Only Living Boy* (Salt, 2009); *A Man Walks Into A Kitchen* (Salt, 2011); and *When You Were A Mod, I Was A Rocker* (Like This Press, 2013). He is the co-author, with Heather Leach, of *Everything You Need to Know About Creative Writing* (Continuum, 2007). He teaches Creative Writing at Manchester Metropolitan University's Cheshire faculty.

Heather Leach has won a number of writing prizes and her work has appeared in many publications, including *MsLexia*, *The Times Higher Education Supplement* and *Best Short Stories 2011*. Her doctoral thesis was on the writing of fiction, and although she is now retired from university teaching she continues to write.

Helen Newall is a Reader in Performing Arts at Edge Hill University, Liverpool. Her fiction has appeared in *Mslexia*, *Pretext* and *Pool*. Work as a playwright includes a new libretto for *The Young Person's Guide to the Orchestra* for the Royal Liverpool Philharmonic; *Remote Control*, an HTV Television workshop; *Dumisani's Drum*, for Action Transport and *Anthem* for the Nuffield Theatre, Southampton. Her experimental performance text, *The Ghost of Someone Not Yet Drowned*, was recently performed in the empty pools of the Victoria Baths, Manchester. Twitter: @HelenNewall.

Robert Sheppard teaches Creative Writing at Edge Hill University, Liverpool, where he is Professor of Poetry and Poetics and runs the MA in Creative Writing. His poetry includes *Complete Twentieth Century Blues* (Salt, 2008) and A Translated Man (Shearsman, 2013). He has also published a book of criticism, *When Bad Times Made for Good Poetry* (Shearsman, 2011). He lives and writes in Liverpool and blogs at www.robertsheppard.blogspot.com.

John Singleton, 1943–2007, was Subject Leader of Creative Writing at Manchester Metropolitan University's Cheshire faculty and taught in schools and universities both in the UK and the USA. He wrote extensively on Creative Writing and his books include *The Creative Writing Handbook* (with Mary Luckhurst, 1999) and *The Creative Writing Workbook* (2001), both published by Palgrave Macmillan. His fiction for young children is published by Andersen Press, and his teenage novels – *Star* (2003) and *Skinny B, Skaz and Me* (2005) – by Puffin Books.

Scott Thurston lectures in English and Creative Writing at the University of Salford, where he runs three MA programmes in English, including Creative Writing. He has published widely on contemporary innovative poetry as a critic and his books of poetry include *Hold* (2006), *Momentum* (2008), *Internal Rhyme* (2010) (all from Shearsman) and *Reverses Heart's Reassembly* (Veer Books, 2011). He is currently researching the relationship between postmodern poetry and dance.

Introduction
Heather Leach

The idea of life as a story and of the story as a journey seems to be hard-wired into our consciousness and culture, which is why this book is called *The Road to Somewhere*. Thousands of years ago, most human beings gave up the nomadic hunter-gatherer life and settled into villages, but perhaps old memories of walking from place to place, of owning nowhere yet belonging everywhere, are still locked into the synapses of our brains. Like dogs, whose legs twitch as they run in dreams, so we still wander the world, the imaginary universe, in our stories of journeys. Each of us must find our own way to the art of writing – to the voice that is ours alone. But writing is a practical craft as well as an art, and like all crafts, it can be learned, given time, effort and motivation.

Who This Book Is For

The book is intended to be useful to all writers: student writers and their teachers in Creative Writing courses in universities, colleges and schools; writing-group leaders and participants; new and experienced writers. All will find plenty here to inspire, stimulate and help. The editors and the majority of the contributors have taught Creative Writing in universities and other settings and are published writers in a variety of forms and genres. There are many practical activities and exercises that can be used by groups and individuals, as well as substantial resources and references.

What's In This Second Edition?

A lot has changed since the first edition of *The Road to Somewhere* was published in 2005. The banking system almost crashed, but survived to crash another day. The climate got warmer, springs got colder, the print-publishing world shivered in a raging digital wind, and writers and readers just kept on trucking. We have revised and updated this second edition to take account of at least some of these changes, added new chapters and expanded others, made improvements to the structure and layout and introduced many new resources and references.

The first part, **Getting Going**, has been reordered and expanded to include the essential elements that all writers, whether beginner or expert, need as part of their writing life: creative process, a place to write, courage and persistence, reading and reflecting.

On the Road offers detailed and practical help with specific skills, forms and genre. There are a number of new chapters. *Style* gathers all the related sections from the first edition into one place, adding useful extra material. *Flash Fiction* and *Memoir* are new to this edition, and these chapters look at forms of writing that have increased in popularity in recent years. *Digital Writing* is a new chapter that attempts to take account of the fast-moving revolution that is changing all our writing lives. The revamped *Scriptwriting* chapter has now been expanded to include writing for screen, stage and radio.

Going Where? Publication, publication, publication! This section tackles the elephant in the creative room in a number of ways. As well as a chapter on traditional print publishing through an agent, there are chapters on *not* getting published, and on writing as personal journey. A new chapter, *Taking Your Writing out into the World*, contains interviews with three contemporary writers: Elizabeth Baines on writing and the internet, David Gaffney on commissioned writing, and James Harker, a recent Creative Writing student, on becoming a professional writer.

Help brings all the *Agony Aunt* pieces of the first edition together into one chapter, so if you're facing existential meltdown, this is the place to go. If you need advice on when to use a comma or a semicolon, you'll find it in *Paragraphing and Punctuation*.

Going Further includes *A Writers' Bookshelf* and a guide to *Writers' and Readers' Festivals*. There is a useful index, including a separate index of writing exercises.

Many Roads

The Road to Somewhere has been written and edited by active writers with active minds and individual philosophies. There are plenty of debates about how to teach and learn the craft, and you will encounter a rich and varied approach in these pages. This is not an A-to-Z plan but a guidebook written by people en route. However, we all believe, and hope you do too, that writing is not just a road to somewhere, it is also that somewhere itself: an activity worth doing, whatever the outcome or destination, a journey to be taken for the sake of the journey.

I
Getting Going

1 Becoming a Writer

Heather Leach

One Writer's Beginning

I used to work in an office. I used to sit at a desk next to a window, which looked out into an odd half-secret space, an inner enclosure. Around the walls were other windows, usually blinded. I was often bored, sifting my way through reports and policies, writing my own in the same rational calm language that slowly gets things done or undone. There was a door at the bottom of the courtyard which I supposed was used by maintenance and repair people, but I never saw them, and so as far as my office day was concerned this strange interior space was inhabited only by birds: pigeons, starlings, sparrows; occasionally a pair of magpies (one for sorrow, two for joy). Throughout a whole year I watched them come flying down out of the trapezoid sky, their anxious fluttering and flapping amplified by the walls as they hustled for space on ledges and buttresses. In the rain and cold they rested there in rows, patient, silent, looking back at me, their thick white droppings staining the already soot-stained stone.

I began to hate my job. Not the point of it, the meaning, which was worthy and honest, but the practice, the necessary but relentless daily discipline, the painstakingly detailed attention that was needed to carry it out. I hated as well the kind of person that this work was slowly turning me into. And the place, the room: that too. It was square with all the usual office accoutrements: desk, telephone, coat-stand, strong overhead lighting, cream cleanable walls. There were no computers then, no fax machines, but you get the picture. Oh yes, and there was also a picture on the wall in front of me, one picture per office, each labelled 'our wonderful rural heritage': unmechanised farms, traffic-free roads, rainless summers.

The more I hated the job and the room, the more I watched the birds. They inhabited their strange interior space with ingenuity, one or two even managing to make a scruffy nest in a corner, although I never saw any fledglings. As the year went by it became a kind of fetish to look out, to say hello to the birds before I did anything else. I found that, with effort, I could climb onto a chair and force the stiff window handle downwards and so lift the latch. The window hinge itself was rigid with years of disuse but I managed a few inches, enough to get my head through, enough to get a breath of acrid feathery air. In winter, when I looked down, there was often a body lying below me on the concrete ground, a small dark shadow, its frozen wings folded. By the next day these corpses had always gone.

In telling this story of the birds, I am trying to put together an account of the year that I started to be a proper writer. But as this is a book about the forms and processes of writing itself, I have to confess that I'm making it up as I go along. What's emerging, I see, is a fairly familiar story: the one about the sad would-be writer/artist/singer/actor who sits day after day trapped at a tedious desk, dreaming of creativity/fame/ riches. The birds, of course, represent – but it should be quite obvious now what they represent – all the slightly embarrassing but pleasantly satisfying clichés that we already know: our wonderful literary heritage; lightness, freedom, flight; somewhere over the rainbow; all that stuff.

This is the way stories go, I find. You begin at the top of the page with a few words, not always quite sure where you're going, but if you persist, if you battle your way through the uncertainty, letting words come by themselves, sooner or later a narrative picks you up, huge rivers of language and form carrying you with them down to a sea of stories. So far: so good. Let's go with the flow, man. Except that each writer needs to find their own direction, to know when to go with the current and when to resist it, not to float or to drift but to swim, sometimes even upstream.

In my office story what should come next is a moment of revelation, clear insight, a bird-inspired epiphany. In fact, as I remember, there was no sudden sense of understanding that year, no dramatic change. I simply began to sit down at a table at home and instead of thinking about how I'd like to be a writer, I actually began to put words onto paper and kept on doing it. If you want to write there's no escape from the desk. Nothing transformed me overnight, and nothing will transform you except *the act itself: writing*. Two things make you into a writer: writing regularly; and reading as much as you can so that you will learn to be aware of the currents of language and culture; aware enough to be able to distinguish between drifting and swimming. There's a lot more to it of course, but that's where we all begin: at the page, the screen. Curious, thrilled, afraid. The words appear one after another. You cross them out, erase them, write more, and gradually something begins to form itself, a knot of thought, an image: the way birds patiently stand side by side, for example, thinking of nothing, their claw feet blanket-stitching a ledge.

This room where I am now is small, square, plain. There's no coat-stand but there is a computer, plus desk, telephone and chair. Sometimes I hate having to sit here day after day; sometimes I hate the relentless discipline, the painstaking hours. I left that other office many years ago and I'm usually sceptical of magical stories but I have to tell you that the birds came with me. They've appeared in a number of stories that I've written, bit parts only, but significant, often shifting the eye of the main character away from the action on the ground, out of the frame, into the sky. Here too, in this writing, they appear again, witnesses, protagonists. I look down at my hands, fingers tapping out this exact word, this particular full stop. To the left is a window and every so often I glance up from the screen, resting my eyes, pausing for thought: just a suburban garden, conifers, bushes, a child's boat-shaped sandpit. But then I look across and see you, reader, looking back at me. Between us is the place where the birds are, a place of beaks and claws. Of wings.

Getting Started

There are many ways of becoming a writer. Some people begin as children, keeping a diary or writing poems that explore feeling and thought. Others get hooked on reading, drawn into fictional worlds that, unlike the mundane and confusing *real* world, offer clear begin-nings and definite endings. You might already have a great plot idea, a detailed plan that is working itself out in your head. Or maybe you have a cause, a strong viewpoint that you want to get over to others, a message to change the world. Some people dream of riches and fame: perhaps you can write a killer script that film studios will fight over, or become the next J.K. Rowling and make millions by writing children's books. Maybe you simply want to write down your life, to pass on everything you know, all the things that have happened to you, your own take on the world, your particular voice. Writers come in all shapes, colours, ages and sizes. There is no right way or wrong way to be a writer.

If you're reading this book, then you've almost certainly put pen to paper, fingers to keyboard and made some kind of a start at writing.

Before you go much further let me tell you something really worth knowing: all you need to do to become a writer is to get the words down: your own words on paper or screen: your own voice. That's all it takes. When you're writing, in the act of writing itself, you're a fully paid-up and welcome new member of a club without any rules and without any rulers. You're the equal of all other writers, dead and alive, from Tolstoy to Tolkien. Let me say it again. It's as simple as this: *writers write.* Full stop.

So why write a book about it? Why join a writers' group or pay somebody's hard-earned money for a writing course? I think the answer is that most of us want to do more than just write. We want to be able to produce something that other people might want to read, that they might even be willing to pay for: a fantastic, unputdownable story; a magical, terrible poem; a great script; writing that's up there with the best; dramatic, emotional, brilliant, funny. This is harder, but a great many of the skills and abilities can be learned if you are willing to put in time and commitment. Below is a list of the absolutely essential activities – five commandments if you like – that you need to develop and practise the actions and attitudes that need to become part of your life.

Write Regularly

Think of writing as a muscle. It needs to get lean and fit. Writing leads to more writing: as you write, new ideas spring up, words lead to other words, stories start, voices speak. Don't wait for inspiration. Like Father Christmas, inspiration knows where you live and if you begin it will eventually find you all by itself. *Regularly* means different things to different people – every day is good, but may not be possible. Don't beat yourself up if you can't manage that, but once a week is probably a minimum. Try writing at different times and in different places and find out which works best for you. Write about anything and everything. Don't think about whether the outcome is good or bad: this is practice not performance. Work that writing muscle. Hard.

Read

The second commandment: *writers need to read.* Stephen King describes reading as the centre of the writer's life. 'If you don't have time to read,' he argues, 'you don't have the time (or the tools) to write. Simple as that'.[1] But *what* should you read? First: read for pleasure. Forget all those rules about 'serious' literature, the classics, etc., and simply read what you like. If, at present, you only like one particular form or genre – fantasy, romance, history, sci-fi, celebrity biography, for instance – then read that form with enjoyment, regardless of what anyone else thinks or says. Try not to get stuck, however, in a reading groove; keep pushing back the boundaries of what you enjoy. If you try something new and don't like it, fine, but make sure you give it a chance. Be aware that difficulty or confusion may be yours, not the writer's, and that greater attention and persistence on your part may light up parts of yourself you didn't know existed. Make a particular point of reading the forms you are trying to write: if it's poetry, read poems; if it's fiction, read stories and novels, if you're writing a blog, read blogs. As you read, not only will you be enjoying the story, poem, whatever it is, you'll also be absorbing the way language works, all the things it can do. Read on the bus, in bed, on your smartphone, on the loo, anywhere and everywhere. Buy books. Use libraries. Writers need your cash and libraries are free. Use them or lose them.

Know Your Medium

Your medium is, of course, language: words, sentences, paragraphs, story, dialogue, image. This is your material – I'm tempted to write *raw* material – but by the time we get our hands on it, it's already well cooked in history and culture. We are born into a world where words shape much of the way we think, feel and understand: an ocean of words, constantly moving, constantly changing. There's far too much language for any one person to know it all, and most of us need a lifetime to grasp even a small part, but this doesn't matter. What does matter is to develop an energetic curiosity about its current and tides, its layers and depths. Reading will certainly help, and the good news is that you have already gained many of the language skills that you need.

The not-so-good news is that to become a writer, particularly a good writer, you need to develop and extend these skills well beyond the average. For many of us, the phrase *language skills* has the stink of grammar about it: all those dry, complicated rules, structures and formalities that make the heart shrivel. Just as the car mechanic needs to know that the name of that thing which mixes air and petrol is the carburettor, so the writer needs a *working* knowledge of many of these forms and structures, to know, for example, what an adjective does and how to use it. The mechanic doesn't necessarily need to have the exact chemical formula for combustion at their oily fingertips, but they have to be able to distinguish, and therefore to name, the parts of the car. You need to be able to name the parts of language, to understand the way it works, to know when something isn't right and to have ideas about how you could make it better.

Play

At the end of this chapter are a number of writing exercises which use random methods to stimulate ideas and generate new work. Many writers have used variations on these methods with surprising and productive results. When the short-story writer, Kathleen Mansfield, was at a loss for an idea, she used to call downstairs to her husband, John Middleton Murry. He'd shout back a word – *table, party* – and this would be enough to get her writing again. The random approach takes away the anxious responsibility of having to think of something 'significant' or 'important', helping you to relax and allowing the associative qualities of mind to develop.

Some people love this kind of exercise and some hate it. A word of warning to the first group. Einstein said that he made some of his greatest discoveries simply by staring out of windows, but even so, he still had to do the sums and work out the theories, and he already knew the language of physics inside out. James Joyce, one of the pioneers of the stream-of-consciousness technique, did not write *Ulysses* randomly: he attempted to write it so that it *appeared to be* the random thoughts of his characters, which is hard. We need playfulness, but it isn't *all* we need.

Perhaps you're one of the second kind of people – you may already know what you want to write about – you've got a definite story to tell – maybe you've got a project planned and you'd really rather get on with that. I'd like to persuade you to at least give the playful method a try. Try it out on a piece of writing that's stuck. Pick a list of words at random and try to integrate them into the next chapter, scene, verse. It could give you a surprising kick-start.

There's a traditional Eastern saying – 'Don't push the river' – meaning that some things have to be left to happen by themselves. The ability to play, to swim in the river of language, may not be all we need, but it's a good place to start.

Try This: Begin with a Word

Take any printed page and, with your eyes closed, let your finger pick out a word at random or ask the person next to you to give you a word. The next step is to follow the word and see where it takes you. Don't try to write cleverly or beautifully. Write for five minutes, then stop.

Try This: Put Words Together

Make a list of words that you like or which are at the forefront of your mind. Use words that refer to things or people, rather than ideas or emotions. Sometimes the simplest words are the most productive. For example, my list at this moment could be:

Shed   Coffee   Tesco   Birds   Rain

Write for five minutes, including all the words. Try not to think too hard. Just visualise what the words represent and write about them. Use my list if you're stuck.

Try This: The Three-Word Trick

Take three words from any source and write a paragraph or two, which includes all three words. The more unconnected these words are to each other, the better. If you're in a group you can have a great time seeing who can make up the weirdest list. Examples:

reindeer; bin-bag; Facebook.
cheese; Superwoman; nits.
brother; rats; room.
valentine; telescope; referee.
Add an emotion to your list:
boredom; hopeless desire; terror; obsession.

Now write two pages weaving all four elements together. Try not to actually use the emotional word – show the emotion through action and implication. You can use the exercise to write in any form: prose, dialogue, poetry.

Further Reading

Natalie Goldberg (1986) *Writing Down the Bones* (Boston: Shambala).
    Lots of playful ideas to get you started – inspirational.
Stephen King (2000) *On Writing* (London: Hodder & Stoughton).
    An autobiography of writing: helpful but uncompromising advice for beginners.
Write Words: What advice would you give to a new writer starting out?, http://www. writewords.org.uk/interviews/answers.asp?qid=8 (accessed 3 September 2013).
    A collection of collated comments from interviews with writers, wide-ranging and detailed. There is much excellent help and advice here.

2 Creativity

Heather Leach

What Is This Thing Called Creativity, and Have You Got It?

That word creative can have the strangest effects: some would rather go apple-ducking in a tub full of spiders than be labelled creative; while others (dream-struck and wild-eyed) are only too eager to set off on the path to Creativity World. If you ask any group of people (even would-be writers) whether they'd describe themselves as creative, the majority will regretfully say something like: 'no, not really, maybe sometimes, not very... I don't think I am.' There'll be one or two brave souls who go against the grain, owning up to a special kind of mind, personality or experience that they label as creative. Yet ask the same people to define what they mean by the word and there'll be a wide range of divergent responses, many tentative and vague, many others dependent on outdated stereotypes and clichés. In this chapter I want to explore some ideas about creativity and to suggest ways of developing your own creative abilities.

Right from the start, let's kill off the idea that creative people possess talents and character traits that the rest of us don't have. Not true. Just as plants grow, so people invent, imagine, create: it's what human beings do. While one person was daubing mud on cave walls, someone else was busy working out a new and quicker method for scraping the hairy bits off meat.

Creativity Wars

There are many definitions of creativity. It's one of those words like love or community that can mean all things to all people, and is often an

ideological battleground. One of the most persistent, sometimes perni-
cious ideas is that you can only be truly creative if you are in touch with
a more mysterious world than that of everyday reality. This idea of the
creative artist as semi-mystical, linked to nature, fairy, dream, and so
forth, gained its greatest power during the eighteenth and nineteenth
centuries, partly as a resistance to what was seen as the overwhelm-
ingly mechanistic power of state and industry. Writers, particularly
poets, became caricatured in the public mind as idiosyncratic creatures,
sometimes thrillingly strange, at other times nerdishly weird.

In the twentieth century (and still going strong in the twenty-first),
the idea of creativity was linked to the Freudian unconscious, hidden
beneath the surface of the mind, and many writers, most notably the
Surrealists, have tried to draw on this unconscious power, using exercises
such as automatic writing and associative wordplay. The idea that the
creative process isn't fully conscious is both nerve-racking and useful.
Nerve-racking because if something is not in your control, how do you
develop or improve it? If writing is something that the hidden inner
self does by itself, then what has it got to do with you, the conscious
sensible person reading this? How does the unconscious learn and
develop? What does it eat, and how should we feed it?

As a counter to this, others have argued for a more rational understanding of the creative process. The novelist Jane Rogers argues that
writers are not arty but crafty: down-to-earth materialists. Rogers says
that writers need to focus primarily on learning the practical tools of
their trade: 'plot and characterization ... narrative structure; poetic form',
and so on (in Miles, 1992).[1] George Orwell, in 'Politics and the English
Language', argues that the more unconscious we are, the more likely we
are to produce sloppy, clichéd writing: 'the worst thing you can do with
words is to surrender to them'.[2]

Consciousness Studies

In recent years, scientists have begun investigating consciousness itself,
and some argue that without the ability to make imaginative leaps,
human beings would never have become human. At some point or other
in the far distant past, one of our ancestors looked at a circular shape
she'd idly made with a stick in the dust and realised that it looked a bit
like the moon. Mark becomes image, image becomes moon: one thing
is imagined symbolically in terms of another, and this ability to associate
ultimately leads us to language. In *Brain Story* Susan Greenfield suggests

that the creative use of language is essential to any understanding of human evolution:

> Language has made us what we are. It freed us from stereotyped gestures and allowed us to use symbols to think metaphorically – to see one thing in terms of something else and to use, not just words but art to represent complex relationships, which in turn, have inspired innovative ideas.[3]

Greenfield, along with many other scientists studying the brain, believes that we are a long way from discovering the roots of consciousness, but that we are uncovering a whole range of insights which can help us understand the way our creative minds work. She uses one example of a tennis player who

> has a serve of up to 120 mph (193 kph) – once the ball has left the racket, his opponent has under 400 milliseconds to work out where the ball is going to land. The decision about how to return the shot has to be made subconsciously. Amazingly, when a player returns the ball they are not even consciously aware that the serve has started…None of the expert players I interviewed claimed to make a conscious decision about how to return a fast serve. Yet such a response is far more than just a reflex – it involves thinking strategically about exactly where to place the shot. Returning a tennis ball is a complex process – all done entirely subconsciously.[4]

There clearly are powerful skills and talents that go beyond our more limited everyday abilities. Think about a skill you already have: driving, for example; riding a bike; playing a musical instrument. It isn't possible to practise at a competent level while thinking in a mechanistic way about every move. You need to learn the skill, and then (this is the hard bit) you need to *allow* some of the skill to become unconscious, to trust that part of the mind/brain to just do it.

Left Brain/Right Brain?

One popular theory of creative consciousness is that the brain is divided into two hemispheres controlling distinct aspects of human behaviour. The left brain is said to be more verbal and analytical, while the right brain is more emotional, visual and musical. Betty Edwards, author of the bestselling book, *Drawing on the Right Side of the Brain*, uses these ideas to set out a programme which can enable beginners to become skilled at drawing. In the first edition of the book, she argues that:

> One of the key discoveries of the research revealed the dual nature of human thinking – verbal, analytic thinking mainly located in the left hemisphere, and visual, perceptual thinking mainly located in the right hemisphere.[5]

In later editions, she acknowledges that more recent research appears to show that the two aspects of mind cannot be precisely located in the left or right side, but that this dual nature is a useful way of understanding the way our minds work.

Dorothea Brande also posits the theory that our mind works in two ways, both creatively and critically. She suggests that the creative energy is best tapped when we are closest to being unconscious: the early moments of waking, or at any time when monotonous activity (music, swimming, walking, mopping the floor, motorway driving) lulls the mind into a semi-unconscious state. The critical sense is needed for evaluation and drafting.

The creative process is only partly under rational, conscious control. We don't fully understand how it works – and most of us feel uncomfortable with things we don't understand. Our education encourages us to be deliberate and conscious and we are expected to prepare for a writing task, for example, in an organised way. In the ideal world, so the received wisdom goes, essays, reports and projects need to be thought out in advance, developed through planning, then written in a form that is ordered and coherent. These learned processes and procedures are central to our education system, and by the time we are adults they've become so familiar and normal that we take them for granted. Of course, many of us fall short of these standards, but the point is that we are all taught, we teach each other, that thinking, planning and rationalising are the best ways of dealing with most writing tasks.

Before we go any further, please note that I am *not* arguing that planning or deliberate methods are *a bad thing* or that too much thinking makes you go creatively blind. My point is that the creative process is a human, non-magical activity like any other, but that most schooling doesn't help us develop it. By the time we are adults many of us have lost confidence in our own inventiveness.

Guy Claxton, Professor of Educational Psychology, says:

> The study of creativity in many areas show that what is required...is a fluid balance between modes of mind that are effortful, purposeful, detailed and explicit on the one hand and those that are playful, patient and implicit on the other.[6]

Claxton argues that we need slower ways of learning and knowing, what he calls 'Tortoise Mind' as opposed to 'Hare Brain':

The slower ways...are not the exclusive province of special groups of people – poets, mystics or sages – nor do they appear only on special occasions. They have sometimes been talked about in rather mystifying ways, as the work of 'the muse', or as signifying great gifts...This is a false and unhelpful impression. A 'poetic way of knowing' is not the special prerogative of those who string words together in special ways. It is accessible, and of value, to anyone. And although it cannot be trained, taught or engineered, it can be cultivated by anyone. [7]

How to Develop Creativity

First of all, relax. You already have many of these abilities. Watch a small child with sand or paints. They just freely make stuff, mess about, try out new things. You're still that child and you can tap into that energy with an adult skill and critical awareness: two kinds of mind activity.

We are all used to making these mind shifts many times a day. We drift, daydream, fantasise, imagine – then we snap back to the task in hand and focus, analyse, think hard. The challenging part is in merging the two modes together into an integrated creative practice. This is challenging for all writers, not just beginners, and we get it wrong some of the time: we daydream and fantasise when it would be better to be critical and analytical; we deliberate and analyse when it would be better to let ideas develop intuitively. Creativity isn't a precise science: because it depends on interaction within complex systems (mind; language), it can't be pinned down exactly or switched on like a tap. However, it can certainly be developed, practised, learned. Remember the tennis player with his impossible return serve. The player's stroke looks 'natural' but we know that such skills and abilities depend, not on magical powers or mysterious forces, but on training, fitness and understanding. I believe strongly that it is the same with writing. There will undoubtedly be limits to learning, different for each of us, determined by genetics and other factors that we can't account for, but there is plenty of scope to go on before we reach those limits.

Try This: Creative Drifting

Look up from this page and find a clear, wordless space to stare at – the sky or a blank wall, table or floor. Gaze at this space for a minute or two, allowing your mind to drift. Sit back, relax and breathe. After a while bring your attention back to this page. Focus down onto the words. Put your analytical brain back into gear and begin to read again. Did you feel the shift between the two kinds of consciousness? Were you aware of a reluctance to move from one particular mode to another? Or back again?

Try This: Stretch the Imaginative Muscle

Take an object – any object available to you right now, a pencil perhaps, and make a list of other uses for it: for example: a tea stirrer; stake for a miniature vampire's heart; chimpanzee's termite gatherer. Keep going with the list (10/20/30 ideas) – the more desperate you get for inspiration, the weirder your ideas may become. Try this again while listening to music and at different times of the day.

Try This: Creative Mind-reading

On a bus or a train, look (discreetly) at the other passengers and give them imaginary names, jobs, lives. Choose one and imagine their thoughts as a stream of consciousness. Later, write up these thoughts into a first-person monologue.

Challenge your own stereotypes: e.g. imagine the man in the bank-clerk suit as a male stripper; the little old lady as an expert in plutonium extraction; the skinhead as helplessly in love.

Try This: Make Things Speak

Take two objects – a book and a mobile phone; a computer and a pen; a table and a chair; a window and a blind; your left hand and right hand; your brain and big toe.

Now make them talk to each other. What would they say? How would they speak? If you're in a group, work with another person to develop a short dialogue. Imagine other encounters. Write down the conversation.

Further Reading

Dorothea Brande (1981) *Becoming a Writer* (London: Jeremy P. Tarcher). Second to none on the creative process. Now available on Amazon, reprinted or second-hand, but many libraries have copies.

Guy Claxton (1997) *Hare Brain, Tortoise Mind* (London: Fourth Estate).

Betty Edwards (2012) *Drawing on the Right Side of the Brain* (London: Tarcher).

Natalie Goldberg (1990) *Wild Mind: Living the Writer's Life* (London: Bantam Books). The title says it all. A creative feast.

Susan Greenfield (2000) *Brain Story* (London: BBC Worldwide).

George Orwell (1948) *Politics and the English Language*. Available at http://www.orwell.ru/library/essays/politics/english/e_polit/(accessed 29 August 2012).

Jane Rogers (1992) 'Teaching the Craft of Writing', in R. Miles and M. Monteith (eds), *Teaching Creative Writing* (Buckingham: Open University Press).

3 Journals and Notebooks

Robert Graham

One of the virtues of Kate Atkinson's award-winning first novel, *Behind the Scenes at the Museum*, was the level of specific detail about the 1960s. Atkinson was able to include details such as the fact that schoolgirls back then wore a particular kind of blouse for games, one covered with pin-prick air-vents that was manufactured by a company called Aertex. It so happens that Atkinson's impressive range of historical data was thanks to the journals she had kept while growing up.

Why Journal?

Nicola Ward Jouve speaks of the journal as 'the beginning of a voice of my own' and a place where a person can find 'a sense of self'.[1] Both of these observations, but particularly the first, hint at the most useful function of the journal: it's a place where you can develop your writing. The writer's journal has been described both as a nursery for creativity and as a creative midwife. But even more fundamentally than that, keeping a journal is an effective way of ensuring that your ideas don't get lost. Here's some advice from a Writing student:

> One of my tutor's sayings inspired me to search for a thrown-away idea and create something new from it: 'The best plays I have written are the ones I have forgotten.' In my case, it was true for stories.

Hallie and Whit Burnett concur with this, with the additional wisdom that recording something at the time it happens captures a certain freshness:

For the writer, first impressions are to be seized upon, and the act of writing in a journal often ensures that these impressions are permanently recorded.[2]

In her books on writing – *Writing Down The Bones* and *Wild Mind*, for instance – Natalie Goldberg promotes the idea of *writing practice*, something the writer should do every day in order to keep writing fit. If you're still not convinced, read Dorothea Brande's wonderful book, *Becoming a Writer*.[3] She strongly advocates the discipline of daily writing; writing as a habit. This is another good purpose for your journal.

In *Writing Fiction: A Guide to Narrative Craft*, Janet Burroway offers yet another function of the writer's journal: 'A major advantage of keeping a journal regularly is that it will put you in the habit of observing in words.'[4]

Here's an example of a writer doing just that:

Feb. 20th, I must canter my wits if I can. Perhaps some character sketches.
Snow:
She came in wrapped in a dark fur coat; which being taken off, she appeared in nondescript grey stockinette & jay blue stripes. Her eyes too are jay blue, but have an anguished, starved look, as of a cat that has climbed on to a chimney piece & looks down at a dog.[5]

Of course, a writer's journal may just be a bolt-hole, a place to wrestle with your demons and insecurities:

November 4, 1959: paralysis again. How I waste my days. I feel a terrific blocking and chilling go through me like anaesthesia. I wonder, will I ever be rid of Johnny Panic? Ten years from my successful **Seventeen** [publication], and a cold voice says: what have you done, what have you done?[6]

Those in full panic mode should consult 'Facing the Fear' in Chapter 6, and the Agony Aunt section's advice on writer's block.

Try This: Character Sketch

Use your journal to write a character sketch. Just for now, don't try to create a character from the ether. Instead, write a description of someone you have encountered in the course of your day. (Flannery O'Connor said: 'The writer should never be ashamed of staring. There is nothing that does not require his attention.') Try to find the telling details. Are the shoes particularly well polished, or not? Is there a moustache which disguises bad teeth? I know a man who, when he's talking to you, repeatedly plucks at the front of his shirt, tugging it upwards and outwards. (Is it to disguise his paunch?)

Write for five minutes.

Forms of a Journal

You could use a hardback A4 pad with blank pages. However, an A4 ring-binder with plastic envelopes, a cardboard box, a cardboard envelope or a filing cabinet would all work as well. Here's another student on her approach to the journal:

My journal is largely an assortment of bus tickets and scraps of newspaper with characters scribbled on them. If a person catches my attention, then they must, surely, be worth writing about:

Too-much-make-up lays her head on her companion's shoulder. She grins up at him cheekily and pretends to bite his fingers off.

In other words, there's nothing in the rules about what constitutes a journal: it's simply the book/envelope/box where you keep your ideas. In a moment, I'll tell you about my own preferences for journal-keeping, but first, consider the habits of Richard Ford, the Pulitzer Prize-winning author of, for instance, *Independence Day* and *Canada*. He begins by filling cardboard boxes with scraps of paper: the backs of envelopes, tickets, receipts – anything on which he has scribbled ideas. From there, he spends months sifting through the boxes and collating the notes into files on his computer – files for individual characters, for themes, or areas of research (in *Independence Day*, one was estate agents). Next, he prints the files and puts them into ring-binders, and from that point he is ready to write the novel. (You can find out more about Ford's writing disciplines in a profile on the *Guardian* website, originally published in February 2003.)

Possible Purposes of a Journal

Just about the most useful book on the writer's journal is *The New Diary* by Tristine Rainer.[7] If you want an exhaustive inventory of the possible purposes of a writer's journal, read her book. (You should read it anyway.) To whet your appetite, here's a list extracted from *The New Diary*:

- Repository for thoughts, feelings and ideas which would otherwise be lost
- Recording dreams – also daydreams
- Spontaneous writing
- Note-making
- Recording overheard dialogue
- Descriptive writing
- Overcoming writer's block
- Creative project journal
- Diary (record of daily events, etc.)
- Paste in photos, clippings, letters, quotes, drawings, doodles, dried flowers, business cards, labels
- Exaggerate
- Pray
- Express love, anger, sorrow, grief, ecstasy, joy, conflict, etc.
- Write to your future self, your past self
- A place for the writer to work out

Jennifer Moon, in *Learning Journals*, a text aimed more at academic than creative writing, suggests some other activities you can try in your journal. She talks about meditating on something (her example is a shell): 'An object can focus attention and provide a starting point.' She suggests asking yourself questions, making lists, and concept-mapping (also known as mind-mapping or making spider diagrams): 'A concept map encapsulates an idea and the themes radiate from the main idea.'[8] For example:

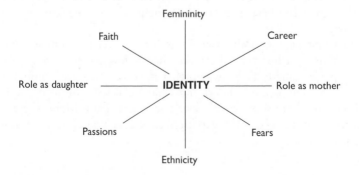

Your Journal

It's all subjective and highly personal, of course. However, you're reading this book, so you are in the market for some advice. My view of what might constitute a bare minimum in terms of notebooks and journals follows.

As we've seen already, your journal doesn't need to be a book – it might be a drawer or a shoebox. The novelist Paul Magrs recommends exercise books:

> I always carry one with me and each of them soon gets filled up with what I'm thinking about or descriptions of scenes I've witnessed or made up: irresistible snatches of dialogue from bus stops and shops. Little drawings, too. The books are my place to file things away.[9]

My preference is for something more appealing to the senses than an exercise book, so I would say go to a good stationers or bookshop and buy yourself an attractive A5 or A4 hardback journal. (Have you noticed? Writers are often stationery junkies who get excited by a visit to Paperchase or Ryman.) The more you like the look and feel of your journal, the more likely you are to want to use it, so choose carefully. Maybe the cover is a Degas reproduction. Maybe it feels soft, but not shiny. When it comes to the inside, you might think about opting for blank rather than lined pages. This frees you up to write in any direction you want, to doodle or draw, and it's ideal for mind-maps and spider diagrams. Think about the quality and feel of the paper. I have some notepads at home with terribly flimsy paper and some which are more sumptuous, and there's no doubt which I prefer.

So what do you write in your journal? Most of the available options have been mentioned already, but let's take a flash through mine. This particular one is A5 and on the cover it has a pretend photograph of Mickey Mouse driving in his car and whistling. The photograph looks as though it has been pasted onto a map of Los Angeles. Don't ask me why.

The first page contains two ideas for a novel that I'm writing; I haven't used either yet. There are then a few pages of notes for a radio play about Billy Fury (which I have yet to write). Sometimes there is a page or more describing what I can see around me. Often this is when I am somewhere new. The point of it is more to practise writing than to record the experience. Nicola Ward Jouve speaks of the journal as a writerly gymnastics. It's like being a dancer or a musician. Unless you practise, you don't develop the muscles, or the suppleness, or the nimbleness of fingers.[10]

Anaïs Nin argues for the same thing, but adds a motivating reason for being 'writing fit':

Writing…as one practises the piano every day keeps one nimble, and then when the great moments of inspiration come, one is in good form, supple and smooth.[11]

Quite often, my journal contains pieces of fiction that end up in a novel I am writing. A cast list for the last one. Something I was told:

Three-year-old to mother returning from hospital after an operation: 'Are you dead, Mummy?'

A lot of pages have sentences beginning with 'How about'. There are some notes on the film *Toto le héros*. Sometimes I have stuck in a Post-it note or notes made on scraps of paper. There's a list of chapters with word-counts from a novel I was working on – very important to fiction writers. A list of possible titles. Some notes on the film, *Don't Look Now* (both the films I've mentioned became points of reference for my novel). Sometimes there will be notes I've made about a piece that I have tabled at my writers' group. Part of a song lyric I was writing. Sketches for the staging of a play I was putting on. And notes on this very book, reader!

The important thing to remember about your journal is that anything can happen there. It's a place of freedom, as Hallie and Whit Burnett contend:

being private, [it] permits us to draw no morals, obey no rules, censure no extravagances. We write for ourselves only and need show no one what we have written.[12]

Your Notebook

Some writers take their journal everywhere with them. Because it won't fit in a pocket and I don't always have a bag to put it in, I mostly keep my journal at home. Instead, I always carry a notebook that's small enough to slide into one of my pockets. I have three different specimens on the desk in front of me now. One is paisley-patterned and covered in stiff card; the second, a Moleskine (a cult notebook amongst writers), is black, with a cotton bookmark and an elasticated strap to keep it closed; the third is spiral-bound and plastic-covered, again with an elasticised strap. All of them would fit in the back pocket of your jeans.

Let's start with the flowery paisley one. At the back are several pages where I have noted down vocabulary while reading, words that I admire but tend not to use. I write them down and then make a point of using them in my writing. 'Fathom (v.)', 'dawdle', 'pzazz' and 'sprightly' are all here. From time to time, I will keep a notebook by my bed solely for the purpose of recording words I find that I don't use and would like to.

At the front of the paisley notebook are pages of notes from a holiday in Israel:

> Israelis blare their car-horns at the drop of a hat. Honk at cyclists – every last, damn one! Different honks: warning; greeting; leching.

One section of these notes recorded an Arab teenager at the Dead Sea who approached women bathers of various ages and offered to cover them in Dead Sea mud, which is reputedly good for the skin. I was struck by how few of the women he approached refused the offer. These notes became 'Mud', a short story I wrote on my return. As Paul Magrs says: 'Think of your notebooks as a way of capturing the things that go through your head.'[13] They might come in useful later. Or they might not: there are scribbled here ideas for many stories that were never written.

There's also a list of things men talk about which ended up merged with notes (under the heading 'Carry On Bowling'), conversational snippets I overheard during a bowling match in my local park. The result was a story called 'The Urban Spacemen', which is about the daft things men talk about, bowling, aliens and John Major.

In the Moleskine I find notes I made on a documentary about British showbiz in the 1960s and 1970s (I was writing a novel partly set in that world). There are the addresses of a number of little magazines to which I was planning to submit my work. And, further on, notes I made on Jonathan Franzen's *The Corrections*, speculations about what worked in it and why. You have to work these things out so that you can emulate them!

The third notebook, the plastic-covered one, contains a list of things I observed people doing at the beach – looking for crabs, taking photographs, drawing their names on the sand, inspecting flotsam. One page is given over to a possible title for the showbiz novel I just mentioned. Another page has this overheard conversation:

I've just been watching this programme about The Beatles. Have you heard of them?

I revised this to suit its new context and used it in the novel I've just been talking about. There's a page that says 'Fray Bentos', because, for an instant, I remembered that in the 1960s people used to eat that brand of corned beef, and I didn't want the memory to slip past. Another page just says 'stodgy burgers' – presumably a term I came across and planned to use.

Try This: Using a Notebook

- Go out and buy yourself a notebook that will fit in your pocket.

- Carry it with you everywhere you go for one week.

- Record any interesting conversations you overhear. If this doesn't seem to be happening for you, go and sit in a busy café and make it happen.

- Jot down any memory that pops into your head during the course of the week.

- Write down any brainwaves you have before you forget them. Most of the ideas for writing that you have in your life won't arrive when you're sitting at your desk. Don't let them escape.

- If after a week you haven't recorded anything you regard as valuable, give up using a notebook, give up writing as well. You won't have to: a week should convert you.

Further Reading

Dorothea Brande (1996) *Becoming a Writer* (London: Pan).
  We recommend this one more than once; that's because it is the book on writing that all writers should have. It doesn't tell you much about craft or technique, but it tells you everything you need to know about harnessing your creativity. As we say elsewhere, it has mostly been in print since the 1930s, which should tell you something. And your journal is the perfect place to work through the exercises in it.
Tristine Rainer (1979) *The New Diary* (New York: Tarcher).
  This isn't aimed especially at writers, but I can't imagine anyone coming up with a more exhaustive list of things for writers to do with a journal.

4 The Necessity of Mess
John Singleton

Creation's Twin

In the beginning was mess, and it was called chaos. And out of it God ordered the world.

Read all about it. The full story's in Genesis, the Hebrew book of beginnings.

In the Bible account, this original primordial mess didn't just pre-date Creation; it was a precondition of Creation. Without it nothing could be made.

Such is the importance of mess.

There's another account of how mess acts as creation's twin. Science, which has its own myths, suggests that the world has emerged out of a rich chaos, or 'primal soup'. The implication of this image is that the 'mess of pottage' (Shakespeare's phrase for oat soup or porridge) is full of goodness and rich nutrients waiting to be transformed (cooked) into something else. Chaos here is a figure for potentiality, promise, possibility.

Try This: Torn Texts

Tear out examples of text from a newspaper, magazine, brochure, manual, book: the more jagged and messy the pieces, the better. Cut these extracts into paragraph- and sentence-sized chunks. Snip out some individual words/phrases. Casually drop them on the floor. Pick up pieces at random and arrange into a piece of writing, editing and repeating and writing in connective stuff as you go.

The Debris of Life

Now let me talk about the chaos/mess in your life. Nothing personal. It's the same for all of us. First, there's the mess we carry around in our heads, the jumble of memories and the stuff down in the far reaches of our subconscious. Then there's the mess we are born into, what E.M. Forster famously called the 'muddle'.

This mess, and the muddle we make of it, is the chaos material out of which we spin our fictions and versions of the world. We all know this. In this sense mess is the *sine qua non* of all creative action. As does God, we start with mess; we've no choice. How we view this mess is the critical point. Most of the time, because we hate, even fear, muddle and mess, we humans are forever trying to make sense of it, get it under control, bring a bit of order back into our lives.

How do we do it?

First, not everyone thinks it's all a muddle. Some think there's a secret plan at work in the world, and despite the mess already here (disease, earthquakes), and the mess we bring with us (war, environmental disaster, crime), there is an irresistible symmetry and purpose beneath. This is what holy men tell us. Others, like scientists and philosophers and investigators of all kinds, tell us different stories about the world we live in and the world that lives in us. None of them are sure they've got it 100 per cent right.

So many stories: such contrary narratives. What a muddle! Back to square one. So what do we do about it?

Well, we could choose the best story for us, a narrative that makes us comfortable and keeps the mess at bay. Or we could reject all 'stories' and take the Rhett Butler line and say we don't give a damn. Or we could say these are all cowardly pretences that turn a blind eye to the real nature of the universe, which is purposeless, unpredictable and careless of humankind. In this world we are strangers to each other and ourselves. Life is pointless; the most we can say is we exist.

Uhhm, that's existentialism for you, the Waiting-for-Godot line. We're just stuck in the mess. Tough.

The Human Endeavour

Now, those who seek order in this so-called disordered universe may be fools to try, but there is one human endeavour that recognises muddle, flux, contradiction and, at the same time, admits the necessity of order and holds the two in gainful opposition. And that is art.

Try This: Story Mosaics

Write a story with ten short scenes. The idea is to write a mosaic of a story. Not one that is bound by cause and consequence, or which follows a strictly chronological narrative and behaves well. In your story nothing striking has to happen. Indeed, your theme may be the untidiness and inconsequence of ordinary life or the arbitrary nature of events.

A Thoroughly Modern Mess

Art does, at times, alarm and upset. Writing, for instance, can persuade the reader that what they took for order and predictability and truth is, in fact, illusion and irrationality – mess, in other words. Then, having led them through the turbulence of change and the anxiety of dilemma and shock, a play or novel can assuage and bring the narrative full circle with a suitable closure so we are consoled and reassured. Mess over: order restored.

Muddle, as both the indisputable subject and unavoidable context of writing, is one thing; muddle, embraced as a wilful part of the creative process itself, is another. I'm thinking here of those modernist experimenters who used chance techniques and forms of spontaneous invention as a deliberate/willed creative strategy. William Burroughs's celebrated cut-ups, Dada experiments with language, the subversive anti-grammar writings of Gertrude Stein were all acts in honour of mess and the uncertainty principle.

In some cases, these twentieth-century modernist artists were either seeking new ways of making or striking new political attitudes in their powerful protests against the dead hand of bourgeois capitalism.

Try This: Messy Business

Consider the concept 'mess'. Babies are messy almost by nature, you could say. Is this the refreshing carelessness of innocence? Old people return to messiness. Is this just a measure of decline, or reflective of a more relaxed attitude to life? As Freud might say, most of us spend our adult lives being analy retentive. Maybe we should be more anally relaxed? Know what I'm saying?

Take 'Mess' as a title and write a messy piece or a piece that takes a very hostile view of mess. Look at the mess in your life and evaluate its importance for you. Is a messed-up bedroom really a sign of teenage rebellion? I blame all this messanthropy on all the anti-mess products on the detergent/sanitary/household shelves of the supermarkets.

Making Mess, Making Poems

To my final point. This is about technique and how to approach the writing process.

We should start with mess and stay with it as long as possible. The mess I mean here is represented by all the initial verbal doodles, half-phrases, aide-mémoires, scribblings that form the fruitful compost of the poem or short story or whatever. Mess in my view is the first and most critical phrase of composition (compostition!). I've learnt to accept reluctantly this necessary stage in my writing: reluctantly, because I like to have things ordered and coherent right from the verb go.

But what I've discovered is that the more verbal mess I create, the more likely a poem or story will emerge: I just have to be patient and wait; attend on events. When Keats advised writers against 'an irritable reaching after fact' I guess he was saying, don't get uptight, go with the flow, relinquish control, give the imagination its freedom.

I see in myself two writers now: one who is a messer, and one who is a controller. It seems to me that the first, the messer, the kid, should have his untidy turn, and then the second, the controller, the parent, can come in and clean up.

A friend of mine used to say good cooks don't bother food. It's the same with writing; let the food cook itself. In other words, don't interfere too much with the imaginative process; maintain a light touch, keep the botherer/controller at bay.

Letting the imagination take its messy unpredictable course is also a good way of getting out of trouble. Often a story or poem hits a dead end. What do you do? Give up? Yes, but only if you intend to come back later. *Or* you can go back to being a messy kid again. Chuck all your ideas up in the air, kick them around, mix them up. It might work and free up the writing. The lesson is: if your work's in trouble, get into a mess.

It's not easy letting go, 'letting your pencil go for a walk', as the painter Paul Klee used to say. Writing being the unsettling process that it is, we have the tendency to play safe, to devise elaborate plots and lengthy character studies as dependable travelling companions, or as road maps to prevent us getting lost. Well, my advice is: 'get lost' – it's the best way of finding out where you're really going.

Butterfly

Here's an instructive example of how mess morphs into something much more: a poem called 'Butterfly'.

What is it with you
you flimsy, wingy thing?
got the shakes?
out of sync?
navigation on the blink?

Just what is it about
this dithering
this aerial stuttering
this er...err...erring
flight?

Is it just a nervous tic
this rapid ricocheting habit?
or some off-beat trickery?
designed to dizzy
predators
make them think you're on the piss
that something's amiss and
stop
pursuing you?
Or is this flighty fashion
just a come-on?
yeah, admit it
with those gamine eyes
the velvets of your wings and thighs
your hems and frills and laciness
tarty lingerie, ma chérie
you play the flirt
i guess
it's a butterfella
and a helluva

good time you're after.
But little pleasure-seeker
your hobbled flight is over
too too soon.
Goodbye bright thing.
As you wither on the wing –
We catch our own breath faltering.

I wrote this in the summer of 2002. I must have spent at least five or six one-hour sessions scribbling in Costa Coffee with nothing happening. I had pages of notes and lists of descriptive phrases such as 'flimsy creature', 'fragile-winged', 'diaphanous', 'tapestried wings', 'damask', 'coiled antennae', 'illogical flight', 'Lepidoptera', 'Red Admiral', 'feelers', 'aerial'. And so on: little more than cliché. But this stock-taking set the poem's agenda. By this I mean it established themes like flimsiness, embroidered colouring, the insect's zany flying habits.

After this bit of route mapping I began to focus on the colouring and shape and texture of the wings, and the notion of flimsy gave way to laciness, which suggested lingerie and flash underwear so come-hither in the Ann Summers shop just round the corner from Costa's in Nottingham. This train of thought led me on to make-up and mascara and blusher and all the vocabulary of slap. I made lists of beauty products, splashed them like rude lipstick all over the pages of my notebook. Nothing came of this in the poem. I decided that shine and gloss was not Madam Butterfly's thing.

In the end, I screwed up all the verbal clutter and tossed it in the bin of oblivion. 'Velvets' was the word that eventually emerged out of all this concern with texture and colour and feel. Its soft richness, when lined up with the word 'thighs', gave me that cheap slightly sleazy-sex feeling I wanted. Actually, I don't know whether I wanted it or whether the poem gave it to me without being asked. Either way, I was glad to have something a step beyond cliché. The point is; I had to work through a lot of dross and mess to get to where the poem began to look minted and fresh.

And the end section is where the controller came in. It's a much larger observation about life, dressed up in metaphor. It's a kind of summation, a steadying of the theme after the ricocheting flights of the poem earlier on.

Looking back over pages of notes and jottings for this poem, I can see a sort of pattern under the messiness. Five stages in the composition seem to have emerged.

First, I started with the obvious, the familiar things. I chucked in everything, anything that came to mind, good, bad and ugly. I censored nothing. And I knew that most of it I would never use. I remember picking up a phrase from a Robert Graves poem where he describes the 'honest idiocy' of a butterfly's flight.[1] I threw that at it. Clichés, borrowings, the lot: I dismissed nothing. The truth is, this poem, like many others, was built on the honest but dull toil of tired phrases. I now try not to be too hard on such hackneyed words – they're good for starters if nothing else. They're the plod from which the poem takes off and learns to fly.

Secondly, after a time, single words began to coalesce into phrases. I tried some odd couplings, a riff here, a riff there. More agglomerations followed as the words began to get the collaborative message. The pages were blotted with huddles of them. Lone words or images that had no partner I listed in the margin. Kept them on the sub's bench for when the going got tough or critical.

In the third phase, I decided I had too many players and one by one began to get rid of the lame and the uninspired – the litter. I gave the hard-nosed accountant/controller something to do. Redundant phrases went. He created a bit of space.

Fourthly, as a result, routes opened up, sentences grouped themselves together in another burst of congress and from then on the poem more or less wrote itself. This stage took about 15 minutes: the earlier messy stage, about a week.

Finally: a fifth phase; a final check over, last couple of lines reworked. Sorted.

Try This: Playing With Clichés

Take any object or animal that attracts you. Write down as many clichés, obvious phrases about it as possible as quickly as possible. Rework some of the clichés, substituting different words or inverting phrases. New ideas will suggest themselves; follow them relentlessly, firing off as many words and images as you can pack into your notebook. I like to work in A4 size so I can sprawl across the page and leave large open spaces for later extensions to ideas already there. Work till the page looks like an ink-bomb's hit it. Now get rid of the dross. It's done its work. Time to get tough and search out the original and arresting under all the word litter. Polish and serve up.

Further Reading

William Burroughs (1987) *The Ticket That Exploded* (London: Flamingo).
    The best of his trilogy of experimental novels featuring his celebrated cut-up
    technique.
Adam Phillips (1999) *The Beast in the Nursery* (London: Faber & Faber).
    An intriguing book to dip into. Adam Phillips is a child psychologist and
    has some thought-provoking things to say about mess.

5 Visions and Dreams
Julie Armstrong

Cultivating Your Visual Imagination

'Seeing' images and having visions is a powerful part of the visual imagination. Some writers naturally have a strong sense of the visual. Others
have to work at developing this sense, much in the same way as a Zen
Buddhist seeks to develop powers of concentration in order to meditate.
Indeed, some writers consider writing, with its senses of heightened
awareness, to be a form of meditation, something we'll return to later.
For now, however, since a strong visual imagination is an asset to any
artist, let's explore ways to develop this, and use it in your writing.

The writer Penelope Fitzgerald has said that her work often begins
with a persistent idea or image. She speaks of one image in particular
which inspired her. On a visit to Cambridge, she saw cows under willow
trees. It was a very windy day, and it seemed to her that they were
almost dancing in the wind. She was so captivated by this one image
that she started a piece of writing.[1]

Remember, it's not what you see but how you see it, and there are
many ways you can develop your visual imagination:

- Collect written images from your daily life in your journal in much
  the same way as an artist collects drawings in a sketchbook. Be alert. A
  writer is never off duty. What do you see that captures your attention?
  A V of geese flying through the sky? Capture the image in your
  journal. Be precise and specific with language.

- Look for images on journeys. Take a train or bus journey. Gaze out
  of the window. Visit art galleries. Jot down anything interesting that
  catches your eye.

- Look at everything from the point of view of a child trying to capture the freshness and innocence children have for the world around them. Try and see things as if for the first time.

- Make sketches of images you find stimulating. Put two different images together and try to connect them in a piece of writing.

Untangling the Mind

Engage with activity that gives you the opportunity to connect with your unconscious mind, perhaps something physical and repetitive like walking, cycling, swimming. Allow yourself to relax as you perform these activities. Absorb what you see. Be receptive to whatever images come into your mind. Can you make any connection between a good writing session and a particular activity, be it swimming or visiting an art gallery? Did you write more easily after taking a bus or train journey? Be sensitive to connections and engage in the type of activity that results in your most fluent writing.

Many view writing as a form of meditation, not least Dorothea Brande, whose book, *Becoming a Writer*, is an essential read for all writers.[2] Some writers, like Zen artists, strive for a contemplative way of life that prepares them for their work. The actual act of writing can become a form of meditation, untangling emotions and cleansing the mind. Through writing, we can cultivate qualities of absorption and self-mastery, leading to spiritual and emotional growth, qualities of value to the budding writer.

When developing our sense of the visual, the powers of meditation cannot be underestimated. Meditating allows a writer to be receptive: it helps to tune the mind and sharpen the senses. In addition, meditating develops our imagination; it also helps us gain control over thoughts and feelings and gives us a sense of order and harmony, which in turn, sets us free to write.

Transforming Your Dreams

Most writers are also dreamers. It is a question of entering these dreams and transforming them into writing. When we engage with images, visions and dreams we are connecting with the unconscious mind. Dreaming is accepted as a plunge into the unconscious. Freud believed the unconscious to be the true reality. Carl Jung saw dreams as a way in which the conscious and the unconscious engaged in dialogue with each other. He believed that dreams are creative symbols. Like visions and images, dreams can be very useful to the writer. They can often be a trigger for the imagination and ultimately a focal point for writing; it is a question of knowing how to realise their potential.

In the early 1980s, Stephen King made a trip to England. He fell asleep on the flight and had a dream about a popular writer falling into the hands of a psychotic fan living on an isolated farm, and wrote the dream down on an airline napkin. Later, in a London hotel, he could not sleep. He got up and went downstairs to ask the concierge if there was a quiet place where he could write. The concierge took him to a desk on a second-floor landing where King filled 16 pages of a notebook.

He says that the *actual* story did not exist at this point. However, knowing the story wasn't essential. He had located the fossil. The rest, he knew, would consist of careful excavation.[3]

Get into the habit of recording your dreams over a period of time, especially any recurring dreams. Always keep a notebook by your bed to write about your dreams upon waking. This way the dream will be captured when it is most vital. Dreams have a tendency to lose their potency as the day moves on, or it may be that we simply begin to forget them.

Daydreaming, too, can allow new thoughts and images to float into your mind. Let yourself drift into your own world, your inner landscape. What do you wish for? Would you like to win the lottery? Do you wish you could be a famous film or pop star? Try out new versions of yourself. If you were granted three wishes, what would it be? To fly to the moon? To sail round the world? Live the wishes in your mind – then write them as if they were actually happening to someone else. Consider the warning *Be careful what you wish for.* How might this impact on a character?

Dream Time

Some writers prefer writing deep into the night. Others like to get up early in the morning. When you are close to sleep, the edges between dreaming and waking are blurred, times when fantasy and the unconscious may become more accessible.

Dorothea Brande says:

> If you are to have the full benefit of the richness of the unconscious, you must learn to write easily and smoothly when the unconscious is in the ascendant.[4]

Morning is a time when you are close to your dream world, a time of quiet and solitude, the space between sleep and the full waking state. Barbara Trapido often sets her alarm for 4 a.m. So why not try it for yourself one dawn. Rise early and, before engaging in conversation with anyone, write freely and uncritically. Write for as long as you are able. Write about anything at all.

The Nightmare

And then I woke up and it was all a dream...

You've probably already been told it's inadvisable to finish a story in this way, as using a clichéd twist like this can alienate the reader, and leave them feeling cheated. But, as with all rules, this one is there to be broken by a skilled writer who can make it work: but it's a dangerous game to play. Reading fiction is already a kind of dream which needs no tricks to make us suspend our disbelief, to sweep us away.

There are, however, plenty of examples of narratives that use anxious or frightening dreams as catalysts: a character's strange dreams can hook the reader or further the plot. Film narratives such as *Solaris* use the strange disconnected quality of dream as nervous characters begin to question the reality around them.[5] And *The Matrix* is built upon the premise that the world we know is a computer-generated dream.[6]

Using dreams in stories is not a new idea: Joseph, clad in an amazing coat, was a dreaming protagonist long ago. Perhaps we like using dreams because it parallels the creative process, something Sigmund Freud commented on:

> Storytellers are valuable allies, and their testimony is to be rated high, for they usually know many things between heaven and earth that our academic wisdom does not even dream of. In psychic knowledge they are far ahead of us, ordinary people, because they draw from sources that we have not yet made accessible to science.[7]

Writers make things up. We explore our minds, conscious and unconscious, for stories and fabricate our dreams. It is important to realise that we can make our visions and dreams *real* through writing and this in turn can create a dream world for the reader.

Try This: Deepen Your Visual Sense

Choose a scene that delights you in some way: a sunset, an urban setting. Study the scene: allow it to fill you with energy. Look at tones and colours, light and shade. Make a list of adjectives that capture the scene visually. Use your findings to develop a piece of writing that brings the scene alive and allows the reader to see it in visual detail.

Choose a piece of fruit. Examine it and describe its exact colour, texture. Taste it. Now write about the experience in as much detail as you can.

Try This: Learn to Meditate

Sit in a quiet place. Relax. Close your eyes. Let your mind drift. Don't force anything but 'see' what images and visions come to you. Open your eyes. Let these images settle for a few minutes, then:

Describe what you saw as vividly as possible. Write freely: don't concern yourself with correct grammar, spelling or punctuation: that can come later.

Further Reading

Sigmund Freud, trans. Helen M. Downey (1993) *Delusion and Dream in Wilhelm Jensen's* Gradiva (Los Angeles: Sun & Moon Classics).
This is a great little novel dealing with dream and memory. It has a commentary by Freud himself, which examines how writers use dreams, and how creative writing assists in dream analysis.
John Gardner (1991) *The Art of Fiction: Notes on Craft to a Young Writer* (London: Vintage Books).
Although there isn't a specific chapter dedicated to writers and dreaming, the index reveals a wealth of comment and advice for dreamers to be found throughout.

6 A Writer's Territory
Julie Armstrong

What Is a Suitable Place for a Writer to Work?

There are no right or wrong answers; the most suitable place to write is the one that best suits you. However, it is important that the place you choose is the one in which you can immerse yourself most deeply in the act of writing. Some writers prefer bustle, others tranquility – somewhere they can *dream* uninterrupted.

Novelists Lesley Glaister and Wendy Perriam both say they like to write in bed. It appears that there is something about the womblike space of a bed that inspires creativity. Maybe because bed is a place where we can withdraw from the rest of the world and enter the fantasy space of our heads. It's a place for dreaming, and dreaming is linked to writing.

Playwright Caryl Phillips prefers to write in hotels, where he can be anonymous. Nobody knows where he is and nobody can get hold of him. This illustrates the need some writers have for privacy, as well as space and solitude. While retreating from the world in order to write is important for some, there are always exceptions. Natalie Goldberg, for example, loves to write in cafés and restaurants; she finds the activity around her increases her concentration. Even in a public space, writing can be a way of creating private space. We can watch the world going on around us and disappear into ourselves.

It's 'horses for courses', and you may still be looking for that special place to write, a place in which you can reach your true potential as a writer. How can you discover the right environment for you?

Experimentation is the key. What suits one writer does not necessarily suit another, and preferences may change with the weather and time of day. Learn to be flexible. Write in different places and circumstances. Working in lots of different places lends itself to changing moods and experiences; it will increase sensory stimulation and enrich your writing, enabling you to step outside yourself and see things afresh. Keep an open mind: trial and error are useful for those who think they've already found the perfect space. Perhaps there's another one out there with an even better atmosphere! Sometimes the place in which you are working will be suitable for short bursts of writing; at other times, for more sustained pieces. What is important is knowing what kind of writing you'd like to do, and finding the best place to suit that activity.

Experimenting with different territories is a way of rejuvenating yourself and your work, a way of experiencing the writing moment and making it full of vitality. The place you ultimately enjoy writing in most will be an environment where you feel comfortable, safe and inspired. Having experimented with different places, try settling with one of them for a while. Whether you have chosen to write in a crowded pub or in an isolated room, you should be able to connect with the place and, more importantly, with yourself. Having a regular writing place means that you will come to associate that place with writing, which will help you to fully engage with the act of writing. And if that place starts to feel stale, move on, or move the furniture.

Virginia Woolf wrote of having *A Room of One's Own*. To have such a space, shut away from the world, would be ideal for most writers, but this may not be feasible for everyone. It is possible, however, to create a writing territory for yourself. It can be as simple as a desk in a corner; a garden shed; a shared room the use of which you negotiate with a partner or friend. Some writers are like bower birds, and their desk space is cluttered with objects pertinent to the work in hand. If you have no room of your own, you might have space for a notice board. Collect postcards, snippets of cloth, stamps, clippings from magazines – whatever floats your boat – and pin it all to the board. And if there's no room on the wall, then a shoebox of treasures will do. Lay them out around you to make a temporary writing environment and put them back in the box when you've finished. Wherever it is, it's the space offering the best internal view: where the dreams and ideas flow unhindered.

Once you've found your place, limber up to work with a few writing exercises and then write! If you are constantly distracted, then the place isn't working for you. Get your mind used to the idea that this is a working space.

Facing the Fear

Why do we go to such great lengths to avoid being alone with the screen?

There are a number of reasons, but fundamentally the answer is fear. This fear is distinct from a writer's block, which tends to interrupt the process. This is the fear that stops writing before it has begun. But fear of what? Awakening difficult memories? Running out of ideas? Sustaining a piece of writing? Writing rubbish?

Don't be afraid that you are the only writer who struggles to write. It's all part of the process, and for many of us feelings of fear and self-doubt are inevitable. Writing *is* introspection. To connect with yourself, to get in touch with your inner world of emotions, thoughts, memories, ideas, can be daunting. You need to find a way of living with the fear, to recognise and acknowledge it, to build up a tolerance and write through it with courage and a steely nerve. What matters is that you make a commitment to your work. You don't have to share it with anyone if you don't want to. And if it is rubbish, so what? Write it anyway. Not every word will be rubbish. Often there's a seed of an idea among the chaff. It is this seed that you have to nurture, to help germinate and grow.

Developing the Writing Habit

One of the best ways to overcome fear and self-doubt is to cultivate useful habits and helpful routines. Some novice writers think that they should wait for divine inspiration before starting. Divine inspiration is a myth. Writers have to work at discovering ideas, even though it is tempting to find all sorts of distractions to avoid writing: you'll just have one more cup of coffee, phone a friend, go to the shops, take the dog for a walk and then you'll write. These are displacement activities: you have to overcome them. (See also our Agony Aunt section.) It can be difficult to get in the mood, but you can't always wait for the mood to be right because the few occasions when it is will not be sufficient to get the work done. Some prolific writers *never* feel like writing, but they are disciplined enough to get on with it anyway and *make* the mood right.

Writing takes time, energy, thought and endurance. It is hard work. If you see it as a job – an enjoyable, but demanding one – then you will realise that, as with any job, you have to put in the effort if you want the rewards. Going to work involves setting your alarm, getting yourself organised and then focusing. Adopt the same approach to your writing. Writing is a daily habit. The trick is to work out how you structure your own habit.

Here are a few suggestions:

- Give yourself permission to be alone at some point during each day. Enjoy the freedom and peace this brings you and allow it to recharge your imagination and fire your creative energy.

- Every day set a time that suits you to write. Start with 15 minutes, then build up to 30 minutes and in no time at all, you will be writing for an hour or more and wondering where the time has gone. The continual act of making time to write and actually doing it will build up belief in yourself as a writer.

- Avoid distractions: if possible take the phone off the hook; don't answer the door; tell family and friends that you don't want to be disturbed, and in time they'll come to respect your writing and treat it as seriously as you do.

- This may be the hardest of all, but, during your writing time, try not to be online, on Facebook, on Twitter, or watching your phone for a text, etc. To get in the writing zone you need to have the single-minded focus of a brain surgeon.

- Be professional: muster up as much concentration, discipline and energy as you can

What Else Can You Do?

Screen to paper/paper to screen

For those studying writing at university or participating in writers' workshops, paper is most likely to be the first point of contact with your ideas. So, if the blank page scares you, scribble onto it; write a sentence, it doesn't matter what. Draw something. Annihilate the white emptiness and then write. Some writers prefer in any case to write in longhand before they write onto the screen, saying it feels more physical and connected. If you're a screen junkie, try paper and pen. If you never write straight onto the screen, give it a try.

Join a writing group

Writing in groups often helps. If you don't participate in workshops, I suggest you do. You'll meet other people who are as passionate about writing as you are, giving you the opportunity to discuss ideas and share work. This interaction will provide stimulus and help develop your self-confidence; it will act as a valuable source of inspiration and motivation. You can read more about this in Chapter 8: 'Writing Together: Groups and Workshops'.

Find a writing friend

Another way of overcoming the fear is to develop a relationship with a writing buddy, someone who shares your enthusiasm for writing. With this person you can discuss the trials and tribulations of writing. Receiving and giving support with a like-minded individual strengthens your resolve to write and gives you support and insight into your projects. By discussing work in progress and reading it aloud to each other, you may unblock your inability to write and progress. You will also develop the art of listening, an essential skill for a writer.

Reduce the pressure

Sometimes writers put too much pressure on themselves: 'today I am going to write a short story'. This pressure creates anxiety. Anxiety creates tension and stress, making it even harder to write. Simply say to yourself: 'today I am going to write and it doesn't matter what I write'. Then write whatever's in your mind, even if it's 'I'm bored with this and can't wait until lunchtime'. Then keep going. Don't censor what you write; don't worry about spelling, punctuation or grammar. *Just do it.* Don't forget that first drafts are allowed to be terrible and no one need ever see them. Don't get it right, get it written. You can always redraft and fix it later.

Acknowledging difficulties is the first step to overcoming them. The second step is writing your way through them. Good luck!

Try This

■ Explore new places. Visit a cemetery, zoo, gallery, funfair, museum. Notice what's going on around you. Record what you think, see, hear and feel. Develop an eye for detail. Be observant.

■ Write about a journey, train, bus, plane, ship. Make the story last only as long as the journey lasts.

■ Put on a piece of music and write as it plays. Change the music to something very different and write again.

Further Reading

Maura Dooley (2000) *How Novelists Work* (London: Seren).
    See especially the chapter about Jennifer Johnston writing her novel, *The Illusionist.*
Stephen King (2000) *On Writing*. New English Library (London: Hodder & Stoughton).
    King gives you the nuts and bolts: he helps take the fear away by demystifying the process.
Virginia Woolf (2000) *A Room of One's Own* (London: Penguin Classics).

7 Reading as a Writer
Heather Leach

Friday morning. It's raining outside and I'm staring through the window at nature grey in tooth and claw. My notes are lying expectantly on the desk close to my elbow. I've typed the title: *Reading as a Writer* at the top of the page and now I'm peering at the screen waiting for words to appear. You have to have a beginning: you have to find a door in the page's wall. Then my daughter comes in with a cup of coffee. She leans forward and reads the title: 'What's the difference?' she says. 'Why can't writers just read like everybody else?'

And that's it: abracadabra; the page swings open.

Why *can't* writers read like normal people? Are there special ways of reading? Are there particular things that writers ought to read?

Read What You Like

The starting point for all of us, whatever our education or experience, has to be reading for pleasure. For many people, this is easy. But for others, reading may have become associated with a whole lot of other issues: serious study, homework, *Lit-er-rich-oo-er*, none of which seem like much fun. Pleasure cannot be forced, and many people have been put off reading as children after being urged to read 'good' books by well-meaning adults. Reading difficult or classic texts simply because they are difficult or classic has nothing to do with reading for pleasure, and will almost certainly not help in your development as a writer, although it might help to impress a few culture snobs. One of the key elements in reading for pleasure is freedom – *you* choose what you read, you and nobody else. Find a writer you like and read as much of their work as you can get hold of. Find out about them; look them up on

49

a website; read their autobiography if there is one. This is how most addictive readers begin: a particular genre, style or voice hooks them in. Read whatever appeals to you: love stories; science fiction; horror; magic; rap-style poetry; nineteenth-century novels; chick-lit. Read until you've had enough, read until you're sick. No shame, no blame.

Jonathan Franzen says that reading teaches us how to be alone.[1] Through reading we slowly become persons, selves: we make up our inner, *imagined* lives from the books we read, from the feelings and thoughts we have about them. This inner space is like the Tardis in *Doctor Who*: small and insignificant from the outside: huge and complex on the inside. Reading alone, buried in a book, you are building a reflective mind space essential for the writer.

But Don't Get Stuck

Readers who want to be writers can't afford to be monogamous. Don't get stuck on one kind of writing. There's a whole world of books, and life is short. There will be times when you need to kiss goodbye and move on. This is not because the Literary Thought Police have decreed that this is A Good Thing, but because to develop your own writing voice you need to have read a wide range of other voices. Good chefs don't just eat burgers or caviar. They try out many tastes and styles in order to develop their own.

There are times and circumstances when you just want to read something easy and relaxing; holiday reading, one of those stories that slips down like strawberry ice cream or cold lager. There are other times when you might want to go back, to reread, *Harry Potter* maybe, or *Jane Eyre, or* Maya Angelou's poems. At difficult periods in our lives we may need to return to stories that are familiar, retracing old, safe ground just as small children like books to be read over and over.

But at other times, we need to push beyond the limits of habit and safety, to read with more attention and effort. This may be hard at first; you may struggle with unfamiliar ideas, strange voices. You may feel awkward and wrong-footed, floundering in what feels like an alien language, designed to confuse and exclude you. This is painful and you might be tempted to give up, to blame the writing or the writer: it's rubbish, you may think, incomprehensible, pretentious or deliberately obscure.

What helps here, I think, is to remember that reading is a process of self-development, of *learning*. Learning – real learning – is not a passive business: you can't become a tennis player by watching Wimbledon on telly. I've tried it – it didn't work. And you can't develop as a reader or a writer without pushing beyond your comfort zone. If everything you read is easy, accessible, straightforward and familiar, you're not working your reading muscles enough. Of course, this doesn't mean that everything difficult or challenging is good, but how will you be able to tell the difference between brilliance and bullshit if your experience is limited?

The Threat of Influence?

Beginner writers sometimes worry that if they read a lot of other people's work then they won't be able to write in their own original voice. On the contrary, if you currently read very little, then what you read when you were younger will probably have the greatest influence. Many beginner poets, for example, find themselves using archaic diction and syntax which *feel* original and natural, but which demonstrate that they are still strongly (and unconsciously) under the influence of the nineteenth-century poets they studied at school. If you read only one writer or form, then you are likely to be strongly influenced by that style or form. There is no way to avoid any kind of influence, and anyway, what's so good about unsullied individuality? We are all part of a complex culture, and by the time we are adults we have already been influenced, like it or not, by a vast range of voices: how else would we learn? Every artist needs to hoover up influences – from past and present – in order to create something new. If, through reading, you absorb a wide range of forms, genres and styles, 'high' and 'low' literature, you will be enriched and much better equipped to speak in your own voice, to write what you like.

I've Seen the Film So I Don't Need to Read the Script

Nice try, but it won't do. By the final edit or performance, a film or stage performance is the work of many – director, producers, actors, technicians, whoever – what you see on stage or screen is a long way from the writer's initial work. The skeleton of the play or script may be clearly visible beneath the body of the performance, and you may get good ideas and inspiration by simply watching, but it will be difficult to distinguish (and therefore learn from), the writer's particular contribution. You need to go to the source: the script itself. Here you will see the initial design, structure, raw materials and layout, how words can be turned into visions: how bones become flesh.

Reading As Reverse Engineering

Reading as a writer is not the same as reading as a literary critic. The contemporary critical reader discusses the text's meanings, its cultural place, use of language, authorship, etc., all of which is interesting, but which often misses what for writers is the key point: which is how the text was *made*, the *process* of writing, the skill, the art. Francine Prose describes how a close reading method helped her to develop her own writing:

> In the ongoing process of becoming a writer...I read for pleasure first, but also more analytically, conscious of style, of diction, of how sentences were formed and information was being conveyed, how the writer was structuring a plot, creating characters, employing detail and dialogue.[2]

The good thing about reading as a writer is that you can have double vision: you can read like normal people – for pleasure, following the story, poem, idea, as a continuous drama or dream. But you can also learn to look beneath the surface of the print for traces of *the making* process, to look at how it *works*. A word of warning: we can never *completely* understand a piece of writing: there will always be some parts that are beyond deconstruction, beyond rational description, and a good thing too. Any creative process involves intuition, emotion, play, all of which, by their nature, are beyond complete analysis. But, hey, we don't need to *know* everything. There is a lot we *can* learn, much that is useful: skills and processes, techniques, *know-how*.

Try This: Close Reading

Take two pages of any piece of writing: fiction, poetry, script.

Look at the title. What kind of expectations does it raise? Does it pull you in? Without reading any further, make a note or two about what you expect to come next.

Read the first two or three lines. First lines are crucial: they set the tone; introduce a voice; give a taste of what's to come. Do they draw you in? Give you information about what is to come? Raise questions? Make you want to know more? The first few lines may be all that someone will read before they either put the book down or take it to the cash till. How does this one work? Do you trust or resist it? Does it make you want to read on? Make a note of your responses.

An example:

"'So now get up." Felled, dazed, silent, he has fallen; knocked full length on the cobbles of the yard. His head turns sideways; his eyes are turned towards the gate, as if someone might arrive to help him out. One blow, properly placed, could kill him now.'[3]

Hilary Mantel's Booker Prize-winning novel, *Wolf Hall,* begins right in the middle of the action, and so hooks in the reader with a number of questions that urgently need answering. Who is 'he'? Who has 'felled' him? Will anyone come to help? We might also pick up a couple of clues about the novel's genre: the words *felled* and *cobbles* imply a historical setting. Can you also glean anything about the character of the narrator from this short extract?

Use of words. Look closely at the first paragraph of your chosen text. Pick out the words that have the strongest impact on you. Use a dictionary if necessary. Ask:

■ why is this word striking?

■ why this particular word in this place?

■ how does the word work with the others around it?

Imagery: metaphors and similes. These terms often make the heart sink. I've watched it happen – simply saying **metaphor** or **simile** can reduce a normally cheerful group of people to anxious shadows of their former selves, muttering stuff about 'a metaphor is a figure of...while a simile uses like...'. Sad. Reading as a writer is not about defining every grammatical term, but recognising a good image when we see one, and learning to use our own to good effect. Watch out for clichés: *to take the bull by the horns, leave no stone unturned, at the end of the day,* etc. David Crystal calls clichés 'zombies of language',[4] images so old and dead that they have lost all beauty and meaning, but which hang around in our minds as if they were alive. A fresh image wakes you up, brings language alive, helps you to see, to hear, to imaginatively experience what is being described. See how many images you can identify in the piece of writing you are examining. You might be surprised by how many there are. Which ones are overused? Which work best? Why do you think this is?

Read for the beat. We all have a sense of rhythm. Even if you can't sing or dance, you can recognise music and movement when you hear or see it. Writing has music in it – all kinds of music: slow or speedy; classic and jazz; rap and rock. Practise reading a few sentences aloud two or three times. Work out where to put the right emphasis and inflection. Can you catch the beat?

Listen for the sound of language.

He clasps the crag with crooked hands
Close to the sun in lonely lands[5]

Notice how in these lines from Tennyson's poem, 'The Eagle', strong effects are created using words which have consonance – close similarity between consonants – clasps/crag/crooked. There is also a pleasing use of assonance – similar vowel sounds – close/lonely, and sibilance – repeated hissing sounds – clasps/close/sun. All of which add to the readability of a text. Look out for such uses in your piece.

Pattern and structure. Look at the way the writing is ordered. Does it move along with an obvious narrative line: a story or argument that unfolds – beginning, middle, ending – as you read? Or does it jump from one voice, idea or description to another, so that you are not quite sure where it's going? Is this writing that carries you along with it like a boat on a river? Or is it more like a puzzle, a maze?

Imagine the beginning before the beginning. Underneath any piece of writing are the ghosts of earlier drafts. Once it may have been just a few notes scribbled on a scrap of paper, two or three ideas still unconnected in the writer's head, a voice whispering, a door opening, a face. The next draft might have been an attempt to write or type it out, but when the writer read it through she saw that it wasn't as clear as she'd thought it was, it didn't say what she wanted it to say in the first place. The next draft may go off in new directions, becoming more solid and real as she writes, as she begins to live in the story, the voices, the place. Later drafts may be about improving and enriching the language, changing awkward expressions, repetitions, clichés, and so on. Final drafts pay attention to spelling, punctuation, and layout. The piece you are examining may look neat and finished, so comfortable on the page that it's hard to imagine it as a vague idea, a few words, some crossed out. Try to imagine these ghost writings, to catch glimpses of them between the lines. Think of your own work in the same way: ghostly drafts slowly becoming solid, alive.

Try This: Turn Reading into Writing

First, read the poem 'Full Moon and Little Frieda' by Ted Hughes.[6]

This one small event (a father walking with his small daughter along a lane in the evening) has long gone, but Hughes has tried to hold it still, the way we would all like to do with perfect moments. Read over the poem line by line, and as you read, close your eyes and try to imagine what they experienced. Conjure up the sights and sounds in as much detail as you can. Don't skim: focus your inner attention, be precise and slow, see it, hear it, smell it, feel it.

Now rewrite the scene in prose, or as a monologue, using the first person. Are you an adult or child? Extend and elaborate the scene; add things Hughes doesn't mention, e.g. the smell of the cowshit; the sound of insects. Use your own imagery to describe these things: focus that inner attention to enable you to go into the scene again and find the right image for your additions. Learn from the precision of Hughes's imagery.

Now write your own 'special moment' in any form. This could be an experience of great happiness or sorrow, or it could be an ordinary moment, as Hughes's is – something that happened often but that was changed by the way you felt about it, or later, in memory. Use as many of the senses as you can. Take us there.

Further Reading

A. Manguel (2011) *A Reader on Reading* (New Haven, CT: Yale University Press).
A collection of 39 chapters examining the crafts of reading and writing.

Ruth Padel (2004) *52 Ways of Looking at a Poem: How Reading Modern Poetry Can Change Your Life* (London: Vintage).
A creative coursebook on how to read poetry, this book is based on Ruth Padel's popular newspaper column. There are 52 poems and 52 readings. Illuminating rather than prescriptive.

Francine Prose (2012) *Reading Like a Writer: A Guide for People Who Love Books and for Those Who Want to Write Them* (London: Union Books).
A detailed, witty and inspirational guide showing how slow, close reading can help you to develop your writing. Examples are taken from Sophocles to Alice Munro.

Francis Spufford (2003) *The Child That Books Built* (London: Faber).
A beautifully written autobiography of reading. Revisits many children's classics and tracks the author's route through teenage books to adulthood.

8 Writing Together: Groups and Workshops

Heather Leach

There are more writing workshops, classes and courses now than ever before. Google *creative writing courses* and you'll get almost six million hits and rising. In the real world, wherever you live, you're almost sure to find a writing group at least a bus ride away. Many universities and colleges have writing options and an increasing number are offering half or even full degree courses in Creative Writing. Some newspapers and publishing houses have started to offer courses: the *Guardian* and Faber, for example, but they are often expensive and London-based, and far beyond the means of most would-be writers living in provincial bedsits.

There's still debate about how much a workshop or course can help, and it's certainly true that a writing course isn't a fast track to the celebrity big-time, if that's what you're hoping for. Matthew Wright quotes Graham Hodge, a second-year student on the part-time MA at Birkbeck, who says:

> some people see a creative writing MA as being a bit like ... an MBA – your passport to a nice pad in Notting Hill ...but I can confirm these perceptions are false ... planning to earn enough from writing to give up the day job will almost certainly lead to disappointment.[1]

On the other hand, many published writers began their careers in writers' workshops, and if you read the biographies and letters of famous and not-so-famous writers, you'll find details of friendships and collaborations, literary groups, university societies and family and friendship connections. This is fine if you live in the kind of world where such networks and connections are common, but there are plenty of places where the likelihood of meeting another writer down the chip shop is as remote as the likelihood of meeting Elvis, dead or alive. Writers' groups and courses offer *everybody* the opportunity to gain from the skill and experience of other writers, and give you a helpful leg-up into the writing world.

Stephen King comments that the main benefit of writing courses and groups is that they take writing seriously:

> for aspiring writers who have been looked upon with pitying condescension by their friends and relatives ('You better not quit your day job just yet!' is a popular line, usually delivered with a hideous Bob's-yer-uncle grin), this is a wonderful thing. In writing classes, it is entirely permissible to spend large chunks of your time off in your own little dream world.[2]

Writer's courses and groups give you ideas, feedback, time to write and motivation, but above all, they give you *permission* to be a writer. Visual artists, musicians, dancers, actors all study on courses – and so do bricklayers, physicists, airline pilots and TV gardeners. It's the modern-day equivalent of the old boys' and girls' network, except that it's no longer open only to the few who know the password.

In the next section of this chapter I'll look at the value of writing workshops and suggest guidelines for getting the best out of them. This chapter refers to real-world classes and groups rather than online ones. See also a discussion and guide to online groups in the *Digital Writing* chapter.

Motivation, Motivation, Motivation

Some writing workshops encourage you to practise writing on the spot: 10 minutes on an opening paragraph; 5 minutes on a quick-fire dialogue; half an hour for a poem with a formal structure. This is a real bonus for many writers. At least you get a start: even if you throw away most of what you produce in those short bursts, it's good practice. Also, for increasing numbers of people, this is the only time they get the chance to use an actual pen or pencil, which is archaic, but strangely moving.

Most structured writing workshops also ask you to produce regular drafts of work in progress, which will then be read and discussed by members of the group. The need to get something, *anything*, written by a particular date and time is a powerful motivator. I should know – the editors of this book are expecting the draft of this chapter by last week – which is motivating me big-time. Writing is hard work, and very few of us work hard unless we have to. Deadlines are the writer's friend.[3]

Your First Readers

The people in the workshop are, ideally, not your close friends, lovers or relations but other writers who are willing to give you honest feedback in exchange for the same from you. If you're lucky, they'll tell you what they really think and feel about your writing. They may not be experts, they may not be clever or literary or even kind. They're readers. Give them respect and attention. Listen when they speak. Carefully.

Confidence

Stephen King is quoted above as saying that being in a group gives you *permission*: it can also give you confidence. This is not the same as praise, which we all need, but which can be both addictive and misleading. Praise is like sugar or alcohol: a lot rots your teeth or makes you fall over, but life without it would be dull. It's often praise that started us on this writing business in the first place: even a brief positive comment by a teacher in the margin of an assignment can be enough to make the beginnings of a writer. Praise in workshops can be very motivating; however, workshops at their best are not mutual backslapping societies, but places where work in progress is looked at honestly and realistically. A group of attentive, honest and interested readers can help you to recognise your weaknesses and build on your strengths. A group's intelligent support can help give you the confidence to keep writing until you produce your best work.

Talking about Writing

This is a rare and precious thing. Let's face it: there aren't many places where it is possible. Normal people don't care *how* books are written: they don't want to know about the nuts and bolts; they just want to read the damn things. The best people to talk to about writing *process* are other writers and the workshop gives you just that. On the other hand, too much talking, even talking about writing, can become a substitute for the writing itself. There is nothing easier than getting carried away on brilliant descriptions of a project, only to find that later, in the quiet silence of your own company, the idea disappears like the ghost of a ghost. In a workshop, the main emphasis of attention needs to focus on words on the page, words actually written. Dreams, ideas, plans are not writing. Only writing is writing.

Reading as a Writer

Most good writing classes also include an opportunity to close-read and discuss a piece of writing in the group and to write in response. You may get something to read that you really like and which stimulates your imagination; on the other hand, you may hate what you're given by the class tutor or leader. However, as discussed in the *Reading as a Writer* chapter, learning from what you don't like, and being able to articulate why, is a crucial step on the way to finding out what you want to write for yourself. Sometimes, trying to write in the manner of a writer you think is pants or pretentious may help you gain a little more respect for what they are trying to do, as well as teaching you some useful tricks and techniques.

Workshop Guidelines

There are many ways of organising and running sessions, some of which depend on the size of the group (6–12 is ideal, but not always possible). However, there are some key factors that I have found promote enjoyable and productive workshops. At the end of this chapter there are samples of handouts which can be copied or adapted to use with your own writing group.

Good Leadership

This doesn't mean bossing people about but ensuring there is a structure to the group that enables everybody to fully participate. Without good leadership, the group may become dominated by talkative, confident people or may drift into unproductive chatting and nicey-niceness. The group leader needs to make a firm but gentle effort to encourage all to be involved – not just at the beginning, but throughout. It helps to establish and agree the guidelines with all group members from the start.

Everyone Should Share Draft Work for Group Discussion

This is so obvious it shouldn't need elaborating. People might read out the work or, in larger groups, share it with one or two others. Some people may be nervous about presenting their work, but like parachute jumping, if they won't jump it's kinder to push them. People usually feel much better after having their work discussed, while those who cop out may feel even more anxious. Face the fear.

Everybody Gives Feedback on Other People's Work

You may feel that the main value of the workshop is to see what people think of *your* writing and that your feedback on other's work is primarily for *their* benefit. But you also learn a great deal by looking carefully at a piece of work in progress, even if it is nothing like your own. People who keep silent, make no comment and don't submit work are acting as an *audience* rather than as fellow writers, which can be experienced by others as intimidating or freeloading. On the other hand, participation does not mean domination. If you're the kind of person who has a lot to say, learning when to shut up can be hard but useful. Listening is a vital skill for writers. The key point is that a group is a group: one jumps; all jump.

Writers Keep Quiet While Their Work is Being Discussed

It may seem strange to suggest that the person whose writing is being discussed should just listen and observe while the rest of the group talk, but believe me, it really does help and, once established, works well for both writers and readers. It helps if you sit back a little from the group, maybe imagining yourself as a fly on the wall or as someone having an out-of-body experience gazing down curiously while the workshop surgeons do an operating job on your draft. It can be frustrating but instructive to hear people misunderstanding your plots or falling in love with insignificant characters. The temptation, which should be strongly resisted, is to jump in and put them right: 'No, this is what I meant, you're reading that wrong ...', and so on. But keeping quiet lets the writer off the hook, and focuses on the work itself, which for many people can be a relief. It helps readers to follow the next good workshop rule, which is to:

Talk about the Work, not the Person

Try to discuss the work as if the writer wasn't there. This may feel awkward and artificial at first, but once established, it avoids giving the writer too much personal attention, which can be uncomfortable, and keeps the attention on the work itself. This means that readers can say something is good or not so good without seeming to flatter or blame the writer personally: it is the draft that is being discussed, and drafts can be changed more easily than personalities.

However, just as writers find it a challenge to keep quiet, many readers also find it difficult to avoid using personal names and pronouns or asking the writer direct questions – 'What did you mean by this word?' 'How did you think of that idea?', etc., etc. – which can lead to distracting debates. It's also best to avoid asking questions or making assumptions about the personal life of the writer unless information is volunteered – 'Is this about your mother, Gemma? Did she really run off with the milkman?' – which may be found intrusive and embarrassing. It also helps if you can learn to use an objective language in discussion: *the* characters (not *your* characters). This practice models the relationship between published writers and readers and it helps the writer to see their work as readers might see it.

Try to Give Fair and Truthful Feedback

In this postmodern age, so many of us mean different things by *truth* that I'm tempted to put speech marks around the word. What I mean is that you should tell the writer what *you* think and feel about their work-in-progress as honestly as you can. This sounds simple and easy, but it isn't. For example, you may not be sure what you think or feel, and you may not be confident about your opinions. This is understandable, particularly if you have not read much in the form of the draft work: if someone submits a sci-fi story, or romance, or a cut-up sonnet series, for example, and you haven't ever read sci-fi or romance and you don't know what a cut-up poem is, then you may think you haven't anything worth saying. Not true.

Another barrier to a truthful response is that you may not warm to the writer, you may not agree with their politics or religion, you may just dislike the woolly jumper they always wear. Maybe they gave your own writing draft the thumbs down and you want to pay them back. On the other hand, you may warm to them so much you're thinking of asking them to go out with you after the workshop. In either case you may be tempted to judge the writing by the way you feel about its writer.

There is also a tendency, particularly within English culture, to be polite, to avoid strong opinions, even positive ones, and also, among many cultures, to conform to what others think. If most of the other workshop members have a particular viewpoint it can be hard to stand against the norm, even if you strongly disagree.

All these difficulties get in the way of an honest response, which is why talking about the work itself and not the person helps. It also helps to remember that you are not there as an expert, but as an ordinary *reader* and you are giving a *reader's* response: a thoughtful, self-aware reader who is open to learning. There's not a lot you can do about liking or not liking people – we're all human – but be aware of the pressures on you to avoid the honest response. Truthfulness doesn't need to be cold, blunt or vaguely nice. The point is to be *helpful and specific* – to find the work's best potential, to describe how and when it works, when it doesn't and what might bring out its best potential.

What Kind of Responses?

The workshop as a whole should pay attention to the work's *big stuff* (themes, story, plot, genre, form, structures, etc.); the *middle-sized* stuff (character, setting, point of view, voice, pace, etc.) and the *small stuff* (vocabulary, sentence structures, imagery, etc.). It may be up to the workshop leader to draw out discussion of elements that haven't been covered. Punctuation and spelling come last. Of course, these must be impeccable on the *final* draft – but we're a long way from that.

The Writer Talks Back

At the end of the discussion the writer could be given a minute or two to respond to any absolutely burning questions, but this has not been a trial, so the writer has no need to defend themselves or their work.

Structured Workshops

Once a group has gained experience and most people are confident about taking part as writers and readers, then you can decide whether you want to structure the process. This doesn't mean that the actual discussion of the work needs to be formal or solemn – just that people give more time and detailed attention to each piece of writing. It is difficult to give honest and realistic feedback off the top of your head, and workshops that over-rely on spontaneity tend to favour already confident people. This is not only unfair to the others but doesn't necessarily produce the most intelligent and creative discussion. These kinds of workshops may take place over a period: say 4 weeks for a group of 12, with each person getting one workshop of 30 minutes each. The above guidelines apply, but there are some added processes that enrich the experience.

Distribute Work in Advance

Ideally, work should be photocopied/emailed/posted on a website and given/sent to the other members of the group a week before, to give them time to read it at least twice and to prepare a thoughtful response.

Writers Ask for Specific Help

Writers should prepare information and questions and attach them to the work. When you give your work to a workshop group you are effectively getting the chance to find out what a group of captive readers think. This is valuable and rare, so make the most of it by asking them to think about the things you want to know the answers to. One way of organising this is to have prepared a cover sheet that all of the group can use and which each person can adapt for their own purposes. I've reproduced one at the end of this chapter, which developed out of one writing workshop.

Readers Give a Written Response to the Questions

It goes without saying that everybody in the group should read the draft carefully and respond to the questions in as much detail as possible, using specific examples from the work. Having to write responses is useful for a number of reasons:

- The writer gets the benefit of all viewpoints, including those of people who may be reticent about *speaking* in groups.

- Written comments may be more considered than spoken ones.

- The effort of paying attention to specific questions and writing down their responses gives everybody in the group good practice in using a critical and creative vocabulary.

- Having to prepare a written response means that readers come to the workshop better able to take part in a discussion.

- The writer can take away the responses and reflect on them later – it can often be hard to take in what is being said in the more heated atmosphere of the workshop.

After the Workshop: What Happens Next?

At the end of the workshop you, the writer, are left with a piece of your own writing plus a lot of feedback. Now you have to go off on your own and look at your work again in light of all this, and this can be difficult. People may have given you contradictory opinions; you may not have agreed with some of them; you may think some are not well founded or that the people who made them lack experience, critical ability or experimental courage. Fine. You don't need to change a single thing if you don't want to and you certainly don't need to incorporate everybody's opinions.

Think of the workshop as a driving lesson: you get lots of good ideas and advice, but once you're on your own in the car with your hands on the wheel, you're in charge. It helps to read the feedback and then to digest it. Take it in, learn what you can, then let it go. You're alone in front of the page again. Time just to write.

Further Reading

John Gardner (2001) *On Becoming a Novelist* (London: Vintage).
   This excellent book includes a substantial section on workshops and classes, which (as long as you ignore the unquestioned assumption that beginning writers are predominantly young men) is inspirational and useful.

WRITING WORKSHOP HANDOUT

Guidelines

- Everybody to present work – how often depends on time and size of group.
- Everybody to give feedback on other people's work.
- Writers to keep quiet while their work is being discussed.
- Discuss the work, not the person.
- Give fair and truthful feedback.
- Allow time for the writer to briefly respond at the end.

Structure

- Each week at least three people should distribute drafts of their work plus Writer's Questions to the group.
- This will be your opportunity to present your writing to the group and get valuable feedback.
- In preparation for this you will need to make and distribute copies of your work in progress. This material should be distributed by e-mail at least ONE WEEK in advance of the workshop.
- In addition, you need to provide a **WRITER'S QUESTION SHEET** – use the model as a guide. All longer projects should also be accompanied by a brief synopsis and a clear indication of where the scene/chapter occurs in the whole. Send a copy of this sheet with your work.
- Each workshop member should give written feedback as well as verbal feedback in the workshop.

WRITER'S QUESTION SHEET

Name of writer

Title of work_____ **Workshop date**_____

FORM, GENRE, etc.? Is this a poem, novel, short story? Is it experimental, romantic comedy, horror, serial drama, detective drama? For longer pieces, add a brief synopsis.

WHERE DOES THIS DRAFT FIT? Beginning, middle, end? Not sure?

WHAT QUESTIONS DO YOU WANT THE READERS TO RESPOND TO?

Dramatic Impact, Narrative Pace, Character, Dialogue, Setting, Time, Language, Vocabulary, Imagery, Voice, Tone, Punctuation, Layout, etc. **The more specific you can be, the better the feedback.**

9 Reflection: Looking Your Words in the Face

Robert Graham and
Heather Leach

We've already learned that writers are readers who write, but perhaps that should be developed further: writers are readers who think carefully about *what* and *how* and *why* they write.

What Is Reflection?

The swiftest source to hand, the dictionary in Microsoft Word, offers eight interpretations of the word 'reflection'. This is the one that comes closest to our meaning:

> Careful thought, especially the process of reconsidering previous actions, events or decisions.

Reflective thinking means stopping and considering what you're doing. It's an opportunity to compare where you are now with where you have come from, a way of discovering how you are changing as a writer and of deciding where you want to go next. Of course, all of us think most of the time about what we are doing – thoughts come and go, some deliberate, some spontaneous. The problem with thought is that it is ephemeral and easily forgotten, which is why we believe that reflection in this context means *reflective writing*. Work of this kind enables you to record, order and shape your thoughts into useful insights and meanings. In this chapter we will suggest a number of ways that you might go about this.

Writers Reflect On Their Work

In an essay called 'I Am A ... Genius!' the American short-story writer Thom Jones talks about the occasion when, after decades of struggle, he sold three stories in the same afternoon – to *Harper's*, *Esquire* and *The New Yorker* – which, in poker terms, is like finding yourself holding a royal flush.

> After getting lost and being found time and again, the writers who don't quit discover the ecstasy within the process of the work itself.[1] They discover the sublime joy of seeing things come together to produce an artistic whole. You read books and love them and someday hope to have the talent and vision to write your own.[2]

Jones is using the space to reflect on the joys as well as the struggle. It's always worth recording the good moments – and, as he says, there will almost certainly be some, if you stick at it.

Next, here's Bobbie Ann Mason commenting on the way she approaches characters:

> I wrote a novel (it was never published) about a twelve-year-old girl, a sort of female Huck Finn. When I was in graduate school I had a wonderful teacher who said, 'in the future you're going to see a shift, where the hero instead of trying to get out of society is trying to get in. I didn't know what to make of that, but I thought about it when I started writing about characters who had never been at the centre, who had never had the advantage of being able to criticise society enough to leave it.[3]

Here's another novelist, Lawrence Norfolk, describing the process of completing his third novel, *In the Shape of a Boar*. Notice how he goes into detail about the structure and form of the book, but also comments on his own state of mind, his anxieties:

> All the editing that is going to be done has been done. The book has to be copy-edited, a process which will be complicated by the presence of the footnotes, and this has to start now. The problems in Part One have been solved (more or less) by reversing the drift of explanatory material towards the back of the section and placing it at the front, which is where readers will find it useful. The tonal shifts in Part Two have been much harder to iron out. There seem to be a lot of different causes (implied flash-backs creating 'false' time-frames, accidents of wording seeming to know more than has so far been narrated, varying distances between narrators and materials) but they all signal strain within the narrative framework as a whole. My instincts about three time frames being one too many seem to have been right, but the structure needs re-engineering, not just cutting. I get to work on that and the tone-problems start to disappear. Two paragraphs vex me in particular, which is usually a sign that the major problem is being solved; the residual anxiety has to go somewhere.[4]

Why do you think he keeps a diary about the completion of a novel? Could it be that he needs to in order to complete?

About 2500 years ago, the Greek philosopher Socrates proposed that the unexamined life was not worth living, the implication perhaps being that by examining your life, you may live it better. A good enough reason maybe, but what we're talking about here is not an examination of your whole life but of your life and work as a writer in order to help you write better. All writers worth the name reflect on their work in some way or other, and they're not the only ones doing it.

If you went through the British secondary education system any time after the late 1980s, you will have been prompted to reflect on your learning as part of your Record of Achievement. If you're a student in higher education now, you will be asked to reflect in a Personal Development Plan. If you work for any largish organisation, you and your line manager will reflect when you have your annual appraisal. If you're a parent, you, your child and your child's teacher are reflecting at parents' evenings. Most of us have already had some relevant experience, although we may not have developed a focused approach to writing about our own work.

For the first exercise in this chapter, you won't need to be an expert in reflective writing, but it will help that you already know how to redraft (and for more guidance see Chapter 10, 'Revision').

Try This: Reading Yourself

Take a draft of a recent piece of writing, ask yourself a series of questions about it, and write down your answers.

■ Why did I want to write this piece in the first place? Where did it come from? Where did I get the idea?

■ Has the original idea changed? In what ways?

■ Why am I writing in this form (short story/novel/script/poem, etc.)? What effect would a change of form make? What would I gain or lose?

■ Which books, texts, films, etc., have influenced or inspired me in this writing? In which ways?

■ What problems have occurred in writing it? How have I resolved them? What problems remain?

Why Reflect?

Writing can be a lonely business. We spend many solitary hours a week looking at the blank screen, and as many hours again buried in a book. As a writer, you need someone to discuss your writing with, and that person will often end up being yourself. (Is it any wonder that the writer Jack Nicholson played in *The Shining* flipped?)

It helps you to look back and remember and it helps you look ahead and dream. It gives you a sense of continuity and authenticity in a hard world. In other words, it makes you real to yourself as a writer, helps you make yourself up as a writer as you go along.

Good reflective writing is a way of thinking; it's a dialogue with yourself. As you reflect, you will find out what you think about your own work, but also about your reading. Reflection makes you write about your writing and reading experiences and thus discover your opinions. The process makes them real and builds interconnections: thought is ephemeral and often vague – writing is more solid and useable. As E.M. Forster said, 'How do I know what I think until I see what I say?'

As we've already seen, reflection is a way of developing your writing; that may be its key function. To reinforce the point, here's Michael Cunningham, reflecting on the way his Pulitzer Prize-winning novel *The Hours* evolved:

> I tried to more thoroughly incorporate [Virginia Woolf's novel] *Mrs Dalloway* into my book. And when I looked at what I had, it felt a little lifeless. It had a certain precision that was more like a Swiss music box than a novel.
>
> I went back and read *Mrs Dalloway* again and was reminded that part of what I love about that novel is its looseness, its riff-ish quality. The way it reads almost like a jazz musician playing improvisations ...And I decided it would be more appropriate, it would be a better tribute to *Mrs Dalloway* if I loosened up my own book, if I didn't insist on strict parallels, if I injected into *The Hours* a rough correspondence to *Mrs Dalloway* and didn't insist upon making it precise.[5]

Reflective writing is complementary. It goes alongside the creative work. A finished piece of reflection is arguably creative writing in its own right. Reflection will help you read and write better. You will learn to be a more self-conscious, more self-critical writer than you might otherwise have been, and you will have a better understanding of the context into which your writing may fit.

But writing reflective pieces about your own work is not only essential to help you understand the kind of writer you are, and it's not only about aiding your growth as a writer; it will also have enormous value to you when you are publishing and promoting your work. For example, in the literary sections of newspapers or websites, never a week will go by without the appearance of features written by authors who have a book to plug. At the time of writing, William Boyd – author of many novels, including *Any Human Heart* – has a new play opening in London. Since the play came out of conflating and dramatising two Chekhov stories, he wrote a feature for the *Guardian* that examined relevant aspects of Chekhov's life and reflected on Boyd's experience of adapting these stories for the stage. Similarly, when the latest big-screen adaptation of *Great Expectations* opened a few months back, its screenwriter David Nicholls (*One Day*, *Starter For Ten*) published a newspaper feature about the challenges of adapting a novel that has had many previous TV and cinema incarnations.

A writer's reflection won't always be written, either: almost all interviews that writers do to promote their work are reflective in tone, and some of the time such reflection will be in a TV or radio programme or a podcast. Just this week, I listened to Kate Atkinson on BBC Radio 4's *Open Book* talking about the writing of her latest novel, *Life After Life*. Everything she said was to do with her understanding of her craft and the particular technical challenges of writing this novel.

Reflection, in other words, is an essential part of the way professional writers promote their work.

Writing a Reflection

Let's unpack the term a little more and look at some of the details.

To produce worthwhile reflective writing, you will need particular disciplines. You will need to be self-critical and self-aware. Self-criticism does not mean negativity, but having a willingness to look carefully at your writing with an open and honest frame of mind: to learn to see what the writing says to you. At a fundamental level, you will need to be able to read as a writer. (See Chapter 7, 'Reading as a Writer'.)

Reflection involves examining the process of writing and finding ways to express an understanding of that process. Here you will explore the experiences that have informed the writing – including, if you are in a class, the stimulus you may have been given to work from.

You might think about what your intentions were at the outset, how well you have fulfilled them and how they may have changed during redrafting. You may discuss any problems encountered and the strategies that were employed to overcome them.

At the moment of finishing it, most writers think a first draft is good – which may be followed quickly by the feeling that it is useless. But how can you revise a draft unless you read it from a critical perspective? In redrafting, you must make decisions about what's good and what needs to change, but the one thing you should avoid is making value judgements about the overall quality of the finished work. You can be fairly certain that you will either overrate or underrate its worth; you aren't in a position to see the wood for the trees.

By now you've got some idea of what reflection is and why you should engage in it. You've read examples of writers reflecting, you've been given some indication of how you might reflect on your own work, and, with the last exercise you've made a start on it. In a moment, you'll get a chance to work on a more substantial piece of reflection. First, let's look at some useful ways to get going (and some potential pitfalls).

Possible Approaches

Reflection is probably connected with the writer's journal. The journal is often the place where you record thoughts and experiences, where you work out ideas, and that may be where you would do much of what follows here.

- Write down the inspirations for this piece of work – where the ideas came from.

- Write a short commentary on any books or films that have influenced you: in what ways can their influences be traced?

- Write about what you originally intended.

- Write about the problems you've come up against and how you've dealt with them.

- Explain why you chose this particular genre or form: script, poetry, short story, and so on. Justify your reasons in terms of narrative, aesthetic, structure, etc.

- Discuss the elements of craft you've studied: dialogue, narrative, structure, pace. How have you applied them to this piece, and what have you learned as a result?

- Describe how the piece has been redrafted and for what reasons.

- If anyone has already read the work or it has been discussed in a writers' workshop, write about the ways that the response has influenced your redrafting.

- Write about yourself as a writer in this place and time: why do you want to write? What kind of writer are you? What kind would you like to be? What is your philosophy of writing; your manifesto?

Possible Pitfalls

- Retelling the story is pointless and won't make very interesting reading, especially where the audience for your reflection has access to the creative work.

- It may be unhelpful to be too self-conscious: you need to strike a balance between self-awareness and overemphasis on inner motivations and emotions. What is important is that the reflective process is meant to help you write better, so keep your eye on the work itself.

- When you read a reflective chapter or article that a writer has constructed for publication, all nicely turned out and tidied up, bear in mind that this is just another narrative. As with recording history, there is no objective truth in writing – only subjective versions of it.

Try This: Reflective Writing

We suggested above that your journal might be where much of your reflective writing takes place, which perhaps means that shorter forms of reflection are more improvised than perfected. However, a formal piece of reflective writing is more polished, more shaped. This may be because you intend it for public consumption, but possibly it is more likely that you shape it and polish it to make it more incisive, more useful to yourself as you refine the work about which you are reflecting.

Write a 1000-word piece of reflection with the focus on your growth as a writer over the past year (or an appropriate period for you).

Use the list above as a way in. You might begin by making a spider diagram, or mind-map, of what you want to include.

Forget about being comprehensive; instead aim to be heterogeneous. Choose the themes or factors that appeal to you at this moment and then mix the ingredients together as you might when baking a cake. It will help if you can construct a narrative or a line of argument that is cohesive, and includes transitions where sharp changes of subject matter occur.

Finally, to give you a model of a learner writer's reflection, at the end of the book we've appended two thoughtful and detailed pieces, which we hope will inspire you to begin writing your own. And, for people in higher education, there's an appendix that looks at research into reflective writing.

Further Reading

As well as the works cited in this chapter, you might find it helpful to look at the following sources of writers reflecting.

Dan Crowe and Philip Oltermann (eds) (2007) *How I Write: The Secret Lives of Authors* (New York and London: Rizzoli).

Sixty writers discuss their writing process in a beautifully designed and illustrated text.

Ten Rules for Writing Fiction, http://www.guardian.co.uk/books/2010/feb/20/ten-rules-for-writing-fiction (accessed 8 November 2012).

An article on the *Guardian* website. Twenty-nine successful writers give their 10 rules for writers, some witty, some tongue-in-cheek, some serious, some passionate, some wise – all entertaining, and essential for the would-be fiction writer. Maybe you could list your own ten rules, as a way to reflect on your own writing practice.

A Painful Glimpse Into My Writing Process [In Less Than 60 Seconds], http://vimeo.com/11840931 (accessed 8 November 2012).

Made and directed by Chel White and written by Steve Poole. Dark, funny, but ultimately encouraging, this film explores territory that will be all-too familiar to most writers.

Example of a Reflection (with annotated bibliography)

Angi Holden (MMU Cheshire student, graduated 2010)

As soon as one reality TV series ends, another begins.

'It's been an amazing journey,' the presenter coos. As a part-time student looking back over my 'journey' I might add, 'And a long one', but that would be no complaint. The major advantage of part-time study is the time it allows for reflection, and the greater opportunity to assimilate what is learnt into the creative process.

During this year my focus for W3 has been short stories, whilst my C3 writing has been for topic-based essays. The modules are not entirely discrete. Nor are they separate from the other writing activities I've undertaken during Year Three – educational placements, courses with The Poetry School, and writing for my Scripts and Media modules. Each facet of my writing life informs the others.

Just as the different aspects of my writing overlap, so the varied elements of my reading influence my work. I continue to read a wide and eclectic mixture of books – novels, short stories, memoir, poetry. And of course, craft texts.

During my first year we researched craft texts, sharing our findings. Based on recommendations, I've developed a growing collection of craft books. Though never a substitute for writing itself, they are invaluable. I consult them regularly, mainly to compare advice on a particular aspect such as dialogue or setting, or to find ideas for resolving a specific problem that I've encountered in my writing, such as transitions between scenes.

Increasingly however, I find that I'm browsing with a more general approach, consolidating what I've learned and reminding myself of things that I've forgotten. Chatting with an online writing buddy I wrote:

> You need to know what your character had for breakfast, whether she caught a bus or walked to the library, what was in her handbag. You don't need to include all the details, but you need to know them.

Then I had to go to my shelf to look for the origins of the advice. Carver? Chandler? Who knows – easily diverted, I spent a pleasurable hour scrolling through my craft books and class notes.

Which brings me to another part of my writing process – notebooks and journals. I always take notes during class and workshops, returning to them later to convert the mess of scribbles into a more functional framework. I have spiral-bound notebooks going back to Year One: a session on beginnings and endings; a spidergram for developing a narrative; an exercise for building characters. Some individual projects – a particular story or a themed collection of poetry – have individual notebooks containing not only the drafts and redrafts of the 'target' writing, but also discussion of the writing process. I will continue to work this way as it helps me resolve problems and later reminds me how I overcame them.

Other notebooks contain ideas for writing. Some of these may be of the 'overheard in a coffee-shop' variety or online stories. The BBC website is a great source of quirky items – today's offerings include an article on official War Artists and another on deactivating Facebook, an obituary of the French Resistance fighter 'Agent Rose' and news of a volcanic dust cloud. Other writing stimuli may come from class exercises or craft books, from artefacts or from visits to museums or galleries.

Websites can also help, such as Jo Bell's blog, which invites responses to topics including 'work' or 'foolishness'. I also use several handmade books of writing stimuli – an overheard conversation, a photograph, a newspaper headline – compiled by my daughter.

Many of the scraps of writing that come from these stimuli go no further, but the basic exercise of moving the pen across the paper is still beneficial.

Occasionally however, a fragment from a writing burst, say a visualisation exercise, may become raw material for a longer piece of writing. More often, a couple of unrelated stimuli interact, and either form the basis of a narrative or provide an alternative angle for looking at a particular theme. Michael Morpurgo describes the way in which the simple image of a watch enabled him to unlock the difficult narrative of *Private Peaceful*.

Morpurgo also discusses the way in which a plot line or character awakens his interest:

> I find I can't leave it alone; it bothers me, provokes me, fascinates me. I research around it, dream around it, let the story weave itself together in my head. I have to give the story the time it needs to develop.

This method of incubating a story is familiar to me. In both W3 short-story submissions, living with the character and ongoing research and reflection were vital ingredients in weaving together the individual narrative threads.

Writing a complete draft at an early stage is also important for getting the maximum benefit from the workshop process. The feedback of fellow writers prepared to take the time to provide constructive comment is a rare gift, not to be wasted on under-prepared work. Having completed, and redrafted, my writing I had to be prepared to redraft again in response to feedback. As a writer, you know what you intend. If the reader fails to get the message you have to take responsibility for that failure.

Sometimes, however, reader response may be a matter of taste, whether in respect of style, genre, content or subject matter. A published short story I read recently had a particularly nauseating storyline and my response was negative. However, reading as a writer I focused on the writing craft. Similarly, when listening to feedback on my work I've paid most attention to craft aspects – inconsistencies of narrative, moments where the action isn't clear or the dialogue is inappropriate – rather than suggestions that a plotline might have a different outcome.

This confidence to stand by my work has been hard-won over a long period. Looking back on my early process notes I find a passage:

I do more than 'accept criticism' – I try to use it to develop, as a focus for improvement.

As I've progressed through the course I've developed a greater sense of my own 'writing voice' and the confidence to redraft in response to feedback without losing ownership of my narrative.

Over the last year I've explored several themes in my writing. What has emerged in any particular assignment is only a fragment, a snapshot of my writing life, and I have a number of ideas that I want to develop further.

I have made an end-of-course promise to myself to continue to read widely, workshop my writing regularly and redraft rigorously.

Annotated Bibliography

Craft texts

Dorothea Brande (1934) *Becoming a Writer* (London: Macmillan).
   As Malcolm Bradbury put it, this 'isn't a book about How to Write a Novel ... it's about the mysterious process of first becoming a writer, acquiring writerly instincts'.

Natalie Goldberg (2000) *Thunder and Lightning* (Boston: Shambhala).
  An inspirational writer, Goldberg has a refreshing approach, and an effective antidote to writers' block. Like Brande, her emphasis is on the process of becoming a writer rather than the mechanics of getting published.
Stephen King (2000) *On Writing: A Memoir of the Craft* (New York: Scribner).
  Split into two parts: the memoir, which he calls 'CV', and 'On Writing', which offers advice about writing practice. 'On Writing' doesn't provide the 'course exercise' approach, but it is interesting and highly readable.
George Plimpton (1989) *The Writer's Chapbook* (Harmondsworth: Penguin).
  This is described as a compendium of 'Fact, Opinion, Wit and Advice', which about sums it up.

Fiction: short stories

Julia Bell and Jackie Gay (eds) (2001) *England Calling* (London: Phoenix).
  Modern stories with a mainly urban setting, that look at the nature of life in the contemporary landscape, by authors such as Andrea Ashworth, Jane Rogers and Joolz Denby.
Nadine Gordimer (1991) *Jump and Other Stories* (London: Penguin).
Laura Hird (1997) *Nail and Other Stories* (Edinburgh: Canongate).
  Neither of these collections appealed to me. However, reading as a writer gave me a different insight, allowing me to learn from the authors' writing craft, particularly their ability to handle dramatic tension.
D. Minshull (ed.) (1992) *Telling Stories* (London: Coronet).
D. Minshull (ed.) (1993) *Telling Stories Vol. 2* (London: Coronet).
  Selections of the best of BBC Radio's short fiction, including gems like Richard Burns's *Perfect Strangers*.
Ra Page (ed.) (1999) *The City Life Book of Manchester Short Stories* (Harmondsworth: Penguin). Includes 'The Afghan Coat' by Heather Leach.
  The collections of short stories that I have found the most interesting and useful during the last year include:

Fiction: novels

Poppy Adams (2008) *The Behaviour of Moths* (London: Virago).
Sara Gruen (2006) *Water for Elephants* (New York: Workman).
Deirdre Madden (2009) *Molly Fox's Birthday* (London: Faber).
Cormac McCarthy (2007) *The Road* (London: Picador).
   Perhaps my favourite reads of the last year. Adams creates a wonderful, eccentric, obsessive protagonist; Madden and Gruen present portraits of intertwined lives viewed in flashbacks during a single day; McCarthy creates a page-turning story from a relentless and harrowing walk along a road. If I read four books as impressive as these during the next 12 months, I shall be delighted.

10 Revision: Cut It Out, Put It In

Robert Graham

The wastepaper basket is the writer's best friend.

Isaac Bashevis Singer[1]

Singer's observation is simply irrefutable. Any committed writer will not only have boxes and boxes of printed-off and discarded drafts but endless digital folders of work in progress. Raymond Carver claimed to do up to thirty drafts of a story, and never fewer than ten. Tolstoy was always revising – right through to the galley-proof stage. And Yann Martel, author of the 2002 Booker Prize-winner, *Life of Pi*, is so bent on getting the words right that he is happy to finish a day's work having written a page.

Fiction is made through a mixture of drafting and redrafting, and obviously there can be no redrafting without the first drafting that precedes it. However, for me, redrafting is where the real business of shaping fiction is done. (And don't forget, this is where you are free to unleash your internal critic, your conscious mind – a fatal inhibition when you're writing a first draft, but you won't be able to redraft without using it.)

The poet John Ashbery claims that

because of my strong desire to avoid all unnecessary work, I have somehow trained myself not to write something that I will either have to discard or be forced to work a great deal over.[2]

I wish I knew how he has achieved this happy knack! Like Bernard Malamud, who says, 'Revision is one of the true pleasures of writing',[3]

I love revision, and I particularly like cutting. Last week I heard a radio programme about James Joyce's *Ulysses*. At one point, the presenter alluded to the fact that Joyce, while revising the galley proofs – in other words, while making a final check before the book was printed – expanded the whole by one-third. *One-third*. I don't think I have always done it, but in recent years, by the time I have finished with the first draft of a novel in manuscript, I have *reduced* it by at least a third. Maybe I'm a sloppy writer of first drafts. Whatever, I love redrafting. One aspect of what you're doing is polishing, finishing off. When you've worked on something for a year or two, what's not to like about polishing and finishing off?

At one stage, the word-count of my last but one novel was 115 000. Later, it had shrunk to 93 000, and the final draft was less than 73 000. In Ashbery's terms, this is wasteful. However, even if I could do anything about the waste, I suspect I would not. I like the story of the sculptor who was asked how he made such lifelike sculptures of his subjects: 'I start with a block of stone and then I remove everything that doesn't look like the subject.' The real shaping of a piece of writing is in the revision process. Furthermore, I would argue that fiction isn't created simply through invention followed by revision: as we have seen, invention leads to revision, but revision leads to more invention.

So. That sounds pretty straightforward: take out the stuff that doesn't belong and leave everything else.

Try This: The Things You Make Them Carry

At the beginning of the story, the writer is giving the reader things. Think of them as things they will need – sleeping bags, a knife, a snack, a compass – as they climb the hill you are sending them up. You don't want the reader getting to the top and being pissed off about the things you made them carry up the hill for no reason.[4]

Using a draft of one of your stories, go to what amounts to the top of the hill in the narrative and see what readers actually need when they get there. Now begin at the beginning and search for and remove all the extraneous information you have burdened them with in the early stages of the narrative.

A Few Words about Revision

I'll get into some detail about revision in a moment, but first a few pieces of general advice. I don't honestly think there is much point in trying to revise until you have a complete first draft. You risk never finishing a first draft if you keep stopping to rework. Revising is a matter of looking at your work and seeing what it says to you – as Jane Smiley puts it here:

> Your only task is to let what you have talk back to you and teach you what is missing or superfluous or not quite right, and then to suggest what would be better than what you have.[5]

A further consideration is that you won't get anywhere trying to revise immediately after you've completed a first draft. You need distance from the story; you need perspective. Revising is seeing the story afresh. Janet Burroway has this advice:

> Put it away. Don't look at it for a matter of days or weeks – until you feel fresh on the project. In addition to getting some distance on your story, you're nailing it to your unconscious.[6]

The main thrust of this quotation is important, and obvious enough. It's probably just worth emphasising the value of the closing point. Revising is perhaps a combination of wrestling with things in your conscious mind and giving up and leaving them to your unconscious mind. It's what people do when they say they are going to sleep on an impending decision.

It's also helpful to remember that you don't have to approach the task of revision all by yourself. When it comes to freshness you will be hard-pressed to beat that which readers bring to your work. They might only confirm things that you knew yourself, but often they will see things that you can't – because they're not you. I think I developed the habit early on of farming my work out to friends who would generously look at it and offer their responses. However, I don't believe I would ever have thought to join a writer's group had I not been thrust into one by the experience of doing an MA in Creative Writing. That was nearly twenty years ago, and I benefited so much from the feedback on my work offered by the workshop members that I have made sure to be in a workshop (see Chapter 8) or group ever since. The advantages are great. It offers you an audience, which every writer needs, and in having one, I think it gives you more confidence and helps you to think of yourself as a writer. For what it's worth, I approach processing this form of feedback in the following way. I jot down everything that everyone says unless it is plain stupid – very rare. Then I live with the advice for a while and eventually use the suggestions that still appeal a few weeks later.

A lot of writers swear by reading the work aloud – even better if it's to somebody else, because as you read it out you will see it through their eyes. In the absence of an audience, you will still find reading aloud to yourself an effective way of finding flaws in your writing. Read it to the wall.

One other thing before we move on: don't think revising is just about eliminating the bad stuff; sometimes you will have to eliminate good material, too. 'Murder your darlings', G.K. Chesterton famously wrote. In revising, you will almost always have to remove phrases, sentences, paragraphs or whole chapters, not because they don't work in themselves – but because they *don't work there*.

The rest of this chapter consists of two lengthy writing exercises, for each of which you will need a first draft. Use the same first draft for both exercises. As you work at these exercises, bear in mind that good fiction is not written, it is *rewritten*. I have yet to meet the Writing student who redrafts too much. In writing fiction, you should do as many drafts of a story as you have time to.

Technical Redrafting

Interviewer: How much rewriting do you do?

Hemingway: It depends. I rewrote the ending to *Farewell to Arms*, the last page of it, thirty-nine times before I was satisfied.

Interviewer: Was there some technical problem there? What was it that had stumped you?

Hemingway: Getting the words right.[7]

Maybe some of what separates Hemingway from you and me is this obsessive attention to redrafting? In *The Fiction Editor, The Novel, and the Novelist*, Thomas McCormack talks first about the 'dermal' flaw.[8] The dermal consists of blemishes on the surface of the novel, and McCormack lists a good many examples of them:

Failures of diction, grace, freshness, materiality, credibility, pace, vividness, under-standability, interest ... clichés, repetitions, stale modifiers, abstract generalities where concrete specificities are needed; phrases, images, and metaphors that simply misfire.[9]

Although 'understandability' is precisely the sort of word you might hope to improve when redrafting, these are all failings that are worthy of your attention when you come to revise. As Jonathan Swift put it, 'Proper words in proper places make the true definition of style.' For my money, however, the most common form of dermal flaw has less to do with style than what McCormack is talking about. The most common form of dermal flaw, and the one that needs your attention first, is when your writing is simply technically wrong. The 'Paragraphing and Punctuation' section in Part IV, 'Help', contains useful advice on technical redrafting – on layout, punctuation and grammar.

Equally common, equally important is the whole area of meaning and clarity. Does what you have written mean what you intended? Are your sentences accurate? Clear? Unambiguous? It's a question of getting the words right and in the correct order. This begins with choosing the correct word. You *lend* a book and your friend *borrows* it – not the other way round. Did you mean *affect* when you wrote *effect*? If you put the words in the wrong order their meaning will be obscured.

Try This: Technical Redrafting in Action

Take a draft of something you've been working on, or something from your journal. If it's on a word processor, print it out: reading for drafting is often easier when the work is on paper rather than the screen. Read it. Apply the above prompts to it. (Now you'll see why double spacing is so useful: it enables you to scribble between the lines, noting the changes you want to make.)

Creative Redrafting

The second kind of flaw that McCormack recognises, the internal flaw, is more serious and harder to diagnose. McCormack lists among its symptoms the following:

> A disappointed sense of its not meeting us at the station, of its having missed some unnameable opportunity, of its lacking a life-supporting temperature, of inertness, of inconsequence, of meaninglessness to events, of something, somewhere in the book, gone profoundly awry.[10]

Internal flaws are not only difficult to diagnose, they're troublesome and time-consuming to fix: you may find yourself having to unravel and remove a whole sub-plot. Speaking of which, it's probably worth saying that many internal flaws concern the plot. So, before you have a go at the next writing exercise, here are a few well-chosen questions that Jane Smiley poses on the matter of revising plot:

Is it clear who the characters are? Is it clear what the conflict is, and whom it is between? Does the reader have a concrete sense of where the characters are in space and time? Is there a climax or is the climax implied rather than depicted? Is the climax dramatic enough, long enough, weighty enough to balance the length of the rising action? Does the denouement get the reader gracefully and meaningfully out of the climax? Does the denouement bring the story to a state of equilibrium?[11]

A Checklist for Creative Redrafting

This might take some time: redrafting is not something you start an hour before a submission deadline.

Narrative tension

- Does your story intrigue the reader at once? What is the first reader question? How soon does it come?

- Does the story begin at the beginning (or towards the bottom of the first page)?

- Is the dialogue dull, or is real conflict expressed?

- Does the dialogue move the plot along?

- Drama is life with the dull parts left out. Have you left the dull parts in?

- Have you told the reader what you should have shown?

- Is there always something at stake? Or are you chewing with no gum?

- By the end of a scene, things will no longer be as they were at the beginning. This is even more the case when thinking of the whole story.

- Have scenes been fully developed? Look for implicit drama in what's written and think of ways to milk it more than you did in the first draft.

- If you have used flashback or exposition on the first page, get rid of it.

- Is the story too internal? (Have you spent too much time inside the character's head?)

- Is the conflict static? Jumping? It ought to rise steadily.

- Does the story end when it should? (Or does it run on after the end has been reached?)

- Does the ending satisfy?

Common flaws

- Are you in viewpoint? (Your reader can only *know, hear* and *see* what the viewpoint character can. Make sure you haven't slipped into another character's viewpoint by mistake.)

- Have you shifted out of one tense and into another?

Characters

- Have you used more characters than you really need?

- Do your characters always speak and act characteristically?

- Avoid giving characters names with the same initial letter.

- Remember that things happen off the page. It's appealing when the reader learns that a character has a life of his or her own, away from the plot of this story.

- Have you told the reader how your characters feel? Don't. Let the reader discover how a character feels through action and dialogue – what the character says and does.

Style

I hope Chapter 18, 'Style', may be of some help to you when it comes to developing your writing, but here are a few further details to consider when looking at drafts to revise the style:

- Is there too much description?

- Is your description static? (The ideal is that description is incorporated into action and dialogue.)

- Is your description specific enough? (*A Ford* rather than *a car*.)

- Is there too much action?

- Are you writing with verbs and nouns?

- Have you avoided clichés?

- Have you removed all superfluous speech tags?

- Are your speech tags plain and without the encumbrance of an adverb?

- Have you written directly? Make cumbersome sentences straightforward. Remove anything that delays the information going straight from your head to the reader's.

- Weed out vocabulary repeats – the same word used twice in quick succession.

- Watch out for redundancies. ('They met at 8 a.m. in the morning.')

- Is there an interpretation of any sentence that is not the one you intend?

- Have you avoided qualifying what you say? (Get it right in one.)

- Have you used active and not passive language? ('He took her to the shops', not 'She was taken to the shops.')

- Any weak intensifiers? ('The dog was totally dead.')

- Do a word search for 'seemed'. If you find it used often, replace it with alternatives.

Try This: Into Action on the Creative Battlefield

Use the same piece of work as before. Or select another. Apply the checklist to it. Some points may be more pertinent than others, or you may wish to track merely for characters, theme or description. You can redraft by scribbling over the printout, or cutting up paragraphs with scissors to reorder them. Use nice pens. Enjoy the process!

Further Reading

Raymond Carver (1993) *Where I'm Calling From* (London: Harvill).

    Carver is the king of economy. If you want to see how bare a sentence can be, read any of his collections of short stories. (This one collects together nearly all his stories.) The language isn't just missing the flab, it has been cut to the bone. Carver's style isn't for everyone, but study him and you will conclude that your prose needs to go on a diet.

James Friel (2001) 'Redrafting Your Novel', in Julia Bell and Paul Magrs (eds) *The Creative Writing Coursebook* (London: Macmillan), pp. 261–70.

    This consists of a list of the things you should be ('Be Kind', 'Be Curious', 'Be Stealthy') when revising. The structure may be playful, but the advice is good, and – as befits the subject matter – succinct.

II
ON THE ROAD

11 Layout for Fiction and Memoir

Robert Graham

Roughly every decade, the conventions of layout for fiction shift. At the time of writing, here's my understanding of the current view of how to lay out your short story, novel or memoir.

- Make sure your work is double-spaced.

- Use one side of the paper only and number your pages.

- Don't indent the first line of your story.

- Thereafter, every first line of each new paragraph should be indented.

- When you go to a new scene or section, press return on your keyboard twice to leave one line's-worth of white space. But do *not* do this after a paragraph in other circumstances – the extra space indicates a break between scenes. Don't indent the first line of a new section.

- Each new speaker requires a new paragraph (new speaker, new paragraph). Malcolm Bradbury, amongst others, abandoned this convention in 1970s novels such as *The History Man*. Personally, I think life is too short and too fast for readers to have to stop and work out which character is speaking.

- Each suggested shift of focus (from one character to another) needs a new paragraph. New person, new paragraph: help the reader easily understand who is acting or speaking.

These are guidelines to help ensure that your prose looks like that you would find in any contemporary book. However, there is more to the way you lay out your writing than simply following conventions. The way your page looks will affect readers, and so it is important to think carefully about the way you design it.

White Space: Page Design

Page design amounts largely to the use of white space, and I regard it as an important element in the reader's perception of the fiction. Mike Sharples, in *How We Write*, argues that page design

> assists in the communication of information…Each choice we, as writers, make in laying out text…on the page generates multiple meanings for its readers.[1]

White space can be used to make the page accessible and inviting to the reader. Sharples articulates this inclination nicely:

> In a novel, the writer's implicit contract with the reader is that, in general, the writer will make it as easy as possible for the reader to keep moving from one word and sentence to the next.[2]

With this in mind, both at the composing and the revising stages, it may be helpful to use short paragraphs and speeches in dialogue that are generally no longer than a line or two. It's also useful – indeed, it's currently a convention of fiction writing – to use extra spacing to show that a scene is over. As Sharples says, white space can be used to 'indicate breaks in meaning [and] signal the macro-structure to the reader'.

In its day, Fay Weldon's use of the page, particularly in her novel *Puffball*, was innovative. She was influenced in this by her background in advertising, where the most effective work carries a minimal amount of text (see, for instance, almost any print advertisement).

The logic behind this awareness of white space is that we live in a visual society. Just as description in nearly all contemporary fiction acknowledges the fact that most readers will know what most things look like, so I think intelligent use of white space acknowledges that contemporary readers aren't nearly as text-friendly as their nineteenth-century forebears. As Sharples writes, 'research suggests that readers prefer text to be set in a more open manner'. However, it is perhaps Weldon herself who best theorises this approach:

> Designers and topographers actually teach you to look upon the page. Words are given resonance by their positions, they must be displayed properly. If you wish to give something emphasis, you surround it by space.[3]

If you want proof that the way you fill your page has an effect on your readers, compare these two pages. (The passages were whole pages in their original context.) The first is from William Golding's *The Spire*:

In this dark and wet, it took Jocelin all this will to remember that something important was being done; and when a workman fell through the hole above the crossways, and left a scream scored all the way down the air which was so thick it seemed to keep the scream as something mercilessly engraved there, he did not wonder that no miracle interposed between the body and the logical slab of stone received it. Father Anselm said nothing in chapter; but he saw from the Sacrist's indignant stare how this death had been added to some account that one day would be presented. A dark night had not descended on the cathedral, but a midday without sun and therefore blasphemously without hope. There was hysteria in the laughter of the choirboys when the chancellor, tottering at the end of their procession from the vestry, turned left as he had done for half his life, instead of right to go into the Lady Chapel. Despite this laughter, these sniggers, the services went on, and business was done; but as in the burden of some overwhelming weight. Chapter was testy, song school was dull or fretful and full of coughing, and the boys quarrelled without knowing why. Little boys cried for no reason ... [4]

The second passage is from Melissa Bank's *The Girl's Guide to Hunting and Fishing*:

Bella says, "We are just here until my stepfather sells the house."
   "How is Alberto?" Jamie asks Bella.
   I ask Yves, "What do you do?"
   Bella stops talking and turns to listen.
   "What do I do?" Yves says. "Take pictures. Write novels. Play the piano."
   I say, "I didn't see a piano."
   He tells me that Europeans are different from Americans – not so single-minded about careers. "The most important thing is to live freely."
   I say, "Live free or die, I guess."

Back at the house, I smoke a cigarette on the veranda before going to bed.
   Yves comes out. "Jane?" he says, and kisses my cheek so slowly it's like his lips are melting onto my skin. "Good night."
   In the bedroom I ask Jamie, "What's going on?"
   "What do you mean?" He's almost asleep.
   "Well, something is."
   He doesn't answer. I wonder if it is because he doesn't know.[5]

Let's be clear: I'm not talking about the comparative quality of the prose or of the narrative in these two pages – and obviously I deliberately chose them to support my case, but you tell me: which one is more inviting, more reader-friendly?

Some basic strategies will maximise white space on a page; dialogue, for one. Golding uses none, while Bank uses quite a bit. The length of the speeches is a factor too: the longest in the Bank extract is only two lines, and most are one line or half a line. Paragraphing is important. Golding has only one, which in fact runs on to almost a further page in length, whereas Bank has many. Not only that; the longest paragraph on her page is three lines. Finally, you can see from the Bank excerpt that page-breaks (an extra space dividing two paragraphs, which denotes a change of scene or a break between sections) also add to the volume of white space on a page.

Try This: Page Design

Examine the first draft of a piece of fiction you have written.

- Dialogue. Look for ways to tighten up dialogue. Is there superfluous material here that should go? Speeches that ought to be shorter?

- Paragraphs. Check that you have taken a new paragraph for each new speaker. Look carefully at any paragraphs that are half a page or more in length – see if you can't split them in two (or three).

- Scenes or sections. Have you left a page-break where one scene or section ends and another begins?

12 Characterisation
Robert Graham

You can't have credible action without characters (although you can have characters without action). However, it may be oversimplifying to see the two as a hierarchy. As Henry James pointed out, the relationship between character and action is too interdependent for that:

> What is character but the determination of incident? What is incident but the illustration of character?[1]

Where Do Characters Come From?

Characters that aren't drawn from life won't be fully realised. We all know enough interesting people to prompt a lifetime's worth of characters for our writing, but you don't need to use that uncle with the allotment in all his complex glory: you might just use the fact that he lives for his allotment. Then you might add in a characteristic you've noted in one of your neighbours – that she will often lock her front door on leaving the house, then go back to check that she really has locked it. Your characters, therefore, may be a conflation of two or three of your family and friends. Here's a student writer explaining how she gets characters off the ground:

> I often write about people I know, or at least use elements of them for characters, and far from finding it restrictive, I feel that it is a strong and familiar way to kick-start my writing. For example: 'Julie Sanderson remembers little of her childhood but the smell of popcorn and petrol. She grew up on a travelling fair.'

There's no rule, however, that characters *have* to be based on people we know well. It could be that you develop an intriguing character inspired by somebody you observed for five minutes on a bus. Here's another student reflecting on the creation of convincing characters:

I have begun to take more notice of people that I see in the street. I take notice of their appearance, their clothes, the way they talk and act. I have also found that through observing people I have developed skills with dialogue. Perhaps I have developed the nosy side of my personality where I have been listening to what people have said or commented on and quite often this has helped me with character development.

Observation is key in this: your characters have to have some basis in reality (and this is where carrying your journal at all times will help you). I would be reluctant to use a character with no recognisable elements of truth about them.

Try This: Visualisation

It's important to visualise characters and settings to make fiction, and that's the purpose of this exercise. I picked it up from the novelist Lesley Glaister, who suggests using a character you're already working with, but if you're between characters at present, then imagine from scratch.

Shut your eyes. Clear a space inside your mind. Inside your head, put a chair in space. Move around it. Touch it. Get to know it. Colours? Texture? Strain to visualise it. Open your eyes. Jot down the details.

Shut your eyes again. Look to see if you've missed anything. Look around the chair to see where it is located. See what's there. Anything incongruous? Time of day? Atmosphere? Write that down.

Shut your eyes again. Go back to the place and check it over again. Have a character enter that space. Have this person look around. Is it strange? Familiar? Will the person sit on the chair or not? If so, watch the movement. Study character. Height. Age. Colouring. Clothing. The way a character moves and sits down will tell you a bit about them. What about attitude? Are they happy, fearful, peaceful? Write it all down.

Close your eyes again. See the space. See the character. Look into their eyes. Look at the hands.

Now, be that person. Sink into the body and feel what it's like to be there. Different body. Different weight, etc.

Write in the voice of this character.

Start with, for example, 'God, I hate it here', or 'One thing I would love to do is ...'. If you're stuck, go back to the chair in the space and visualise.

Flat and Round Characters

There are many more aspects to a real person than a fictional one, however multifaceted you've written them. Some fictional characters, however, are less complex than others. It was E.M. Forster who first distinguished between flat and round characters, but René Warren and Austin Wellek have expanded on these concepts:

> 'Flat' characterisation...presents a single trait, seen as the dominant or socially most obvious trait...'Round' characterisation...requires space and emphasis; is obviously useable for characters focal for point of view or interest.[2]

In Will Ferguson's novel, *Happiness,* Edwin Vincent de Valu is a clear example of a rounded character. Being the point-of-view character obviously helps; it offers the 'space and emphasis' to which Wellek and Warren refer. Edwin is disorganised, not terribly competent, ambitious, intelligent and critical of the world of publishing in which he is employed. He is a comic character, but he certainly has tragic undertones.

His wife, Jenni, is a useful example of a flat character. If we set aside the fact that she is stupid, she really only has two 'character-indicators': she is shallow and very enthusiastic about sex. The best example of the former characteristic is the way she adopts a magazine article ('Better Living Thru Post-It Notes') and makes it a philosophy of life:

> Yellow Post-It Notes were everywhere: in the kitchen, in the dining room, even, no doubt, in the washroom. There were Post-It Notes on the lampshade ('Energy consumption! Think about the big blue planet!'), above the dishwasher ('Clean dishes! Clean mind!'), and on front of the fridge ('Better health and a more beautiful body').[3]

Jenni is a pretty flat character, but the flattest I know of is the chauffeur in Richard Brautigan's *Dreaming of Babylon*, whose one characteristic is the back of his neck, which appears to threaten C. Card, the novel's hapless private-eye protagonist.

Unlike a major character – who says and does and changes enough to appear rounded – a flat character is no more than her character-indicators. This is fine. You will hope to create characters as rich and complex as Madame Bovary, but you will find that you have room for, and need of, characters who would not be out of place in the *Mr Men* books. Dickens's novels are full of them: Tiny Tim in *A Christmas Carol* and Joe Gargery in *Great Expectations*, for instance.

Saying, Doing, Appearing

There are a number of ways of creating character.

In Maggie O'Farrell's novel, *My Lover's Lover*, the reader gets an initial idea of what the character Marcus is like from descriptions of his physical appearance:

> The curve of his bicep is a pale, milky white, his forearms a deep brown. His fingers are stained with green ink.[4]

But he is also characterised by the things he does, in this case, with Lily, whom he has only just met:

> He moves nearer and, without speaking, slides one arm around her shoulders and the other around her waist. The length of his body rests against hers. He bends his head and presses his lips to the dip just below her cheekbone.[5]

We now know that Marcus is decisive, forceful and, depending on your viewpoint, forward. We know it and, more importantly, we worked it out for ourselves; nobody told us. We were *shown*.

The way characters look and what they do is informative to the reader, but so too is what they say. A little later, Marcus holds a piece of paper out for Lily and says:

> 'Do you want it?'
> They look at it together, a tiny runway on his outstretched hand. She keeps her face serious. 'Not really.'
> 'How about if I write my phone number on it?'

Now we know that Marcus is quirky and a bit of a tease. And again, we have reached these conclusions by inferring. O'Farrell hasn't said that Marcus is a tease, or eccentric.

In the case of Marcus, we come to understand his character not only through what he says, but also though what he doesn't say. When Lily moves into his flat, into what has been his girlfriend Sinead's room, he is so reticent about her that Lily comes to the conclusion that Sinead has died. And from this we may deduce not that Lily is slow, but that Marcus is manipulative.

As we've just seen, the best ways of creating characters are showing what they say and do; but it doesn't hurt to let us in on how they appear. A few tips on the latter, though: it's generally a good idea to describe a character's appearance on the hoof. Incorporate description into action or dialogue. Fiction more often than not resembles a film rather a photograph; it's a moving picture, and if you stop to describe things, your readers may lose interest. A head-to-toe description of a character's appearance is unnecessary: let the reader fill in from some choice pointers, and if you give details of appearance, do it early on in the narrative, before the reader has had time to imagine Freddie having dark hair, when on page 341 you suddenly announce his hair is red. Readers find this very disturbing!

Characterisation by Association

Characters aren't defined just by what they do and say: the setting in which we find them may say a great deal about who they are. This is what the novelist Jane Rogers describes as conveying character by association with 'place, mood or occupation'.[6] It can work in several ways. At its most literal, characterisation by association may be as functional as the relationship between character and setting. If we meet a character lying in a hospice bed, she is defined as a dying character because she is in a hospice – nobody says she is dying.

If setting is the stage in the theatre of fiction, then I suppose what characters wear is their costume. This too is a means of characterisation. In Michael Frayn's novel *Spies*, Stephen Wheatley, the young protagonist, is presented to us wearing a 'too-short grey flannel school shirt hanging out of too-long grey flannel school shorts' and an elastic belt 'striped like the hatband of an old-fashioned boater, and fastened with a metal snake curled into the shape of an S'.[7] His clothes tell us at the very least that he is a schoolboy from another era.

At a slightly more sophisticated level, the physical objects associated with a character may have connotations that are helpful to the reader. Which brings us back again to Henry James.

Solidity of Specification

Writing of Henry James, Robert Scholes and Robert Kellogg famously coined a term, which well describes the aspect of fiction writing I want to discuss next:

> the air of reality (solidity of specification) seems to me to be the supreme virtue of a novel – the merit on which all its other merits helplessly and submissively depend.[8]

Solidity of specification: I take this to mean that specification creates solidity, and naming the names – 'a *Finding Nemo* bag', not just 'a bag' – is a priority when you're writing. Why? Because a plain bag is nothing in particular and a piece of Disney merchandising says something about both character and setting. To Jane Rogers's list of 'place, mood or occupation' I might add that character may be conveyed by association with mode of transport – or record collection, choice of shop, taste in coffee. And, speaking of record collections, Nick Hornby's work illustrates the power of solidity of specification. In the space of one page in *About a Boy*, Hornby manages to specify the following: Laura Nyro's *Gonna Take a Miracle*, afternoon reruns of *The Rockford Files*, *Countdown*, Nirvana. If you just flick through the book at random, you might find, amongst many, many other specifications, Snoop Dogg, *The Simpsons*, Bruce Springsteen, shaved parmesan, flavoured condoms, polenta, Nottingham Forest, *Pinky and Perky*, Mozart and Joni Mitchell. All of these specific details function as little jewels embedded in the narrative; little jewels which light up for the reader. Solidity of specification does what it says on the packet: it makes the world of the story *solid*. 'Amy drove her car to the shop' tells us nothing much. 'Amy drove her MX5 to Harvey Nichols' tells us quite a bit about Amy.

Try This: Data

In *On Writing*, the novelist George V. Higgins puts the case for research in fiction writing. He contends that the novelist should have as much data to hand as the best feature writer.

Think of someone you know well. You will know a fair amount about this person's tastes: the cereal boxes in the kitchen cupboard; the designer labels in the wardrobe; the TV set; the music system, and so on. You may not use all these details, but you need to know them. This exercise won't produce a fully formed character for you, but it will get one started. It's an easy way of focusing on your character's tastes.

■ Your character is at a supermarket checkout. List ten things in his or her trolley.

■ List ten books on your character's bookshelves.

■ List ten records in your character's collection. (Are they CDs, LPs, 78s?)

■ Log your character's broadcasting week. Which radio and TV programmes does she listen to or watch?

■ List your character's five favourite apps.

Double the Effect

What a viewpoint character notices about other characters almost doubles the effect. It amounts to a list of connotations about the characters in question, but it also reveals something about the viewpoint character. In this passage from *Nice Work* by David Lodge, Vic Wilcox, the managing director of an engineering firm, is accompanying Dr Robyn Penrose, a Women's Studies lecturer, to the car park:

> Wilcox shook his head impatiently. 'Where's your car?'
>
> 'The red Renault over there.'
>
> 'Why did you buy a foreign car?' he said.
>
> 'I didn't buy it, my parents gave it to me, when they changed it.'
>
> 'Why did they buy it, then?'
>
> 'I don't know. Mummy liked it, I suppose. It's a good little car.'
>
> 'So's the Metro. Why not buy a Metro if you want a small car? Or a Mini? If everybody who bought a foreign car in the last ten years had bought a British one instead, there wouldn't be seventeen per cent unemployment in this area.'[9]

Here we clearly learn as much about Vic as we do about Robyn. We already know that he opts for a Jaguar rather than a German marque for his company car, and thus, cars here become a means of characterising.

Change

One of the fundamentals of storytelling is that there must be change. Often, the change has to do with action, with what happens. But sometimes, change may be about perception. Somebody whom the author has presented as unsympathetic may later be presented as more appealing. Usually this will be to do with the perceptions of the viewpoint character altering.

In David Park's novella, *The Big Snow*, Detective Sergeant Gracey is initially presented as a thug, a man who goes about his duties as a policeman in ways that would not generally impress Amnesty International. Early in the narrative, through the eyes of the tyro Detective Constable Swift, we see Gracey interacting with a criminal in the toilet of a pub:

> Through the gap he saw Brown on his knees, his long thin fingers holding on to the rim of the wash basin, an open razor glinting like a grin in the grime on the floor, his eyes fixed on Gracey staring back at him as he raised his wooden truncheon high in the air above his head, then without breaking their locked gaze brought it drumming down on Brown's hand.[10]

Later, when Swift has been showing too much initiative, Gracey lays into him:

> 'Swift, from the moment I met you, I could see you were a snotty-nosed little twat with your education and your head full of half-baked ideas from too many films and detective books. A regular little Sherlock Holmes who thinks on the basis of five minutes in the job he's got it cracked.'[11]

During the early and middle stages of the narrative, Gracey is portrayed in the least sympathetic light, but as the final stage begins, Swift and Gracey have a punch-up and come to some kind of understanding. Thereafter, they work on the murder case as a team, and the reader begins to see that Gracey may not be so villainous after all. Due to changes in the presentation of a character, the reader's perceptions have altered, and this is good. Readers like change. They also like a villain who has some charm.

Pitfalls

It's all subjective, horses for courses, and so on. The particular course that yours truly trots round is dramatic fiction, where exposition is execrable and introspection is invidious. Allowing for the fact that I'm speaking from a rather extremist perspective, allow me to suggest a couple of things in the area of characterisation that I think it's good to avoid.

You think, to a greater or lesser extent, all the time. It's desirable in a human being, but in a character in fiction, I would argue, it's a turn-off for the reader. When marking student writing, I always respond badly to internal monologue. As Rob Watson puts it:

> introspective writing...may strike you as more literary and less reliant on the disciplines of form (easier, too, since you just have to open up and let it fall), but few novelists have done it well. Most introspective stuff is miserably inept.[12]

Such writing feels claustrophobic and it isn't dramatic: no other characters are involved, nobody acts and nobody speaks. Maybe human beings and characters in fiction are really not that different: aren't you interested in what other people say and do, and not particularly energised by what they're thinking about?

The other thing to avoid wherever possible in characterisation is simply telling the reader about a character. Say you're introducing us early on in your novel or short story to the narrator's family:

Mother had been born to a rich family in Sydney and lived at home until she ran away at the age of sixteen with my father, Peter. My Dad, the son of a storekeeper from Alice Springs, was not an ambitious man. He was happy to sit on the porch all day listening to early Birthday Party records and smoking dope, which irritated my mother no end...

This isn't terribly dramatic or engaging, especially on the first page of a novel. I would never argue that it is possible to avoid telling the reader things; I'd just recommend trying your best to do so. The reader wants to be intrigued and to be put to work. When you explain, you are handing it to the reader on a plate and you don't want to do that.

Finally

If you stick to what a character says and does, your fiction will stand a good chance of being readable. A word of warning, though: you won't get far in the task of characterising on that alone. Before you write a word, you need to know your character in detail.

Robert McKee, the screenwriting guru, has ten commandments for writers, one of which is that the author should know his world as God knows his. You can't spend too much time preparing characters before you begin to write. The creators of Alan Partridge spent hours and hours developing the finer details of Partridge's life. It's crucial to them to know that he wears Pringle sweaters and drives a Lexus. It may even be important to know things about your character that never get mentioned in the fiction. Hemingway had a theory that what you knew about a story but omitted made the story stronger, whereas that which you omitted because you simply didn't know it weakened the story.

Further Reading

Richard Bausch (2009) *Peace* (London: Tuskar Rock).
Read this short Second-World-War novel for the impressively understated characterisation of the old Italian man who acts as a guide for three American soldiers trying to cross a mountain in enemy country. Both the Americans and Bausch's readers constantly have to deduce whether or not this guide is on their side. The old man may or may not be complicated, but part of the author's skilful characterisation of him is that readers are kept in sustained suspense trying to decide what kind of character he is.

John Gardner (1991) *The Art Of Fiction: Notes on Craft for Young Writers* (New York: Vintage).

This is essential, which is why we've put it in *A Writer's Bookshelf.* Read it yourself and find out why.

John McGahern (2002) *That They May Face the Rising Sun* (London: Faber & Faber).

Turn to page 23 and read the story of John Quinn, as recounted by other characters in this masterful novel. It won't take you long; it lasts 14 pages. Quinn is a monster, but a human monster. You can learn a couple of important things here. The first flies in the face of most of the chapter you have just read: all you really need when it comes to creating memorable characters is to keep your eyes and ears open. The second lesson is that rounded, convincing characters are complicated. John Quinn is a thug who abuses the women in his life, but at the same time, his kids think the world of him. It's the Tony Soprano lesson: a villain has to have his redeeming features.

13 Point of View
Robert Graham

'Nothing', Ethan Canin says, 'is as important as a likeable narrator. Nothing holds a story together better.'[1] If the narrative is the end product of the fiction-writing process, the starting point is the narrator. The reader of a novel or short story is entering into a relationship with the narrator.

Shlomith Rimmon-Kenan differentiates between narrators who participate in the narrative, and those who don't.[2] As an example of the latter, the realist novels of the nineteenth century employ what David Lodge, in his essay, '*Middlemarch* and the Idea of the Classic Realist Text',[3] refers to as 'the convention of the omniscient and obtrusive narrator'. It's a matter for debate whether such a convention has fallen out of fashion in contemporary fiction, but my advice would be to avoid it. While Margaret Atwood, Angela Carter and Salman Rushdie all use an ironic version of the omniscient narrator, I would suggest to you that this approach is not for every writer. You need to have a good deal of control to pull it off. Instead, why not plump for having a narrator who participates in the narrative, as exemplified in this extract from Sarah Waters's *Fingersmith*?

> We were all more or less thieves, at Lant Street. But we were that kind of thief that rather eased the dodgy deed along, than did it.[4]

Sue Trinder isn't a narrator sitting in an armchair telling you about the action, she is immersed in it.

Pip in *Great Expectations* and Holden Caulfield in *The Catcher in the Rye*: they play a central role in the story they narrate; they are protagonist-narrators – they tell their own story. Narrators whose role is subsidiary, such as Lockwood in *Wuthering Heights* or Nick

Carraway in *The Great Gatsby*, are described as witness-narrators in that they narrate someone else's story. Thus, Sue Trinder in *Fingersmith* is a protagonist-narrator. Sue is present for nearly every-thing that happens in the course of her narrative and involved in it up to her neck:

> My stomach ached from the nurse's fingers. My mouth was cut by the spoon. I had an idea that, once they got me into a room, they would kill me.

Point of View

The handling of point of view (or POV) is key to the way a narrative will function. In place of viewpoint, Janet Burroway offers the term 'vantage point',[5] which I like. I think it is helpful to regard viewpoint as the place from which you experience the story. Whether that is within a character or over her shoulder, and whichever person – *I, she, you* – you write in, your choice of point of view will affect the way your story is told and the way in which it is perceived. Point of view is the perspective from which the story is told. *Great Expectations* is told from Pip's perspective, *The Catcher in the Rye* from Holden Caulfield's.

Presentational Fiction: Addressing the Reader

'In a good presentational story,' Orson Scott Card says, 'the audience will forgive a certain shallowness of story because they so enjoy the writer's style and attitude.'[6] *The Catcher in the Rye* is very much a piece of presentational fiction, where the narrator addresses the reader directly:

> I'm not going to tell you my whole goddam autobiography or anything. I'll just tell you about this madman stuff that happened to me around last Christmas just before I got pretty run-down and had to come out here and take it easy.[7]

The voice, the style are very much more important than the story. A narrator who wasn't opinionated would neuter a presentational style. Apart from giving a potent view of the narrator, the fact that the narrator has strong opinions and expresses them also delineates his presence.

In *Catcher*, the narrator's voice and strong opinions are more signif-icant as characterising devices than his actions. In the course of the novel, Holden Caulfield doesn't do much, but he expresses a good many extreme opinions and does so in an idiomatic and stylised way:

> The reason he fixed himself up to look good was because he was madly in love with himself. He thought he was the handsomest guy in the Western Hemisphere. He was pretty handsome too – I'll admit it. But he was mostly the kind of handsome guy that if your parents saw his picture in your Year Book, they'd right away say, 'Who's *this* boy?' I mean he was mostly a Year Book kind of handsome guy.[8]

If you are less confident in the creation of plot, you may aspire to a presentational style and voice in the hope of winning over just the kind of reader that Card has described: one who is willing to forgive your shortcomings.

Try This: Presentational versus Representational

Rewrite the first two pages of *The Catcher in the Rye* so that Holden never addresses the reader directly. This alters it from presentational to representational fiction.

When you've finished, compare the two versions and try to say what the effects of making the change are.

Single-Viewpoint

In their respective novels, Holden and Pip are the sole point-of-view character. The advantage of having a single narrator is that he or she becomes, in Oakley Hall's term, the 'central authority'.[9] Hall's belief is that since Henry James, the establishment of a central authority is 'the chief means to believability'. The contemporary reader is perhaps less likely than the nineteenth-century reader to accept the author as the central authority. Perhaps the difference between a central authority and the intrusive narrator of the classic realist text is worth noting: it's the difference between a point-of-view character – the one through whom we *experience* the narrative – and an omniscient narrator – the one who *recounts* the narrative. Showing versus telling again. Nevertheless, the narrator as central authority only succeeds if the chosen narrator – however unsympathetic he or she may be – compels the reader. Pip and Holden Caulfield are narrators most of us would find sympathetic. It's just the opposite with Barbara Covett – more of her in a moment – in Zoë Heller's *Notes on a Scandal.*

Who is Your Point-of-View Character?

Before you make a decision about which person your viewpoint will be in, it's important to decide which character will make the best narrator. Choosing the viewpoint, according to David Lodge, 'is arguably the most important single decision that the novelist has to make, for it fundamentally affects the way readers will respond, emotionally and morally, to the fictional characters and their actions'.[10] To illustrate, look at the example of Heller with *Notes on a Scandal*. She has admitted that she completed a first draft before it occurred to her to use Barbara Covett as her narrator. Read the novel and you will see that any other viewpoint choice would not have generated the narrative power of the final draft.

In Which Person?

As it happens, the examples I have been talking about so far are all first-person narratives – throughout, it's 'I did this' and 'I said that' – but your point-of-view character might just as well be written in the third person: 'She did this' and 'She said that.' First-person singular and third-person singular narratives are most common, but Jay McInerney's *Bright Lights, Big City* uses the second-person singular:

> You are not the kind of guy who would be at a place like this at this time of the morning. But here you are, and you cannot say that the terrain is entirely unfamiliar, although the details are fuzzy.[11]

And Jeffrey Eugenides's *The Virgin Suicides* is written in the first-person plural – quite a rare viewpoint choice. The book is narrated by a group of teenage boys in a suburban neighbourhood:

> We saw the gangly paramedic with the Wyatt Earp moustache come out first – the one we'd called 'Sheriff' when we got to know him through these domestic tragedies...[12]

At What Distance?

I'm going to stick my neck out here and disregard much of the available advice about the various points of view. The distance from which a narrative is pitched – which John Gardner calls the 'psychic distance...the distance the reader feels between himself and the events in the story'[13] – may be more significant than the choice of viewpoint – as you are about to see. I would also suggest that whether you opt for single or multiple points of view may be more important than which person – first, second, third, etc. – you write in. But for the moment, let's consider that choice anyway.

First-Person

This option – 'I saw the dog' – may invite more direct engagement from readers, because it allows the character to address them directly.

There are problems with single-viewpoint narratives and the use of the protagonist narrator. One of them is the drift towards the monolithic: the reader will have to spend 80 000 words or so in the company of the narrator, and with one narrator, this will be unbroken time. First-person narrative – and especially single-viewpoint first-person narrative – is quite a limiting form. Writing in his preface to *The Ambassadors*, Henry James says: 'the first person, in a long piece, is a form foredoomed to looseness'.[14]

One snag with first-person narration is that the novel or story is going to be limited to what the POV character is present for, and it's difficult for one character to witness everything that may need to happen in a novel.

There are other reasons to believe that in first-person mode, fiction writers are affording themselves an apparent freedom that opens up a variety of pitfalls. It allows for self-indulgence, and to some extent it has a tendency to work against dramatising: it is easy for the first-person narrator to tell the reader about events he ought to be showing. In the same preface, James writes of the potential for dullness: 'the question of how to keep my form amusing while sticking so close to my central figure and constantly taking its pattern from him had to be faced'. It's also easy in the first person to slip into internal-monologue mode – which, after more than a paragraph or two, can make readers feel a bit too much like they have been trapped in a lift with someone who talks too much.

Limited Third-Person

This POV – 'she/he saw the dog' – has many of the same advantages and limitations as the first-person. It is, however, more flexible in that you can adjust your focus, edging, for instance, away from limited third-person to detached or omniscient third-person and even to omniscient third-person. Jennifer Egan's use of limited third-person in this extract from *A Visit from the Goon Squad* is fairly representative of this viewpoint option: 'Sasha leaned against the tub beside him and took a tiny sip of grappa. It tasted like Xanax.'[15]

According to Card, 'the overwhelming majority of fiction published today uses the third-person narrator'.[16]

Third-Person Detached and Third-Person Omniscient

These variations on third-person viewpoint are little more remote from the viewpoint character, a little less subjective. If limited third-person is looking from within the POV character, detached is looking right over his or her shoulder. Here, in *Half-Lives: The First Luisa Rey Mystery*, one of the novellas that make up *Cloud Atlas*, David Mitchell is using detached: 'Judith Rey, barefoot, fastens her kimono-style dressing gown and crosses a vast Byzantine rug to her marble-floored kitchen.'[17] Third-person omniscient is written from a more panoramic vantage point, which you might think of as the God perspective. It's equivalent to the long shot that establishes the setting in a film. David Mitchell uses it in this passage, also from *Half-Lives*: 'A young woman emerges form the next-door party and leans over the neighbouring balcony. Her hair is shorn, her violet dress is elegant, but she looks incurably sad and alone.'[18] Third-person in both detached and omniscient form are the points of view most conducive to what David Lodge calls 'staying on the surface', and you are less likely to slip into telling when using either.

Second-Person

This addresses readers as though they were the POV character – 'you see the dog at last and you whistle her over' – and is thus very similar in effect and limitations to first-person and limited third-person. But it's a little difficult to pull off without seeming mannered; you have to be an accomplished fiction writer to succeed in this viewpoint.

First-Person Plural

As mentioned above, this viewpoint – 'we saw the dog' – is Jeffrey Eugenides's choice in *The Virgin Suicides*. It's also used in Josh Ferris's

2007 novel *Then We Came to the End*, and, much earlier, by William Faulkner in *A Rose For Emily*. There's an element of objectivity in first-person plural, which lends the narration authority. It may also result in an impersonal feel; it's perhaps more objective than subjective.

Multiple Points of View

This narrative strategy has several advantages. The move from single to multiple viewpoints affords the possibility of a quilted text (see Chapter 16, 'Plot', for more on quilted narratives). A shift in viewpoint is change, and narrative tension, narrative itself, is all about change. But that is not the only advantage of deploying more than one point of view. Another is the fact that the single-viewpoint character doesn't have to witness everything. However, be aware that multiple-viewpoint needs to be used in a controlled and considered way. As John Gardner says, the author has to establish 'the expectation that, when he likes, he will move from consciousness to consciousness'.[19] In other words, the author needs to establish at an early stage a pattern of moving between viewpoints. If you write in one viewpoint and then, three-quarters of the way through your story, adopt another, you will undermine the credibility of your fiction.

A word about dual-viewpoint: one drawback to having two viewpoint characters in novel or story is that the reader will almost always prefer one to the other. For example, in Carol Shields's *The Republic of Love*, which looks at a love affair from both points of view, I preferred the sections narrated by Tom, the easy-going disc jockey, to those of Fay, the more highly-strung folklorist. Maybe there's an argument for saying, then, that if you're not using single-viewpoint, more than two POV characters is preferable.

Try This: Point-of-view Shift

Pick a novel or short story you like and rewrite a page of it, changing the point of view: if it's first-person, change it to third, and so on.

How does the change affect the piece?

Further Reading

Anne Lamott (1995) *Bird by Bird – Some Instructions on Writing and Life* (New York: Anchor Books, 1995), p. 49.
   This is one of the most enjoyable books on the writer's craft. Sure, there's wise advice, but I recommend it mainly because Anne Lamott's world-view is very engaging and she makes you feel good about being a writer.
Jay McInerney (1985), *Bright Lights, Big City* (London: Jonathan Cape).
   You shouldn't need me to recommend *The Catcher in the Rye*: reading it ought to be a writer's reflex action, so instead I'm sending you in the direction of *Bright Lights, Big City*, the progenitor of a Hollywood sub-genre: the yuppie nightmare. The second person narrative here is a virtuoso performance. Major laughs, too.

14 Dialogue
John Singleton

Dialogue Is an Unnatural Practice

Sometimes you hear writers praised by reviewers for their 'natural' dialogue. Such and such has a 'real ear for dialogue/ordinary speech/conversation', they write approvingly, as if the ability to capture actual speech is a gift. It's not. It's a misunderstanding of the true nature of dialogue.

Fictional dialogue for the most part is very unnaturalistic, full of contrivance and artfulness. It has to be to avoid all the defects of ordinary everyday conversation. I say 'defects' simply because what is acceptable in the oral is not in the literary. Just eavesdrop on any conversation in a pub or café and you'll see the obviousness of what I'm saying.

Literary dialogue is shorn of all the hesitations, repetitions, fractured grammar, fragments, 'ums' and 'ers' and all the other unofficial alphabet of sounds and additives that feature in daily conversation. Such dialogue is crafted. It is cleaned up and shaped and articulate. Only when characters are inarticulate or under great emotional stress does written speech begin to take on the rawness of the 'natural'.

It's not that dialogue in novels and scripts shouldn't be naturalistic, if by naturalistic is meant it *sounds like* the real talk of actual characters. And that's the trick: making the artificial and crafted appear natural and unforced; hiding the art in artlessness. Even those writers who believe in *actualité*, who write it as it is, do, nevertheless, manage to subtly shape their dialogue, creating underlying rhythms and patterns and echoes.

In this sense I'm being unfair to the critic who recognises and praises a writer's *ear* for dialogue. It is absolutely essential for a writer to have such an 'ear', by which I mean having a feeling for the tune and melodies of conversation. It's easy to write tuneless and flat dialogue, but the best is full of the music and expressiveness of the spoken language.

Dialogue Is More than Just Me and You

Like all utterance, dialogue is expressive of both the individual's personality and the social context in which they operate. I remember once an old Potteries' man describing his thirst to me with the phrase: 'I'm so parched I could go licket mop stick.' The expression here is graphic and so indicative – of character, regional distinction (note the dialect omission of the 'and' between 'go' and 'lick' so typical of a local grammar), class (my middle-class businessman father would never have used such a phrase), and of a cultural moment that has passed with the advent of sponges, detergents and Dyson vacuum cleaners. But if you are writing a regional novel set in1960s' Stoke-on-Trent, or one of your characters is a grandfather from Hanley with a typical working-class turn of phrase, then this will influence how you write him into dialogue.

Try This: Dialogue and Conflict

Write a scene in which you have two contrasting characters. One is from a different social circle and class from the other. Invent a situation for their encounter and develop a scene through dialogue that expresses their different social and class cultures. Remember that some people regard regional language as an inferior mode of expression, while others consider it a sign of authenticity and grass-roots reality. How strongly do your characters feel about language and how regionalism defines identity?

Dialogue Is 'Voices'

All this means that not only do you have to have fine-tuned antennae for the sounds and rhythms of language – what I have called the music of speech – but also an inner ear, an awareness of the social and psychological resonances of speech. What I mean by this is that each person has an individual 'voice', or particular vocabulary and verbal mannerisms that identify and distinguish them from other people. But this voice changes according to circumstance: the way a teenager talks to her mates is different from the way she talks to the headteacher in her school, to her brother, or her grandmother. In one situation she may be boastful, gossipy and slangy, in another she may be respectful, subservient-seeming and more formal in her speech. If she has to talk on the phone to a counsellor, or respond in an interview, her 'voice' will change yet again. Writers need to note these differences and have that 'ear' not just for their character's voice but for all the nuances of that character's 'voices'.

Now if one of your characters uses the phrase 'the social and psychological resonances of speech', just what kind of person would you have in mind, and in what context have you placed that character? Is s/he trying to impress, even browbeat a listener with this sonorous phrase, with the academic voice? Imagine a tutor in college talking like this in a tutorial to a naïve young student. Could you convey the academic detachment – even the self-importance – of the tutor, while at the same time mocking/implying the gullibility of the student? The student could use a hybrid academic/colloquial vocabulary and hesitant expression to show they do not quite have the appropriate voice for academia, and the tutor could be shown 'performing' through the use of extended rounded 'speeches' with lots of subordination in the sentences, and some jargon.

This contrast of 'voices' could create real punch and point to your scene. So make it even more resonant and have your characters of different sexes. And what do you get? A young working-class woman, grappling with the intellectual challenges of higher education, wanting to impress, and an educated, middle-class, middle-aged tutor grappling with a sense of his own dullness and aware he is just going through the motions. Willy Russell, of course, has written *Educating Rita* out of just such an encounter. But the tutor could be boundlessly enthusiastic and the student tired and cynical, in which case the dynamics of the scene would change and the dialogue with it.

Try This: Active Dialogue

Write a scene that takes in some of these elements. Decide whether to first 'place' your two characters, or launch straight into dialogue relying on the spoken word to communicate the situation and location to the reader. You could of course start with three or four lines of dialogue and then try some narrative in-filling and scene-setting before picking up the dialogue again.

Dialogue Belongs to Characters, Not to Writers

Some writers treat characters as if they were alter egos, or use them as mouthpieces for their own views, or just as mouthpieces. This is not to say characters should not express political, religious or philosophical views or opinions, but that these should be as much a *part of them* as temperament and disposition. It's worthwhile, then, creating characters who speak very differently from the author. If you're a male writer create dialogue for women characters. Ask a female friend to read your work for hints of gender bias and stereotyping. If all your female characters seem passive in their expression, liberate them from your own obsession and create something more feisty, or better still create a number of female characters expressing a range of characteristics and attitudes. Set one character or group of characters to challenge others and create diversity and drama in your fictional discourse.

Dialogue Is Multi-Purpose

To some extent what you as a writer want from a scene will dictate the kind of dialogue you write for it. Back to the tutorial. If you want to ridicule the jargonising that passes for understanding in education then this will show in the vocabulary you put in the mouths of tutor and student. The key to good dialogue and successful scenes is *that more than one thing should be going on at the same time.* So, for instance, in our tutorial scene, the satirising of modern education can be developed at the same time as the theme of innocence and seduction, sexual and institutional power, etc. And the two characters will be revealed, their contrary motives, their backgrounds, their temperaments, aspirations, anxieties etc.

Much of the composition of this fictional complexity, which only reflects life's own variety, depends on the writer's intention/purpose/position with regard to the characters. For instance, the writer may decide on a strategy that juxtaposes simpler student language and the magisterial tutor voice for the purpose of puncturing the latter's pretensions. But then you may not be on the side of your student character. As a writer you may want to be more balanced, and this will affect how you shape the exchange between your characters.

As well as revealing character, back-story and charting themes, dialogue impels the narrative. Out of one scene comes the impetus for the next. Suppose that, at the end of their tutorial, the tutor offers to give the young student extra help with assignments, and lightly touches her knee as he leans to pick up a fallen book: this then becomes a topic for a subsequent conversation between the student and her flatmate. Here the tutor's reputation maybe an issue, etc.

Whatever the upshot of their talk, the student now has a dilemma (Is the tutor making a pass at her? What should she do about it?), which will, in turn, influence her behaviour in the next meeting.

Dialogue Is Contextual

Dialogue isn't an isolated feature of fiction. It exists in context, the context of the whole story and the context of the scene. Many fictional scenes mix dialogue with narration of action, with description of location, with interior reflection, with authorial commentary, with reported speech, and the art is to keep all or some of these elements in the air and balanced at the same time.

By now our tutor character is getting tired. He's been running end-to-end tutorials for two hours and is dying for a coffee. How do you communicate bored? Do you have the author simply state the fact to the reader? That's the most precise method. But you may feel it is better to show, not tell, and thus you interleave between passages of speech little gestures like pencil-tapping and window-gazing. And you write a final summing-up by the tutor which sounds like a well-worn script, mechanical and mainly cliché and jargon.

One of the dialogue arts, then, is that of complementing and juxta-posing contrasting physical images with spoken words. After all, many of us use language not to reveal but to conceal things, to say one thing but feel/think another. Words often counter and contradict body language. It isn't true when I say 'watch my lips' that all else follows. So remember your characters are communicating not just through speech, but through gesture, pose and mannerism, and dialogue is only one element in a rich communicative context: the automatic nervous system, for example, gives an observant person plenty of information by manifesting itself through sweating, trembling, palpitations and other involuntary signals. Dialogue is more than the words that characters say.

And there's yet another crucial element supplementing, modifying and often contradicting the oral and the autonomous, and that's the cerebral – the mental and perceptual world. The thoughts of your characters represent another 'voice' in the conversation of any scene. Indeed, they may represent more than one 'voice' because so often our interior world is riven by opposing feelings, ideas, sentiments, opinions, realisations. And so often it is though conversations with our inner selves that dilemmas are resolved or debated or highlighted or exacerbated. Good page dialogue gives some hint of this busy clamorous interior life.

Try This: Dialogue Gives Information

Write the opening of a story with a passage of dialogue in which you aim to give as much information as possible about two characters without making it obvious and sounding like a synopsis.

Dialogue Is the Kiss of Life

Speech is a sign of intelligent life, and though dialogue is not an inevitable constituent of fiction, it is if you want to create convincing characters and dramatic situations. Up to 18 million people watch weekly soaps on UK television. Visuals may dominate the medium, but dialogue is more than just an add-on. Try watching serial drama with the sound off. You'll be lip-reading like mad. In fact, the best soaps are those that rely primarily on neither dialogue nor visuals, but balance the two modes of communication. In this, they bridge the gap between film and theatre.

Nevertheless, good dialogue does give *immediacy* to fiction. It shows things as they happen. A scene of convincing dialogue in a novel or short story is like the curtain going up to reveal a well-lit stage; it creates anticipation and excitement; it animates characters. Until they speak they are stiff, hardly more than cardboard cut-outs. Put words on their lips and they come to life. Listening to dialogue puts us readers on more intimate terms with characters, draws us in by invitation, as it seems to share dilemmas and predicaments, heartache and triumph.

Now, take a look at the following extract from Dave Eggers's bestselling novel, *A Heartbreaking Work of Staggering Genius*.

Beth and her brother are talking to their dying mother, trying to persuade her to go into hospital and have her nosebleed treated before she starts choking.

'They're waiting for us.'
'Call another nurse.'

'Mom, please.'
'This is stupid.'
'Don't call me stupid.'
'I didn't call you stupid.'
'Who were you calling stupid?'
'No one. I said it was stupid.'
'What's stupid?'
'Dying of a bloody nose.'
'I'm not going to die of a bloody nose.'
'The nurse said you could.'
'The doctor said you could'
'If we go in, I'll never leave.'
'Yes you will.'
'I won't.'
'Oh, Jesus.'
'I don't want to go back in there.'
'Don't cry, Mom, Jesus.'
'Don't say that.'
...
'Fine, bleed. Sit there and bleed to death.'
'Mom, please?'
'Just bleed. But we don't have enough towels for all the blood. I'll have to get more towels.'
'Mom?'
'And you'll ruin the couch.'
'Where's Toph?' she asks.
'Downstairs.'
'What's he doing?'
'Playing his game.'
'What will he do?'
'He'll have to come with us.'

The characters are by turns exasperated and distressed by having to play out of character and adopt uncomfortable parental roles. Uncertain, they become wound up and overheated. Though the mother uses her illness as a bargaining tool, her attempts at resistance only serve to highlight her vulnerability. The short, tight phrases and sentences underscore the tensions in the encounter and give it that jerky apprehensive feel. And then the scene collapses, as does the mother's resistance, into the prosaic ending, and her sudden acquiescence confirms the air of inevitability that hangs over the whole episode.

Throughout, dialogue captures emotional intensity, delineates character, hints at the complex dynamics of family life and insinuates some strong visual moments. These are inferred, for instance, from the exclamation, 'Don't cry, Mom' and from the comment about needing 'towels for all the blood'. This latter image shakes the reader, and at this point the tension collapses into ironic banality as one of the children points out that the couch will be ruined. The domestic rises above blood and death, and normality makes a show of reasserting itself. In the same way the mother's innocent question, 'Where's Toph?' is her way of seeking solace in the ordinary and mundane, a return to the comfort her caring maternal role. The scene finally ends in quiet acquiescence.

Dialogue in Practice

Attribution – 'he says', 'she says' – can be a problem. Some hesitant writers try and avoid repetition of the common verb 'to say' by using alternatives such as 'reply', 'respond', 'answer'. As these options run out, more and more exotic alternatives are tried such as 'aver/concur' for 'agree', or 'ejaculate/expostulate' for 'exclaim', or 'pronounce' and 'articulate' for 'say', or even 'adumbrate' for 'explain', or 'interject' for 'interrupt'.

The art is to keep it simple: don't be frightened of repetition; make your voices so distinct you don't need constant attribution.

But you could use more descriptive/image-based attributions such as 'murmured', 'whispered', 'sighed', 'wept', 'hissed', 'smiled'. There's a whole auditory and visual vocabulary out there. Poor dialogue resorts to the needless adverb and the adverbial phrase to gloss speech. An example:

> 'Get out of my sight,' he shouted angrily.

The spoken words suggest anger, which makes both the attribution 'he shouted' and the adverb 'angrily' redundant. The art of good dialogue is to make the spoken words carry tone, emotional force and even gesture, if possible. The general rule is: reduce attribution to a minimum.

Another way to handle attribution is to place it in the middle of a sentence or passage of speech and not at the end. This way a dramatic pause can be created. Compare:

> 'No,' he hissed. 'I will not have it.'
>   *with*
> 'No, I will not have it,' he hissed.

Isn't one more dramatic and forceful than the other? Consider the pacing of the two sentences and the stressing of syllables. Do you notice anything significant?

Or, put the attribution at the beginning of a line of speech like this:

He stood up, and looking in her eyes said, very slowly, very quietly, 'I'm going to kill him.'

Now that's how to delay crucial information till the last syllable and thereby create suspense. No sentence you ever write should be complete till the last syllable sings.

Dialogue and Exposition

Try and avoid using dialogue to 'set the scene' or explain action. Dialogue should not be the equivalent of stage directions in a play. Certainly it is important to contextualise action and say where characters are coming from, account for their present situation, appearance, etc., but if you have to do it through dialogue, make it so 'natural', so seamless, that the reader doesn't realise s/he is being fed vital preliminary information.

Pacing

As with all writing, pace and rhythm are critical. Consider how you can alternate passages of emotional intensity with those where you relax the reader. If you're writing a scene between two old friends reminiscing, it has to be gentle and slow-paced, probably with interludes of interior reflection, and gestural and descriptive moments. Pace may be expressed in terms of long sentences with plenty of qualification. On the other hand, if you're writing an action-packed thriller, pace and sentence shape in dialogue are altogether different. Scenes of high tension feature sentence fragments, short phrases, plenty of monosyllables, exclamations! And no dialogue lasts more than half a page before we are off on another high-speed scene.

Banality Is Avoidable

Some writers mistake realism for naturalism, thinking that the nearer you can get to normal daily speech in fictional dialogue the better and more convincing, i.e. real, it will sound. No way. The dullness of transcribed speech is a glory to behold. Some writers also believe, with justification, that the ordinary and everyday should be as much a preoccupation for artists as the unusual, the hidden and the extraordinary. Indeed, the one does not preclude the other. Thus a scene where two soccer fans discuss team selections over a pint may be a common experience in fact, but in fiction it is fraught with cliché and platitude.

Of course a good writer creating a pub scene will turn cliché to advantage, as Graham Swift does in his Booker Prize-winning novel, *Last Orders*.[1] Read the second chapter. Ray, a bookie, Jack, a butcher, and Vince, a garage owner, are drinking late in the Coach and Horses. Ray keeps repeating his dull joke about the horses never going anywhere. However, though the repetition may bore his listeners, it works a strange magic on the reader, and by the end of the chapter the images of Coach and Horse take on an ominous and prophetic power. The writer has turned brash bar-room cliché into gold. Read how he does it.

Dialogue Begins Anywhere

New writers are often hesitant about writing dialogue. I think the best way to write good dialogue is to read good dialogue, and then have a go yourself. So, study Graham Swift, Dave Eggers, David Mamet. Now set yourself a limited number of characters in a recognisable location and write their talk. Go for it.

Further Reading

Jean Saunders (1994) *How to Write Realistic Dialogue*. London: Allison & Busby.
    A basic but very useful guide.
Lewis Turco (1991) *Dialogue*. London: Robinson.
    A useful general introduction to a range of dialogue-writing techniques.

15 Setting

Helen Newall

If narrative is a journey, character being the driver, and plot the vehicle, then setting is the scenery along the way. The big mistake, however, is to think that it's merely the backdrop: if you use it well, setting can powerfully amplify theme, show character, advance the narrative. It creates atmosphere; it is the world in which your characters exist; and in some cases, it's the story itself. Some writers have even gone so far as to say that they treat landscape as another character.

Whether you're writing from memory, or from your imagination, places need to be as vivid as possible to you as you write, otherwise, how will you convey them to your readers? Because part of the pleasure in a text concerns not just the unfolding of events, but the evocation of the environment in which events occur, it's worth spending as much time knowing your setting as you would one of your characters. Just as in a journal you note remarkable characters or images, 'collect' places. Read and think about how other writers use environments.

Graham Swift's novel *Waterland* is a haunting portrayal of the East Anglian fens. The carefree atmosphere of Gerald Durrell's *My Family and Other Animals* depends not just on the comic portrayal of his mother and siblings, but on his fond evocation of long-ago Corfu summers bejewelled with insects and animals.[1]

Circuits of Connection

The pleasure in a text's sense of place often occurs because, just beneath the surface, there's an intrinsic connection between events and setting: just as it's risky for a writer to ignore setting altogether, it's a waste for a writer not to exploit the potential of such connections. Think of them as circuits conveying power, and you'll see how setting can light up characters, or illuminate actions.

Consider Thomas Hardy's *Tess of the D'Urbervilles*: when Tess's fortunes are high, Hardy presents her in a rural idyll, milking cows in lush, summery meadows: however, after she is rejected by her husband, we see Tess picking turnips in the bleak desolation of Flintcomb Ash. Even the name of the place is telling.

The panoramic opening to Alan Paton's *Cry, the Beloved Country* is an elegiac foundation for the rest of the novel. It sets the tone. The prose has the lyric rhythm of a song, and is structured almost in contrasting verses. The early paragraphs present the riches of the landscape: the voice says (or sings):

> Stand unshod upon it, for the ground is holy, being even as it came from the Creator. Keep it, guard it, care for it, for it keeps men, guards men, cares for men.[2]

But the latter paragraphs detail the decay, which was the daily lot of a disenfranchised people.

> Stand shod upon it, for it is coarse and sharp, and the stones cut under feet. It is not kept, or guarded, or cared for, it no longer keeps men, guards men, cares for men.

In the final paragraph we learn that

> The men are away, the young men and the girls are away. The soil cannot keep them anymore.

And the song has become a haunting lament, and a powerful cry for justice.

Try This: The Great Outdoors

Go somewhere: a park; a city street; a hillside. For as long as possible write down everything you see, hear, smell, feel, taste. Note the changes as time passes: clouds might darken the far hillside; a street might grow busier as dusk falls. Look for the mood of the place. Watch the people in the place. Observation is a powerful tool for a writer, so doing this as many times as you can will help your writing when you want to visualise a place back at your desk.

The Secret Unity of Words and Place

Unity of place usually refers to the playwriting notion that too many scene changes are disruptive. While the setting potential of the novel is generally wider than it is for the stage, the concept is useful as a guiding principle when applied to more abstract systems of imagery.

Take, for example, E. Annie Proulx's novel *The Shipping News*. The protagonist, Quoyle, has moved from a disastrous and tragic relationship in New York to the remote coastal wilderness of Newfoundland. Sense of place is evident beyond descriptions of the setting: it is evoked in the field of Proulx's descriptive devices. At the start of the book, when Quoyle receives the awful news of his wife's fatal car crash, Proulx depicts it thus:

> Quoyle gasped, the phone to his ear, loss flooding in like the sea gushing into a broken hull.[3]

There are any number of images Proulx could have used, but the one chosen concerns the sea and a stricken ship; it reflects the nautical landscape of Newfoundland and the broken and sinking state of Quoyle's mind.

When Quoyle and his kids stay in a run-down motel, Proulx describes it thus:

> Room 999 was ten feet from the highway, fronted by a plate glass window. Every set of headlights veered into the parking lot, the glare sliding over the walls of the room like raw eggs in oil.[4]

We have been given enough to imagine the unsettling movement of light down the walls, the tawdry greasiness of the motel, and perhaps queasily, the half-cooked breakfast that awaits them. All very suitable: all very complementary. To have described the Newfoundland sky as being the colour of television, as William Gibson does at the start of *Neuromancer*, might have been accurate, but inappropriate, however brilliant a comparator it is for Gibson's fictional world of virtual realities and computer hacking.[5] This agreement is part of the grammar of sense of place. Writers exploit it.

Similarly, in Anne Michaels's *Fugitive Pieces*, the chance discovery of a photograph precipitates the devastating revelation of a family secret, after which the narrator notes that

> The snow gradually disappeared from under the trees, leaving wet shadows. Detritus hidden all winter lay strewn across lawns and floating in gutters.[6]

And it seems that after the silence of snow, all things hidden are suddenly, painfully exposed.

The more you look for these examples, the more you'll find. It's unlikely that your readers will consciously note every example, but there will be an unconscious acknowledgement as layer upon layer is laid down, deepening the sense of place. Perhaps discovering examples is like snow melting, revealing a writer's secrets, but the magic is not lost if you start making the connections work for your own writing.

The Pathetic Fallacy

This is John Ruskin's famous phrase for the poetic convention whereby inanimate things are imbued with human emotion (from 'pathos' for emotion, and 'fallacy' because it doesn't really rain when we're sad; sometimes it just feels that way).

Ernest Hemingway once said:

> Remember to get the weather in your god damned book – weather is very important.[7]

It is the texture that brings setting to life, and it can either contrast or complement the action. A word of caution, however (with which Ruskin would wholeheartedly agree): it doesn't do to use the pathetic fallacy in the vocabulary of setting. Rain falling 'like heaven's tears' tends to sound overblown, and if your daffodils are 'happily fluttering', and your fluffy bunnies hopping joyfully, your story has crash-landed in Greetings Card Land. Get out now!

The fact remains: you can make the weather do whatever your story needs: the funeral scene might gain more pathos if everyone huddles under black umbrellas, or perhaps what is required is spring sunlight to conflict with the sombre anguish of the mourners.

It's no accident that it rains in films: pavements become beautifully shiny and reflective, rain is dynamic, it makes noise, and characters behave in interesting, active ways, rushing to get inside, papers or coats shielding their heads.

The same principle is true of prose: the action of L.P. Hartley's *The Go-Between* occurs in the oppressive heat of an Edwardian summer. As the heat builds, so does a secret and illicit passion, until it is certain that violent storms of many kinds are imminent, and, as the heat breaks, the circuits of connection between setting and plot are the lightning strikes that destroy so many lives.

Sense of Place

The trouble with sense of place is that it's tempting to achieve it by dropping in chunks of description, but if it doesn't actually bring a narrative to a dead stop, description certainly slows down the pace, so care is advised. Incorporate description into action and dialogue: keep the action moving. Conscious use of pace, however, is a vital part of a writer's arsenal: Umberto Eco, author of *The Name of the Rose*, notes:

> There is no doubt that at times an abundance of description, a mass of particulars in the narration, may serve less as a representational device than as a strategy for slowing down the reading time, until the reader drops into the rhythm that the author believes necessary to the enjoyment of the text.[8]

If you want to slow the action – perhaps one character is waiting anxiously for another to make a decision – then the inclusion of a visual detail, just as a character might be seeing it, might help you make the moment stand still. For example:

> "Did you do it?" she asked.
> A gull hung in the air, keening into the wind, and for a moment, the expanses of sea glittering behind him seemed so brilliant that she had to close her eyes. She could imagine him shaking his head. She was sure that as the gull screamed, he shook his head. She opened her eyes, and he opened his mouth to speak...

The moment of resolution is delayed to maximise suspense. Let's hope the answer lives up to the build-up of tension, or there's the danger of a terrible moment of bathos.

In contrast, if your character is too rushed to notice scenery, then it's likely that the narrative pace won't have time to stand and stare either: generally, when there's too much setting, the narrative is static, besides which, given too much description, readers have no imaginative leap to make; it's all been done for them.

If in doubt, imagine the setting as directions for the journey the reader will make through your narrative: given too few details, the reader may miss a vital turning because the route is unmarked, the landmarks are not distinguished, the writing is bland: too many, and the description of the route becomes cluttered, and noting all the various landmarks becomes a laborious and complicated task.

Try This: Street Building

Use the cues to picture a street. Get someone to read the cues to you one by one while you sit dreaming or writing. If you're working alone, read them one by one and shut your eyes and try to see what the words suggest.

- The street is cobbled.
- It is dusk.
- The wrought-iron gas lamps are beginning to glow.
- A neon sign in a window stutters on and off.
- Snow falls.
- A man runs past...
- chased by a pack of dogs.

Rewrite the above, embellishing the narrative with details of action and place, trying to keep it as visual as possible. But bear in mind when pace dictates that such details drop away.

A Place to Practise

Some writers start from somewhere that inspires them and find a narrative in it; others create characters and plot and then build suitable environments around them. Louise Erdrich (*Love Medicine*) begins with landscape, and says of her response to it:

> It has a lot to do with where I grew up. I set myself back in that pure, empty landscape when I am working on something...[because] there's nothing like it...it's the space where everything comes from.[9]

If this doesn't sound familiar, don't panic. Perhaps your characters drive the first draft: the second draft can then be about interweaving the setting. You have to find your own way of working: do whatever works for you, but as you draft, open yourself up to the possibilities of character influencing setting, and vice versa. Each new draft is about adjusting the balance between aspects of character, plot, setting, till they seem holistic and inseparable, but they don't often start out that way: when you read a novel you're watching the polished performance; you're not seeing the moments when the writer got it wrong and had to start again.

Try This: Be a Collector

Start building a reference collection of places that inspire you to write: you could even build a virtual collection via Pinterest, or by making galleries in Flickr. Visual information is as valuable as any other form of information.

Visual Writing

Having chosen somewhere to locate a story, budding screenwriters may think that, having labelled the setting for each scene, they need not weave setting through their narratives to the same degree as fiction writers do, after all, the camera will fill in the rest; but consider the fact that before they are filmed, all screenplays are read, and to get filmed they have to be a damn fine read. Jane Campion's award-winning screenplay *The Piano* is a wonderfully dark and lyrical read: the prose is visual but spare: it gives just enough for the reader (and the camera) to fill in the scene.[10] Perhaps the most famous image is the piano abandoned on the wild beach, but having given us this, she merges visual and environmental details into the action descriptors:

31. EXT. BUSH AND CLIFF ABOVE BEACH. DUSK
Again ADA stops to look at her piano from the cliff top. The sky is darkening and the air is full of bird calls. She turns from the cliff top, her face grimly set. She walks past BAINES, oblivious of his curiosity.[11]

The darkening sky and the bird calls are the details that bring the printed information to visual life. They are the keys which can unlock for the reader the power of the mind's eye, making the scene more vivid and immediate, and since the darkening reflects Ada's mood, this immediacy concerns character as much as environment.

Similarly, in *Apocalypse Now*, Francis Ford Coppola's 1979 masterpiece about the Vietnam War, the link between narrative and setting is inextricable. But such visual detail is impossible to give in full in a screenplay: nevertheless, the prose in scene descriptors needs to be as taut and evocative as in any novel. Help your reader imagine the scene, but don't 'see' it for them by describing every last blade of grass. As with a novel, too much detail is as boring as none.

Based on *Heart of Darkness*, Joseph Conrad's 1902 novel, *Apocalypse Now*, is a quest narrative: the protagonist, Willard, must travel up the Mekong River to find and 'terminate with extreme prejudice' the renegade Colonel Kurtz, but, as with all good quests, the journey itself is as important and transformative as the final goal.

As Willard journeys, the river changes from a wide, open place where the American army controls and surfs and destroys at whim, to a narrower, more winding course through a darker, more thickly tangled jungle, which the army finds harder, if not impossible, to deal with: although the weapons with which Willard's boat-crew are attacked grow more primitive, they are picked off one by one. At one point, contrasting with the American air superiority seen earlier, the boat passes under the crashed wreckage of an American bomber, still smoking, in the trees. Upstream, it seems, things are darker, less sure, more mysterious, and as in all good forest myths, the advice is not to get out of the boat.

As he gets physically closer to the mysterious Kurtz, Willard tries to understand him by reading his file, and ponders on what Kurtz has done to so enrage High Command (and this is where the narrative of setting comes into its own, since sitting in a boat reading classified papers isn't exactly active stuff). Yet the closer he gets, the more intangible and atavistic everyone's motives become. When Willard finally reaches his destination he explores Kurtz's camp in an overgrown temple ruin. At one moment, the camera pans over a desk showing that Kurtz has a copy of James Frazer's *The Golden Bough*, a book that seeks to collect together world stories and mythologies to thereby find a source which will show how the primitive mind operates, and what Frazer offers is that to become the god, you kill the god.[12]

Willard is seeking the source of the river, and the heart of darkness: and in the very end the only way he can fully know Kurtz is by becoming him. The setting *is* the story, because travelling upriver has become a metaphor for this journey into the brutal and primeval darkness of the human psyche.

Words: The Building Bricks of Place

If all this seems hard, then remember that even the best writers work at it: Ernest Hemingway, whose prose seems effortless, wrote:

> What I've been doing is trying to do country so you don't remember the words after you read it but actually have the Country. It is hard because to do it you have to see the country all complete all the time you write and not just have a romantic feeling about it.[13]

Bear in mind that unless you're writing autobiography in the strictest sense, you need not be true to how the place really is: if need be, let details shift to accommodate the narrative you're weaving, but if you use a famous place, get the salient details right: there's nothing more annoying to a reader than an error that breaks the frame (and nothing more annoying to a writer than receiving endless pedantic readers' letters about it!).

The setting for a sustained piece of writing should lodge itself in your mind as clearly as if it were a memory of an actual place, even if it does not in fact exist. It is built, developed, landscaped, changed, rather in the manner of a virtual makeover, according to the demands of characters and plot. And if there is a secret, it is to see the setting so vividly that you can run the film in your head, without giving it all to the reader: offer instead tantalising descriptors which suggest, and your readers will fill in the rest, and think you've told them more than you have. This is the ultimate circuit of connection; between writer and reader, and it is the most powerful of all.

Further Reading

Larry W. Phillips (ed.) (1999) *Ernest Hemingway on Writing* (New York: Touchstone/Simon & Schuster).
 A book to dip into again and again, and, with chapters such as 'What Writing is and What Writing Does'; 'Advice to Writers' and 'Knowing What to Leave Out', who could fail to learn something from it?
E. Annie Proulx (1993) *The Shipping News*, various publishers.
 If you haven't already, it's time to read this stunning and powerful evocation of people and place.

16 Plot: Your Vehicle

Robert Graham

Yes, you're on a journey as a writer, but don't forget that you want to send your readers on a trip, too. Plot is the vehicle in which you roll them down the road.

For many authors plots are difficult, and it would be nice to think that you could write fiction that relied on voice or characterisation alone. Sadly, that isn't possible, and a plot of some kind is a necessity. How do you come by one? The same way as every other writer – by, in Anne Lamott's phrase, 'flail[ing] around, *kvetching* and growing despondent, on the way to finding a plot and structure that work'.[1]

Character

All the best plots begin with character. In the concluding episodes of the Danish TV drama *The Bridge*, the crucial relationship between character and plot is emphasised not once but twice. As the story's conclusion approaches, we discover that it is police detective Martin Rohde, one of the two central characters, who has caused Sebastian Sandstrod, the 'Truth Terrorist', to embark on his murderous spree. It emerges that Rohde, who we already know has a problem with monogamy, slept with Sandstrod's wife several years before. The other central character, Rohde's colleague Saga Norén, suffers from Asperger's syndrome and has been learning with some difficulty to tell white lies to spare others' feelings; at the story's climax, everything depends on whether she has been successful in that. In other words, the genesis of the plot lies in the character of one of the protagonists and its resolution depends on that of another. So before you do anything else, get to know your characters.

Henry James says character will determine plot, and plot will illustrate character, but it's not clear whether the chicken or the egg comes first, and you may complain that you will only get to know your characters as you write your fiction, as you develop your plot. Not so long ago, I wrote a short story which involved one character being in love with another, who kept most of her life a secret from him. At the outset, I didn't know that she was married, but quite far into the writing it occurred to me that the reason for all this secrecy could be that she was married. In other words, I learned the one key thing about this woman when I had three-quarters of a first draft under my belt. Your characters will develop as you write.

The Inciting Incident

A good place to begin the creation of your plot is with what Robert McKee calls 'the inciting incident'.[2] Amy Tan's novel, *The Joy Luck Club*, uses the death of the central narrator's mother as its inciting incident. Perhaps your protagonist's husband has been abducted: or a son arrested on drugs charges: or maybe a protagonist has just been unfaithful to his wife. Coming up with an inciting incident is not a bad way to start planning your plot.

But you might think about establishing the characters and the setting showing the status quo – before going to the inciting incident. If somebody is going to be abducted, the impact of the abduction on readers will be greater if they know and like the people who are left behind. If you want to maximise reader involvement, you will introduce characters and setting in a dramatic fashion before getting to the real meat of the narrative. This will hook the reader right from the start. Just about any James Bond film you care to name does this in what is often called the pre-title sequence, a brief, cliff-hanger episode which pulls viewers to the edges of their seats.

The Hook

If you look at how other writers snare the reader early in their narratives, you will see something similar. Perhaps the best hook you could find in a short story is the opening sentence of Russell Hoban's 'Telling Stories':

I wonder if this happens to a lot of men?[3]

This raises, in a confessional tone, an engaging reader-question. The initial sentence of Richard Ford's novel *Wildlife* has the strength of being very definite. It is also packed with information:

> In the fall of 1960, when I was sixteen and my father was for a time not working, my mother met a man named Warren Miller and fell in love with him.[4]

We know right away that this story is going to be told from the first-person point of view, which, for most readers, is appealing. The first sentence of the novel introduces us to the narrator. It also tells us his age. It tells us when these events occurred. It gives us an efficient synopsis of the novel. It introduces us to the four main characters. In addition, the first sentence establishes a simple hook, one which will keep the reader engaged for some time: if the narrator's mother fell in love with Warren Miller when the father was away, what was the outcome? Did the family break up, or did it stay together? And, either way, what was the effect on the narrator?

Ansen Dibell argues that every effective opening to a novel does three things:

> The chief of these is to get the story going and show what kind of story it's going to be. The second is to introduce and characterise the protagonist. The third is to engage the reader's interest.[5]

Richard Ford's short, clever opening to *Wildlife* seems to me to fulfil these three things.

So, let's say you now have an opening hook, followed by an inciting incident. That might take you through the first ten per cent of your story. Somehow or other, flailing and *kvetching*, you now need to gestate a plot that builds on what you've achieved so far. That last sentence contains two crucial notions. One is that you have to gestate your plot. You need to live with it. You need to let the plot thicken. That may be a passive process: you live with the story and listen to what it tells you. But it can also be active, as Patricia Highsmith shows us here:

> When I am thickening my plots, I like to think 'What if...What *if...*' Thus my imagination can move from the likely, which everyone can think of, to the unlikely but possible, my preferred plot.[6]

The second crucial notion in that sentence is flailing and *kvetching*, Anne Lamott's memorable phrase. I'm no expert on Yiddish, but I can tell you that *kvetching* means complaining chronically, and I know I flail and *kvetch* all over the place when I work on my plots. So will you.

Try This: The Simple Linear Plot

First get yourself a couple or more characters. If need be, use the exercises in Chapter 12, 'Characterisation'.

Plot a series of events using the simple linear structure: a person (or persons) has a wish, desire, need or objective. The fulfilment of this wish, desire or need, the gaining of this objective, meets an impediment. The impediment is overcome. The objective is gained or the wish is granted.

Variations:

■ The pursued aim is either unattainable or, when attained, not worthwhile.

■ The protagonist fails to overcome the impediment – to comic effect.

■ The impediment is established and nothing progresses until the very end of the story. (The plot put off.)[7]

You don't have to write them out in full: use rough journal notes, or write the events on a series of index cards.

Use these notes to write the first draft of a workable short story. Don't try to write it all in one sitting: spend time letting the ideas gestate. Take them for a walk. Daydream about them in your bath. Stare out the window with them.

Steadily Rising Conflict

One of the ways in which you may ensure that your plot is an engaging experience for the reader is by trying to create steadily rising conflict – a concept which has been explained by James N. Frey:

> conflict which fails to rise is *static* – any kind of conflict which is unchanging. Conflict which rises too quickly is *jumping* – it leaps from one level of intensity to another without adequate motivation or transitional stages. What the dramatist wants is slowly rising conflict which reveals more facets of character because the characters will react differently at each stage of the conflict. As the character responds to rising conflict, he changes, showing all of his colours. Conflict proves character.[8]

Frey suggests that a rising conflict should take place in what he calls a 'crucible – the container that holds the characters together as things heat up'.[9] In John Fowles's novel *The Collector*, the crucible that holds the characters together is the cellar in which one holds the other captive. In Yann Martel's *Life of Pi*, Pi and a Royal Bengal tiger are adrift in a lifeboat – their crucible.

Steadily rising conflict is not, in my view, well served by an authorial presence. For more on this see Chapter 17, 'Immediacy'. As David Lodge explains:

> The intrusive authorial voice...detracts from realistic illusion and reduces the emotional intensity of the experience being represented, by calling attention to the art of narrating. It also claims a kind of authority, a God-like omniscience, which our sceptical and relativistic age is reluctant to grant to anyone.[10]

Nor is steadily rising conflict well served by lengthy passages inside this or that character's head, by exposition or (much) flashback. Narrative tension is, however, served by brevity and economy; by being straightforward; by description being incorporated into action and dialogue; by dialogue that builds tension and advances the narrative; by sharp beginnings that hook the reader and endings that resolve the conflict and don't outstay their welcome.

Remember, narrative tension is not something you worry about later. It should be there from the very start. So leap into your narratives *in medias res* – that is to say, in the middle of things. In other words, your story should begin with the blue touchpaper burning – not with the trip down to the shops to buy fireworks.

How do you achieve steadily rising conflict? Well, it's hard to go wrong if you follow the second of Robert McKee's 'Ten Commandments': 'Thou shalt not make life easy for the protagonist.'[11] This, in a sense, is most of what any plot is about, and it seems to me self-evident that in a story, things will often progress step by step from bad to worse and that in so doing they should raise the tension for readers. I don't foresee much future for a plot where things just keep getting better and better.

To Plan or Not to Plan

Much has been said and written about the extent to which writers should plan their stories. One – good – argument against too much planning is that if you sit down to make a plan it will come out of your conscious mind, which is good at organising and criticising, but not at creating. On the other hand if you don't plan, but allow the plot to emerge from your unconscious mind, it may be more organic, more natural – better. Many writers are either good at planning with the conscious mind *or* at tapping the unconscious; being able to do both together is the trick that's hard to master. However, if you can't tap the unconscious you won't be able to write anything worthwhile – and you won't have anything for your conscious mind to edit and restructure – so let's look at how access to the unconscious works.

Have you ever had one of those dreams which feel like the best story you've ever encountered? Made in your unconscious mind. All your best ideas, from the solution to a knotty problem through to that perfect birthday present for your nearest and dearest, will pop up from the unconscious. 'I don't work with plots,' John Cheever said.[12] 'I work with intuition, apprehension, dreams, concepts.' So that's the argument against planning too much and for writing to discover. I would recommend the latter, but with the qualification that you do need to have some idea of where the whole thing is going. 'I work away a chapter at a time,' Aldous Huxley said, 'finding my way as I go. I know very dimly when I start what's going to happen. I just have a very general idea, and then the thing develops as I write.'[13] How does it develop? It will feel as if you are listening to your unconscious, waiting to hear your story signalled to you. Graham Greene wrote in *The End of the Affair:* 'So much of a novelist's writing, as I have said, takes place in the unconscious: in those depths the last word is written before the first word appears on the paper. We remember details of our story, we do not invent them.'

Completion?

Almost any writer you talk to will admit that the execution of a piece of work never lives up to the original conception, the vision of what the piece will be. So, while we're talking about the way work is composed, it might be comforting to look at part of an essay on the subject by Annie Dillard:

> You are wrong if you think that in the actual writing, or in the actual painting, you are filling in the vision. You cannot fill in the vision. You cannot even bring the vision to light. You are wrong if you think that you can in any way take the vision and tame it to the page...Words lead to other words and down the garden path. You adjust the paints' values and hues not to the world, not to the vision, but to the rest of the paint...And so you continue to work, and finish it. Probably by now you have been forced to toss

out the most essential part of the vision...The work is not the vision itself, certainly. It is not the vision filled in, as if it had been a coloring book. It is not the vision reproduced in time; that were impossible. It is rather a simulacrum and a replacement.[14]

The end product is always a pale shadow of the original idea.

Mike Sharples includes a diagram[15] which 'shows composing as a cycle of contemplating ideas, specifying plans and intentions, composing text and interpreting the text, leading to further ideas and continued composition'.

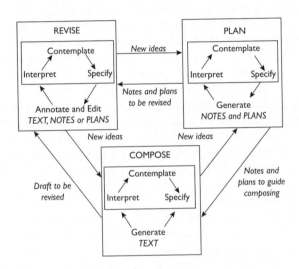

What may be most interesting to you here is the idea that the three stages of writing – planning, composing and revising – are spiral, not linear. Any one stage is as important as the others: more than this, each stage is dependent on the others.

Sharples's cycle may be helpful for you to bear in mind as we approach an aspect of narrative design which I regard as important to the overall effect on the reader: pattern. The creation of pattern may take place during planning or composition, at the revising phase, or during all three. Sharples says of revising that looking at the first draft 'prompts the writer to interpret it and contemplate ways in which the plan could be extended, leading to a new round of planning'. Or as Rob Watson puts it in his *Extracts from a Work in Progress: Writing Life*:

thoughts only exist with time. They need time to find their shape and size, and time to establish contacts and continuities.[16]

Pattern

Pattern may be one of the results of this process, and one kind of pattern involves creating repetition in much the same way as rolls of wallpaper use a repeated image. Let's look at one example of this.

In her novel *Sweet Desserts*, Lucy Ellmann creates a structure where the narrative is often interrupted by a number of different kinds of asides. Some of these have no relation to what goes on before (or after) them, while some in a strange way do comment on, or add emotional colour to, the narrative in which they are embedded. One of these strands consists of recipes, or sometimes just fragments of recipes:

> Bone two large eels, fill them with diced truffles. Wrap in a piece of muslin and tie with string. Cook in wine and well-flavoured fish stock. Drain, unwrap, and cool under a press.

Another strand is letters sent or received by the narrator, Suzy Schwarz:

> *Dear Suzy, I don't want to hear any more talk about killing yourself. It would be a terrible loss to the world, and to your family. Cheer up! Make friends! Don't be sad.*

Sometimes Ellmann incorporates found texts:

> THE MUSK-DEER inhabits the steep slopes of the Himalaya. He lives an active but lonely life and feeds on grass and lichen.

At one stage, she even uses a found text to theorise this approach:

> Many artists have used Chance and ready-mades in order to obscure their exact involvement with the work of art.

Other patterns in *Sweet Desserts* include tick-box questionnaires, snippets from language textbooks, snatches of song lyrics and jokes:

> Goldberg's a private in the army. His mother dies, and his superior officers don't know how to break the news to him. His sergeant volunteers to do it. He calls the whole platoon out, makes them all stand to attention, and then says:
> 'All those with mothers still living, step forward!'
> They all step forward.
> 'Not so fast, Goldberg!'[17]

What Lucy Ellmann is up to is a form of collage. Unconnected images create an effect when they are placed next to one another in a visual collage, and so too do unconnected pieces of text. Often one piece of text can be used to comment on another: the joke just quoted is a way for Suzy Schwarz to deal with the fact that her father is dying. Taken all in, Ellmann's use of pattern helps her construct a novel that is the very opposite of monolithic.

Pattern has a positive effect on the reader because it is a means of making sense. When readers come across the second example of a pattern in a novel, they may think, 'Aha – I've seen one of these before. I know what they are.' This may give readers the impression that they are making sense of the text, that they know to some extent what is going on. It may also give readers an indication that *the writer* knows what is going on. The pattern shows that the text has been designed. It shows that there is a design and, therefore, a designer. The text is not just something that tumbled unformed from the writer's mind. On the contrary, it has been shaped with a purpose. These are positive responses to elicit from a reader; responses along these lines are the kind the writer wants; if nothing else, a responding reader is an active reader.

Try This: Creating Pattern

(You'll need a first draft for this.)

Look out for flourishes that you could turn into recurrent motifs or running jokes. Alison Moore, in her novel *The Lighthouse*, uses a lighthouse key-fob as a recurrent motif. In her novel *Things To Do Indoors*, Sheena Joughin makes frequent use of the small, but appealing, device of rendering song lyrics as reported speech: 'Dylan [was] singing that someone must say hello to his girlfriend, who might be in Tangiers.'

See if you can create pattern in a piece of fiction you're writing by looking for potential motifs and making them recur *or* by developing a witty device into a running joke.

Plant and Pay-Off

Perhaps the most efficient illustration of plant and pay-off is Chekhov's much-quoted observation that the gun in the first act must go off in the third. The plant is the first (or second, third, and so on) mention of whatever it is. The pay-off is when whatever it is used at a key moment in the narrative.

Halfway through *Toy Story*, Sid, the nasty kid from next door, sets Andy's cowboy doll Woody on a barbecue and jams a match in Woody's empty holster. It is clear he means to torch the doll. However, Woody escapes. Then, at the climax of the film, Woody and his friend Buzz Lightyear have the chance to catch up with their family, the Davises, if they can light a rocket attached to a roller-skate. And Woody remembers the match – textbook plant and pay-off. (Except, in this case, the screenwriter chooses to play with the convention: once ignited, the match blows out and the dolls have to find another way of lighting the rocket.)

A word to the wise, though: beware guns that don't go off. I once tried to be clever at the outset of a novel in manuscript. I thought I'd let the reader discover the name of the first-person narrator by having him read his name on an envelope. However, instead of revealing the character's name without telling the readers, I made them wonder what was in the letter – and the answer was, of course, nothing important to the plot. So the letter was a gun inadvertently planted, which would never go off.

In the examples described so far, pattern has been achieved by using a straightforward, brief form of plant and pay-off. Rose Tremain's *The Way I Found Her* is exemplary in its use of plant and pay-off. Three major elements of plot are sustained through the use of this device: the ability of Lewis, the narrator, to play chess; his growing skill at negotiating the rooftop of the Paris apartment building where he is staying; and the construction, by his father back in England, of a garden hut.

Lewis and his mother Alice are staying with Valentina in Paris for a summer while Alice works on the English translation of the novel Valentina is writing. Lewis's father, Hugh, is left at home, where he is planning a surprise for his wife when she returns from Paris:

> Hugh said: 'Lewis, I'm going to build a hut in the garden ...It's a secret between you and me, OK? I'm building it for Mum. We'll put a desk and a chair in it. It'll be a place where she can sit and read or work in the summer.'[18]

The garden hut is mentioned a handful of times and it seems as though Tremain's intention is comic relief: in these references to the building of the hut, Hugh appears ridiculous:

> Because I knew exactly what was going to happen to the hut: it would remain empty forever. A desk would be put in it for Alice and a gas heater, even. But Alice would never spend any time there, not even in summer.[19]

All the garden hut planting is paid off with considerable resonance when we learn, in the book's penultimate page, what happened to the hut:

> So I tell Hugh, I don't want to sleep in [my bedroom] any more; I want to sleep in the hut…So that's more or less where I live now, separate from the house, separate from Alice and Hugh.[20]

In effect, the hut has become a kind of symbolic home for Lewis, and with a fetching poetic justice: it was intended to be a place of solitude for Alice, but by the end of the narrative, it is in fact Lewis who needs to be solitary.

And let's not forget Saga Norén. Every time *The Bridge* shows her learning to say what will be tactful rather than what she thinks, the screenwriters are planting in preparation for the big pay-off, when her ability to tell a white lie will decide the outcome of the plot's climax.

Alternative Narrative Strategies

Aristotle believed a plot required a beginning, a middle and an end. Wayne C. Booth argues that this notion fell out of fashion during the twentieth century. It is unrealistic, he says, to 'begin at the beginning and plod methodically through to the end'.[21] In support of this, Booth points to Ford Madox Ford, who promoted a model which involved moving backwards and forwards over the protagonist's past – the non-chronological approach that is a hallmark of modernist fiction. Just such a narrative strategy can be seen in postmodern fiction, too: Peter Barry contends that for the postmodern writer, fragmented narratives are

> an exhilarating, liberating phenomenon, symptomatic of our escape from the claustrophobic embrace of fixed systems of belief.[22]

One of many possible ways to create a fragmented narrative is to break up what might otherwise be a monolithic text.

Breaking up the Monolith

You might break up the monolith by creating breathing space for the reader. Even in eras where readers may have had longer attention spans, there has always been a need for breathing space in fiction. At a fundamental level this begins with allowing the reader to participate in the text by letting them do some of the work – in what, for instance, remains unexplained.

Creating breathing space for the reader also involves, as Laurence Block explains in *The Writer's Digest Handbook of Short Story Writing*,[23] making use of the passing of time, geographical movement, leaving one set of characters and focusing on another, pulling back the focus. Also the use of what he calls collage – which I call quilting – rather than linear plot to tell the story.

In creating breathing space in my own work, as in the more general aim to avoid the monolithic, my ambition is to keep the contemporary reader – and myself – stimulated. This may be achieved through page design: breaking chapters into brief sections, making chapters and paragraphs and sentences shorter. It may also be achieved through using a range of narrative techniques. More variety, more complexity.

Another way of breaking up the monolith is using multiple viewpoints and flashbacks. Speaking of time, gaps in the chronology of days, months or years is another way of creating breathing space. Alternating between main plot and sub-plot also contributes to creating a various text.

Masculine Narrative Strategies

I'm simplifying here, but what I would call masculine approaches – and all writers use both masculine and feminine narrative strategies – tend to be task-oriented and target-related. For example, the simple linear plot, the reversal plot – anything, in fact, that could be defined by a plot structure, which consists of hook, steadily rising conflict, climax and dénouement.[24] Most Hollywood films use this kind of narrative structure. If you want to know how to vary your simple linear plot, Ronald B. Tobias's *20 Master Plots*[25] is a useful guide. If you want a quick understanding of the difference between masculine and feminine narrative strategies, watch the Spike Jonze/Charlie Kaufman film *Adaptation*, the first two-thirds of which are arguably more feminine in approach and the final third more Hollywood, more masculine, in structure.

In linear plotting, it's helpful to bear in mind that you can slow down the changes that are taking place. In Alison Lurie's *The Truth About Lorin Jones*, narrative tension is sustained throughout the concluding sections by negotiating change sparingly: the suspense is kept tight; the resolution comes an inch at a time, while the level of drama is maintained and often increased. For example, Lurie is able to keep us guessing about whether or not the protagonist will get her man. (For more on how pace is related to description, read Chapter 15, 'Setting'.)

Try This: Dual-viewpoint Story-building

Find an object and think about the following questions and make notes. It may be helpful at times to close your eyes and ponder the situation.

■ Where are you?

■ What you can see?

■ What can you smell?

■ What can you touch?

■ Is anyone else there?

■ What are the weather/atmosphere/mood like?

■ How do you feel?

■ What do you wish?

■ What does the object mean to you?

■ What is the problem at the moment?

■ What has led up to this moment?

■ What do you think will happen next?

Your notes should create a character in a situation. You'll need at least two characters, so repeat the exercise to create your second character, making the responses very different to make the second character distinct from the first.

Use the notes to write the first draft of a short story in which you write scenes, alternating the viewpoint, so that the story is seen through both your characters.

Don't try to write it all in one sitting: let the ideas gestate. Though it may not amount to a spree, a dual-viewpoint story is a first step on the road to being polyphonic.

Feminine Narrative Strategies

Feminine approaches tend towards plurality: of viewpoint and of narrative strategy. These approaches offer an alternative way to achieve what every narrative must do: maximise reader involvement with the text. In any number of contemporary novels, feminine narrative techniques are deployed: in Toni Morrison's *Beloved*, Louise Erdrich's *Love Medicine*, Amy Tan's *The Joy Luck Club*, Anne Tyler's *Dinner at the Homesick Restaurant*, Alice Walker's *The Color Purple*, Carol Shields's *Larry's Party* and Cristina Garcia's *Dreaming In Cuban*.

Tyler's family saga, *Dinner at the Homesick Restaurant,* is a tour de force in the use of multiple viewpoints. Each member of the Beck family has at least one chapter written from his or her point of view. An earlier model for this multiple-viewpoint approach is William Faulkner's *As I Lay Dying*. Multiple-viewpoint fiction offers more variety: the author may well be removed from the text and no one point of view is given credence above any of the others, thus suggesting that no one character's reality is the objective truth. For the writer, it's very stimulating: like an actor in a one-man show, you have to adopt a series of personas.

The use of multiple viewpoints is a prominent feature of Tan's work. In her novel *The Joy Luck Club,* for instance, the author has no overriding or unifying plot in the traditional sense. Instead, the novel is divided into four thematically linked sections, in each of which four viewpoint characters have one chapter apiece. Jing-Mei, the central character who links the other characters, has the most chapters. She is the unifying thread linking other viewpoint characters.

The Joy Luck Club, and other similar texts (those cited above, for example), may occupy the middle territory between a novel and a collection of short stories, but their appeal is that they offer an alternative to the traditional narrative. It's something like the pleasures of a compilation tape over those of a whole album by one artist.

Another interesting feminine narrative strategy is quilting, which is used in all of the novels mentioned so far. It amounts to fashioning a textual patchwork, whether through altering viewpoint, moving through time and space in a non-linear fashion, or, like Lucy Ellmann's *Sweet Desserts*, using a collage of writing modes (in this example, jokes, recipes, letters, personal ads and other found texts).

Elaine Showalter has written about narrative quilting in some depth. She notes Judith Fetterley's argument that nineteenth-century American women writers were freed from the pressures of the novel form[26] – the one 'most highly programmed and most heavily burdened by thematic and formal conventions'[27] by, as Showalter puts it, 'working with the piece or the story'.

Let me try to summarise her account of the history of this development. Women found that the short-story form – 'the short narrative piece' – allowed them more freedom. The growing importance of the book and novel form in America at the time led them to collect their stories together. In some cases, the collections later evolved into novels 'with narrative structures developed out of the piecing technique'.[28] She goes on to examine a short fiction by Kate Chopin, 'Elizabeth Stock's Story'.

Stock wants to write, but is daunted by the masculine, linear narrative form which she describes as 'original, entertaining, full of action, and goodness knows what all'. The feminine narrative form, which she attempts, is made up of patches in the manner of literal quilt-making, and according to Showalter, 'seems to offer a more authentic, but less orderly plot'. Chopin's story ends with Elizabeth Stock dying and her work being edited, condensed and preserved according to the consecutive and linear models of the male tradition, with all their craziness and originality lost.[29] The male editor in question prefaces Stock's patchwork narrative with an explanation of his task:

> I was permitted to examine her desk, which was quite filled with scraps and bits of writing in bad prose and impossible verse. In the whole conglomerate mass, I discovered but the following pages which bore any semblance to a connected or consecutive narration.[30]

In many respects this is how I think the quilted narrative works: the author acts as masculine editor of his or her own feminine text. On the one hand the narrative may be various, making use of multiple viewpoint, collage, the epistolary; on the other, the author needs to give it some structure that causes the whole to cohere and compel.

Further Reading

James N. Frey (1988) *How to Write a Damn Good Novel* (London: Macmillan). For all that it has a tacky title, this is a very helpful book. It's a particular kind of novel that he theorises, the dramatic novel. Frey covers much of the necessary ground in quite a short space and summarises some essential wisdom – such as Aristotle's *The Poetics*, which may be the earliest advice on writing. He has memorable chapter titles like 'The Three Greatest Rules of

Dramatic Writing: Conflict! Conflict! Conflict!' I found it more useful than many other texts on writing.

Joyce Carol Oates (2001) *Middle Age: A Romance* (London: Fourth Estate).

A highly structured approach to the multiple-viewpoint novel: there are three major sections to the book, each consisting of five chapters, each of which is written from the point of view of one of the five main characters. In each section we meet these characters in the same order. The book traces the effects of the death of Adam Berendt, a mysterious bohemian sculptor, on each of five his friends. We read on because the multiple narratives promise to unravel the mystery of who Berendt was.

Mike Sharples (1999) *How We Write* (London: Routledge).

This is an academic text, but written in an accessible style. If you're interested in thinking about how we write, it's well worth a look.

Rose Tremain (1998) *The Way I Found Her* (London: Vintage).

Tremain is one of the finest contemporary British novelists. Apart from what I've said about her use of plant and pay-off, much can be learned by studying her work. Hers is always a beautifully realised fictional world, finely textured without ever being dense.

17 Immediacy: It's Showtime

Robert Graham

I once heard a BBC radio documentary on which a researcher for Ace Records was talking about being in the vaults of the major label that owns Otis Redding's recordings. He was ploughing through tape-box after tape-box, sifting for recordings to lease for reissue, when he came across a box labelled 'Otis Redding – Dock of The Bay – Take 1'. He described playing the tape for the first time. He explained that the sound effects – the waves washing onto the shore, seagulls – had not yet been added and the whistling solo was fluffed: 'Otis wasn't actually a very good whistler.' What the researcher said of the experience was, 'It put you right there on the studio floor.'

Writing immediate fiction puts the reader 'right there on the studio floor' – right there in the action. Rather than recounting the narrative, you want the reader as close as dammit to experience it. This is perhaps the reason that, in Percy Lubbock's words,

> the art of fiction does not begin until the novelist thinks of his story as a matter to be shown, to be so exhibited that it will tell itself.[1]

Showing Not Telling

I've touched on showing and telling in Chapter 12, 'Characterisation', but in my experience, students find the difference between the two confusing, so I'm going to say more on the subject now.

Telling, Wayne C. Booth contends, amounts to 'summary' and is 'inartistic'; showing involves the use of 'scenes' and is 'artistic'.[2] Like most writers, I have often found it difficult to spot when I am slipping into telling. The difference between telling and showing, according to Monica Wood, can be expressed thus: showing involves 'using vivid details and engaging the senses ... painting a bright descriptive picture for the reader', while telling is 'uninspired narrative that only serves to explain what is going on in the story'.[3]

But what's the point in me telling you about it when I could show you?

Telling

> ALL THIS HAPPENED, more or less. The war parts, anyway, are pretty much true. One guy I knew really *was* shot in Dresden for taking a teapot that wasn't his. Another guy I knew really *did* threaten to have his personal enemies killed by hired gunmen after the war. And so on. I've changed all the names.[4]

This isn't immediate. It's somewhat an author's note, but Kurt Vonnegut (whose work I like) has put it in as his first paragraph – possibly the one paragraph in a novel that has to work harder than any other. No doubt Vonnegut did so deliberately. Maybe he was challenging the boundaries of truth and fiction, I don't know. Whatever the author's intention, the register of this passage is narration, or explanation, or monologue. It's the author addressing the reader directly, and when that happens, you can be sure that, rather than being shown, you are being told something.

There's more to it than the author addressing the reader directly, though. Telling comes in a variety of forms. When the author explains, it's telling. When the author lectures you, it's telling. Authorial summary is telling. Here the author is giving you a shorthand version of a series of events. This may be because the events are not so important, or it may be because the author wants to speed up the pace. And there are several ways in which you can fail to show, which for my purposes here might as well be classified as telling. Generalisations are not showing; when an author generalises, he is telling you about what tended to happen. A scene, showing, is something that happened in a particular place at a particular time. When the author analyses or interprets the behaviour of his characters, it is not showing; it is not taking place anywhere. Abstractions, as we're about to see, cannot be shown. Interior monologue is only taking place in the viewpoint character's head, so it is not showing.

You will find passages of telling in any great novel you care to name. Henry James does it. Richard Ford does it. And Carol Shields. And on and on. Is it a bad thing? All I know for sure is that showing is more dramatic and dramatised fiction is more engaging. And I also know that nobody will read your novel if it is entirely told. Not even your doting mother.

When to Tell

It's tempting to think that there's a quick-fix rule that will make your life as a writer straightforward, but there isn't. Sometimes telling will be desirable. Renni Browne and Dave King[5] have come up with three separate reasons a writer might have for using authorial summary:

1. When you want to vary the rhythm of your writing.

2. When you need to include a good deal of repetitive action.

3. When you want to include plot developments that are trivial enough not to need showing.

The first point here is more or less that variety is the spice of life. Showing is the optimum mode for writing fiction, but you can get too much of a good thing.

On the second point, it's to do with making the material you show have the maximum impact. At the moment, I'm writing a novel about a comedy double-act. The story will often feature the characters on stage or on television. If many parts of this story are summarised, it means that the ones that are presented as scenes will have a greater impact on the reader.

Browne and King's final point here: one way of reading it is that if something involves only minor characters or amounts only to a minor event, it may be better to summarise it.

Showing? Or Telling?

Still, most learning writers find it difficult to tell showing and telling apart. Renni Browne and Dave King's definition of a scene is helpful: 'In scenes, events are seen as they happen rather than described after the fact.'[6] Another way in is the illustration I often use in workshops: which would be more engaging, watching Martin Scorsese's *The Departed* or listening to me recount the film blow by blow? You might almost say that it's the difference between experiencing something vicariously and being told about it.

Perhaps Bernard MacLaverty's litmus test may help. MacLaverty is an Irish writer who has proven himself a master of the art of showing. His novel *Grace Notes* was shortlisted for the 1996 Booker Prize. His short stories have been compared to Chekhov's. In the field of short fiction, compliments don't come any better than that.

Imagine, says MacLaverty, that you are pitching your story to the film producer David Puttnam. If he thinks your material can be filmed, he will be offering you a million-pound contract. If he thinks your material is unfilmable, he will boot you out of his office.

You have two versions of the material. One goes like this:

Jimmy was in love with Jane.

Short and sweet. The other goes like this:

Every morning, Jimmy waited at his bedroom window for the moment when Jane would emerge from the house opposite. And each day as she walked out to the bus stop, he would stare as she walked by and sigh when she disappeared from view.

Which version of the material should you pitch?

Try This: Showing? Telling?

Read the first chapter of any novel you can pluck from your bookshelves. Using MacLaverty's litmus test, go through the chapter, highlighting the places where the author has told rather than shown. (As you are about to find out, I don't believe it's always wrong to tell; plenty of successful novelists do so plenty of the time. But my view, for what it's worth, is that it's advisable to keep telling to a minimum.)

Showing

That evening, Cody went out to the porch and looked northward some more in the twilight. Ezra came too and sat in the glider, pushing back and forth with the heel of one sneaker. 'Want to walk toward Sloop Street?' Cody asked him.

'What's on Sloop Street?'

'Nothing much. This girl I know, Edith Taber.'

'Oh, yes. Edith,' Ezra said.

'You know who she is?'

'She's got this whistle,' Ezra said, 'that plays sharps and flats with hardly any extra trouble.'

'Edith *Taber*?'

'A recorder.'

'You're thinking of someone else,' Cody told him.

'Well, maybe so.'[7]

This is immediate fiction. There are just two registers present here: what the characters do and what they say. Note also that there is conflict. Cody and Ezra, who are brothers, are also rivals. How is the conflict communicated to the reader? Indirectly. Look at the line where Cody, clearly rattled, says, 'You know who she is?' It shows us that Cody did not expect Ezra to know Edith, and that it bothers him to discover it.

There are two other things to note about Tyler's scene. First of all, it takes place somewhere, and this is a useful indicator of whether a piece of writing is showing or telling. Authorial summary and exposition come to you out of the ether. They don't take place anywhere. But a scene always has a setting. More importantly – and this is so obvious, it wouldn't be hard to miss it – a scene always has characters. (Of course, authorial summary has characters, too, but they aren't present: they're just being *talked about*.)

The Senses

I said earlier in this chapter that you want the reader almost to experience your story. Experience comes to us through the senses, through feeling. As the Pulitzer Prize-winning novelist and short-story writer Robert Olen Butler puts it, 'emotions are experienced in the senses and therefore are best expressed in fiction through the senses'.[8] Butler's view is that fiction engages readers when the author focuses on the viewpoint character's 'moment-by-moment sense-based events and impressions'.

As I said a few paragraphs back, your fiction will be immediate when you stick to what your viewpoint character does and says. Butler's insight fills out this advice. There is more to being in the moment than action and dialogue, and that *more* is what Butler calls the viewpoint character's moment-by-moment sensory impressions. If your character is outside in sub-zero temperatures, the experience of that is not an action, but it is crucial to immediacy. Dickens, in Chapter 2 of *Great*

Expectations, re-creates Pip's sensory impressions as he describes the boy's sister, Mrs Joe, cutting bread and buttering it:

> First, with her left hand she jammed the loaf hard and fast against her bib – where it sometimes got a pin into it, and sometimes a needle, which we afterwards got into our mouths. Then she took some butter (not too much) on a knife and spread it on the loaf, in an apothecary kind of way, as if she were making a plaster – using both sides of the knife with a slapping dexterity, and trimming and moulding the butter off round the crust. Then she gave the knife a final smart wipe on the edge of the plaster, and then sawed a very thick round off the loaf; which she finally, before separating from the loaf, hewed into two halves, of which Joe got one and I the other.

You feel you could reach out for that slice of bread and butter and take a bite out of it, don't you?

Here are two further examples of writing that is centred on the viewpoint character's moment-by-moment sensory impressions. The first is from the title story in Jhumpa Lahiri's terrific (and – again – Pulitzer Prize-winning) short-story collection, *Interpreter of Maladies*:

> He could smell a scent on her skin, like a mixture of whiskey and rosewater. He worried suddenly that she could smell his perspiration, which he knew had collected beneath the synthetic material of his shirt. He polished off his mango juice in one gulp and smoothed his silver hair with his hands. A bit of the juice dripped onto his skin.[9]

This is felt writing that inhabits the viewpoint character's senses so fully that they almost become the reader's, too.

Another example we all might aspire to is the way Alice Munro, in her story 'Walker Brothers Cowboy', makes us vicariously experience the narrator, a girl perhaps in her early teens, dancing with her father's old flame:

> Nora laughing and moving with great buoyancy, wrapping me in her strange gaiety, her smell of whisky, cologne, and sweat. Under the arms her dress is damp, and little drops form along her upper lip, hang in the soft black hairs at the corners of her mouth.[10]

Dickens's handling of Mrs Joe producing bread and butter for her husband and her brother focuses on what the viewpoint character sees. Jhumpa Lahiri and Alice Munro include not only what the viewpoint characters see, but also what they smell. And the Munro story adds to that the physical experience of movement, or rather of being moved: 'Nora laughing and moving with great buoyancy, wrapping me in her strange gaiety.' In other words, the sense of touch – which is the single sensory perception in this sentence from Cate Bailey's story, 'Concessions', which won *Mslexia*'s 2011 short-story competition. Here, the viewpoint is reluctantly having sex with a brutal ex-lover: 'The cast-off wool … scratched the backs of your thighs as he pushed your dress up.'[11]

Try This: Immediate, Moment-by-Moment Writing with the Senses

Write a one-page scene, in which the setting is a dentist's waiting room. John walks in, sits down and spots a woman he knows on the other side of the room. They say hello. He can't remember her name.

Try to incorporate these methods of achieving the immediacy just mentioned:

- Use characters.
- Record what the characters do.
- Record what the characters say.
- Have your dialogue demonstrate conflict *indirectly*.
- Record the characters' moment-by-moment sensory impressions.

Offstage, Paring Your Fingernails

Suspending the narrative to address the reader is a sure-fire way of destroying immediacy. Apart from the collapse of the sense of immediacy for the reader, the other problem with this device is that the story has stopped. You do a lot of work to get your reader interested in your story; why would you want to have to begin that work all over again? The author and the narrator are not usually the same person – but keeping the author or the narrator offstage 'paring his fingernails', as James Joyce put it, promotes immediacy. This is a matter of showing the reader how a character feels by the way he behaves and, often less directly, by what he says. Showing will begin with what the characters say and what they do. Immediacy is also promoted by avoiding the use of exposition, explanation, lecturing – anything which would bring the author on-stage.

The Scene

One way to maximise your chances of producing immediate fiction is to think in scenes. This is fundamental. If a piece of fiction doesn't have scenes, it isn't immediate. It may be exposition, or a lecture, or a monologue, interior or otherwise, it may be recounting or summarising – but it won't be immediate fiction.

The word 'scene' makes you think of films or plays, which is only right, as a scene should be *dramatic*. Something is dramatic when it has been dramatised. You dramatise when you use conflict to reveal character. If the author tells the reader about it, it has not been dramatised. It won't have much impact, either. Remember the often-quoted wise words of the American short-story writer, Flannery O'Connor: 'Readers aren't going to believe something just because you tell them.'

Dramatising is showing. If you show them something, readers will believe you. If you dramatise your material, it will have impact. You've already learned enough to make the basic elements of a scene. (Record what the characters do. Record what the characters say. Have the dialogue demonstrate conflict indirectly.)

The Function of a Scene

A scene moves the action forward. At the end of a scene, things are no longer as they were at the beginning. The way a scene moves the action forward is by having characters *act* and *speak*, and demonstrate conflict indirectly.

A scene also explores and reveals character and motivation. By the end of each scene the reader should know more about the characters. The way we learn more about them is by seeing what they say and do in response to the conflicts they face.

A scene must happen somewhere. When writing a scene, you have to make clear where and when the action is taking place, the setting of the action. A scene will have an emotional mood or atmosphere: funny or tragic, hopeful or desperate. For more on this, see Chapter 15, 'Setting'.

Advice on Making a Scene

■ The scene begins when the blue touchpaper has already been lit – not on the trip down to the firework shop.

- A scene, especially an opening scene, may well have a hook to snare the reader.

- A scene will often have a reversal. If it starts with a plus, it will often end with a minus. (Jill asks Jack out at the start of the scene; Jack falls down the hill and fractures his skull at the end of the scene.)

- Narrative tension in a scene will rise steadily. (It will not be static. It will not leap from low-level tension to nuclear-alert tension.)

- As a scene develops it will often start to read faster – achieved though shorter sentences, dialogue and paragraphs.

- The scene will have some kind of climax – a revelation, perhaps, a cliffhanger situation or a hook that pulls the reader on to the next scene.

- As soon as possible after the climactic moment, the scene will be over.

Try This: A Scene

Using the list immediately above, have a go at writing a scene. Here's your starting point:

'I was aiming for a punk look.'
'You missed.'

Exposition

If you are using the pluperfect tense you are failing to create a sense of immediacy. Exposition (background information) often comes in the pluperfect, by far the weakest tense – since it is most removed from the immediate – for the fiction writer. The pluperfect is the 'had-been' tense:

> For as long as she could remember, Louise had hated bus stops. She had once been mugged at a bus stop, and it had been at a bus stop that Dan, the great love of her life, had told her it was over between them. Bus stops had always been bad news.

And if you want to know what's wrong with exposition, think of it this way: a reader wanting answers to questions creates narrative tension;

in seeking answers, the reader is working. Exposition provides the reader with answers to questions they haven't even asked and requires them to do no work. The skills and techniques you use in immediate fiction create narrative tension. Introducing exposition is only going to undermine that tension.

Narrative Distance

A further factor in the creation of immediacy is the distance between events and the way in which they are brought to the reader. It's the distance between the narrative and the story or between the narrator and the story. The narrower that distance, the more real, the more convincing the fiction will be.

To look at some of the ways in which this distance may vary, it will be helpful to choose a novel where the narrator participates in the action – J.D. Salinger's *The Catcher in the Rye*, for instance. Some of the time Holden Caulfield, the narrator-protagonist, will address the reader directly:

> If you really want to hear about it, the first thing you'll probably want to know is where I was born, and what my lousy childhood was like, and how my parents were occupied and all before they had me, and all that David Copperfield kind of crap, but I don't feel like going into it, if you want to know the truth.[12]

In this celebrated opening, Holden, the narrator, is talking about the story at some distance. Here, before the narrative gets going, Holden isn't anywhere. Readers have begun the novel, but there isn't any action or setting, just a narrator addressing them. Thus, to put it in terms that you already understand, the reader will not feel very close to the story, because the author, in the guise of his creation, Holden Caulfield, is telling rather than showing. (Of course, the reason readers stick with Holden in their millions is because of his idiosyncratic voice, and voice is a way in which you may compensate for shortcomings in your narrative – but that's a whole other point, and one for another book.)

I first described Holden as a narrator-protagonist, a narrator who participates in the action. As such, in addition to suspending the action to address the reader directly – in the example given, the action hasn't even begun, but it amounts to the same thing – Holden will sometimes comment on the action as it is taking place, as we see here in a scene where he meets up with Sally Hayes, an old girlfriend, to go to a matinee:

> 'We better hurry,' I said. 'The show starts at two-forty.'
> We started going down the stairs to where the taxis are.
> 'What are we going to see?' she said.
> 'I don't know. The Lunts. It's all I could get tickets for.'
> 'The Lunts! Oh, marvellous!'
> I told you she'd go mad when she heard it was for the Lunts...
> Then, just to show you how crazy I am, when we were coming out of this big clinch, I told her I loved her and all. It was a lie, of course, but the thing is, I *meant* it when I said it. I'm crazy. I swear to god I am.

Twice here, Holden breaks off from the scene to address the reader: when he says, 'I told you she'd go mad when she heard it was for the Lunts' and when he tells us that he's crazy. The rest of the time, Salinger keeps Holden to his day-job: conveying a scene through action and dialogue.

You can see that there is a difference between the fiction in the two passages cited, where the narrator addresses the reader some or all of the time, and that which is going on during the rest of the novel, when Salinger writes immediate fiction from the viewpoint of Holden Caulfield:

> Finally I got out of bed with just my pajamas on, and opened the door ... Old Sunny and Maurice, the pimpy elevator guy, were standing there.
> 'What's the matter? Wuddaya want?' I said.
> 'Nothin' much,' old Maurice said. 'Just five bucks.' He did all the talking with the two of them. Old Sunny just stood there next to him, with her mouth open and all.
> 'I paid her already. I gave her five bucks. Ask her,' I said.

In a strictly show-don't-tell world, this third passage is what you would be aiming for. However, there are advantages to having the narrator address the reader directly. For one, as a narrative stance it amounts to an invitation to the reader to enter into a relationship with the narrator. The narrator is implicitly appealing for sympathy. The reader cannot help but feel more intimate with the narrator. In *Catcher*, whether Salinger has Holden addressing the reader out of the ether, commenting on a scene while it's happening, or presenting with immediacy – in a scene – the aims are the same: to make him engage the reader. At the same time, using these three forms of discourse offers variety, or possibly complexity, which is one of the attributes of real life.

> **Try This: Varying the Immediacy**
>
> Write a page or so in which you include the narrative modes just listed (addressing the reader out of the ether, commenting on a scene while it's happening and writing a proper, immediate scene. Your stimulus: three people who have been in a car too long.

Further Reading

Jennifer Egan (2011) *A Visit from the Goon Squad* (London: Corsair).
   With Jonathan Franzen's *The Corrections*, this is widely thought to be one of the best American novels of the century so far. Is it a short-story collection or a novel? Well – both. But if you want to see how to combine showing and telling to consistently strong effect, look no further.
Anne Tyler (1992) *Dinner at the Homesick Restaurant* (London: Vintage).
   Nick Hornby has called Tyler the best novelist at work today, but of course, there is no best. Anne Tyler on form, though, is a guaranteed page-turning read, and if you want to learn how to write immediate fiction (and how to avoid exposition) you won't go wrong studying the work of the bard of Baltimore. She is also a mistress of characterisation. She has been turning out skilful novels since the early 1960s, so if you become a convert, there's plenty of good reading ahead of you. For my money, *Homesick* is her finest achievement – and it's on record that it's still her favourite of her own novels – but *Ladder of Years* and *The Amateur Marriage* are very good reads, too.

18 Style
Robert Graham

Narrative craft is important, but even more important is the ability to write well and with style, so that each line is a pleasure for the reader. What is style? According to Jonathan Swift, it's not much more than proper words in their proper place. The writing in a decent instruction manual might achieve that – Hemingway talked about getting the words right – without being what you or I might think stylish. So there has to be a little more to it than clear expression. The novelist Henry Green said that a writer's style is 'himself, and we are all of us changing every day'. Perhaps writers' styles emerge from the rhythms of speech where they grew up, from the style of authors in whose style they aspire to write, from the lyrics of songs they know, from writing they find in print, online and in the media. It may well be to do with the sound of language, as well as its meaning. The foundations of style lie in some of the aspects of writing we're about to examine: language, syntax, vocabulary choice, grammar and punctuation. Let's look at the style of a couple of contemporary writers.

Richard Ford is a fiction writer with a pronounced style and a man unfazed by the long sentence with several sub-clauses and more than one or two detours:

> Falling property values now ride through the trees like an odourless, colorless mist settling through the still air where all breathe it in, all sense it, though our new amenities – the new police cruisers, the new crosswalks, the trimmed tree branches, the buried electric, the refurbished band shell, the plans for the 4th of July parade – do what they civically can to ease our minds off worrying, convince us our worries aren't worries, or at least not ours alone but everyone's – no one's – and that staying the course, holding the line, riding the cyclical nature of things are what this country's all about, and thinking otherwise is to drive optimism into retreat, to be paranoid and in need of expensive 'treatment out-of-state.'[1]

You don't have to be able to control a very long sentence to be stylish, though. Ann Beattie's prose is crisp and efficient, so that her style is almost the opposite of Ford's:

> He sipped a beer. At seven-thirty he opened the paper and looked through the theatre section. A quarter to eight he got up and left.[2]

You may feel that either of these styles is beyond you or that neither is for you. Either way, most of us are interested in developing our style. This chapter is not going to turn you into Richard Ford overnight, but there are some simple steps you can take which will improve your prose.

Simple and Direct

As in life, in several aspects of creative writing, less is more, plain and simple are best. Certainly this is the case with style. In *The English Style Book*, Robert Clark argues for simplicity in written expression: 'Look closely at the sentences of most distinguished writers and you will invariably find that the words chosen and the syntax used are fundamentally simple.'[3]

In the Bible, in the Gospel of John, when Jesus arrived at the tomb of his friend Lazarus, the narrator captures the moment in one short sentence (the shortest verse in the Bible): *Jesus wept.* Would more words have helped us understand the moment? No. It's a cast-iron certainty that adding to this two-word sentence would only detract from its effectiveness. We can be pretty sure that Anton Chekhov would have endorsed John's style. For good and ill – search the Net for Michael Chabon on the subject – Chekhov was arguably the greatest influence on twentieth-century short-story writing, and in part this was to do with style. Here he is advising a peer, in a letter of 1899:

> You understand it at once when I say, 'The man sat on the grass'; you understand it because it is clear and makes no demands on the attention.
>
> On the other hand, it is not easily understood, and it is difficult for the mind, if I write, 'A tall, narrow-chested, middle-sized man, with a red beard, sat on the green grass, already trampled by pedestrians, sat silently, shyly, and timidly looked about him.'
>
> That is not immediately grasped by the mind, whereas good writing should be grasped at once – in a second.[4]

Chekhov is widely thought to have known what he was talking about, and what he is talking about here is cutting out the flab – removing the superfluous. In the illustration he gives, this is a matter of concentrating on just the essential detail, on giving readers a level of detail that they can absorb. There are other reasons for being concise, though. When you come to redraft your work, distillation is desirable. You might begin with a statement like this, which you could refine in the ways that follow:

⇒ The process of learning to write with concision can take years.

⇒ The process of learning to write concisely can take years.

⇒ Learning to write concisely can take years.

Sometimes removing the superfluous is just a case of not saying things in a roundabout way. For instance, in this sentence, *I was unaware of the fact that she did not drink coffee*, the author is beating about the bush by including *of the fact that*. This phrase is unnecessary. I was unaware that she did *not drink coffee* is more concise and therefore more effective. (Bringing craft as well as style into it, though, the phrase *I was unaware* inserts an intermediary you ought to ditch, too.) Sometimes examples of the superfluous in writing might be better described as redundancies. You should avoid using clunkers anything like the following: continue on; return back; bald-headed; forests of trees; merge together.

Concision is key to good style, but so, too, is directness. In narrative writing, in order to intrigue, you will often want to keep your reader in the dark. However, when you do want the reader to understand something, you shouldn't leave anything to chance. You want the information you wish to transmit to travel as directly as possible from your mind to the reader's. Here are a couple of suggestions.

Writing with verbs and nouns is desirable. This means as far as possible avoiding adjectives and, especially, adverbs. (See what Robert Sheppard and Scott Thurston say in Chapter 22, 'Poetry', about the effect of adjectives on nouns.) It has to do with hitting the nail on the head first time, so that the information goes straight to the reader's head. It has to do with finding a verb that conveys what you want to say without the need to qualify it with an adverb. If you want to write in a direct, clean and concise style, adverbs are more often than not superfluous. Compare these two expressions of the same information:

(a) Selina walked angrily out of the room.

(b) Selina stamped out of the room.

'Stamped' conveys 'walked angrily' in one word.

Another way of ensuring your prose is as direct as possible is to avoid qualifying phrases. The rationale here is similar to that in my last point: part of the secret to direct communication is getting it right first time. If you make a statement and then qualify it, you are not getting it right first time. Compare the following versions:

(a) The Beatles came out of Liverpool and conquered the world, having first become the most popular band in Merseyside and then in Britain.

(b) The Beatles came out of Liverpool and conquered the world.

In other words, make your point and leave it alone. Get it right first time.

Now take a look at Australian novelist Helen Garner keeping it simple and direct and eschewing qualification:

> I boiled the kettle and wrapped the hot water bottle in its cloth. Her door was shut. Was I supposed to knock? I opened it and slid in. She was lying on her back on the bed, fully dressed, with her eyes closed. The late sun glared off the wall next door, making the room comfortless and harsh.[5]

Try This: Develop Your Style 1

Using the word 'Lost' as a stimulus, write the first 500 words of a piece of fiction. When you have a first draft in place, use the advice above on writing simply, concisely and directly to produce a more polished second draft.

Concrete Detail

It's hard for readers to engage with abstractions, as this passage from Thomas Pynchon's *Mason & Dixon* illustrates:

> As relentless in his hatred of those he hunts down as they are indifferent, in their love of God, to the passions driving him. Jansenist Convulsionaries, Crypto-Illuminati, and the Neo-Quietists alike have cultivated his wrath.[6]

Nothing too wrong with Pynchon, of course; he's a novelist with an impressive reputation. But compare the above to this:

> He washed his face. He put the soap and towel in the shaving bag. Then he put in the soap dish and the glass from over the sink and the fingernail clippers and her eyelash curlers.[7]

Concrete as granite, and not an abstraction in sight. The result? We access the information at once, and in terms of style the prose has the virtue of being as utilitarian as a spanner. Pynchon's style may well be more revered than Carver's often bare-bones sentences. I'm not saying one is a better writer than the other; just that the Carver passage is much more direct and so much more accessible.

Being specific – being precise – sharpens your writing: *The shrub was dying* tells us much less than *The hydrangea was dying*. And *We went to Aldi* communicates more than *We went to the supermarket*. It's also useful to include the detail of what you are focusing on: *We used to build go-karts out of planks and pram-wheels*. This includes the useful specifics of the planks and the pram-wheels, and they bring the sentence, the moment, alive.

However, here's another aspect of being specific. The words *We used to* makes this statement related rather than immediate, because it suggests that building go-karts was something that happened on several occasions. It's a generalisation, not a specific event. Much better if the action appears to be happening in front of us: *That morning, we built a go-kart*. Now it's something that happened on a particular occasion, which has more impact, more immediacy.

Syntax

The organisation of words in a sentence – syntax – will have an impact on the effectiveness of your writing. One very basic way of improving your sentences is to make sure that you group related parts of a clause together. The reason for this is that words which connect with one another to form meaning work best when keeping each other company – for instance, the subject and verb of a clause. Compare these two versions of a sentence:

(a) Stephen Spielberg's influence in late twentieth-century Hollywood was almost unrivalled.

(b) In late twentieth-century Hollywood, Stephen Spielberg's influence was almost unrivalled.

'Stephen Spielberg's influence', 'was' and 'unrivalled' are connected and so work best when grouped together.

You can also use syntax to control the effect a particular part of a sentence will have on the reader: another straightforward technique is to remember that the sentence ending packs the most punch, so push the information you want to emphasise as far back in the sentence as you can. Compare these two versions:

(a) Morrissey would sell more records and play to bigger crowds if he reformed The Smiths.

(b) If he re-formed The Smiths, Morrissey would sell more records and play to bigger crowds.

Stylish Dialogue

You can learn a lot by studying John Singleton's Chapter 14, 'Dialogue', but don't forget that the way you write dialogue is part of your style, too. That style can consist of being smart and witty, like this from Raymond Chandler's *The Big Sleep*:

> 'Tall, aren't you?' she said.
> 'I didn't mean to be.'[8]

Style can emerge from repetition and a certain ping-pong rhythm, as it does here, in Elmore Leonard's *Freaky Deaky*, where Greta has just received a proposition and Chris is quizzing her about it:

> 'What're you doing, thinking about it?'
> 'No, I'm not thinking about it.'
> 'What're you doing?'
> 'I'm not doing anything, I'm sitting here.'
> 'What about the settlement?'
> 'I go back, tell him I've thought about it...I guess, and then he gives it to me.'
> 'You mean you're going to think about it?'
> 'No, but I have to tell him I did.'[9]

Dialogue writing like this is concocted and shaped. It isn't an attempt to record the way real people speak. Rather, Leonard's aim is to create narrative tension and to do so with sheer, fizzing, eye-catching style.

It might be true to say that you can't be a good fiction writer if you can't write good dialogue, so (a) I hope you will find examples of good dialogue in the work of any writer cited in this book and (b) you can develop yours by studying dialogue used by the authors you like best.

Grammar

One central factor in writing well is to ensure that your prose is always grammatical. There are too many ways of being ungrammatical to go into, but here are a couple of errors I come across often – and I realise that for some of you the fact that they are errors will be obvious. But not all of you.

If the subject is plural, then so is the verb.

> *Wrong:* The schoolchildren was very well-behaved.
> *Right:* The schoolchildren were very well-behaved.

Another example of flawed grammar is subject and object confusion. When the first person is the subject, it's *I*: *I kicked the ball*. When the first person is the object, it's *me*: *The ball thumped me in the face*. The same thing applies with *who* and *whom*: *This is the woman who loves me*. And: *This is the woman whom I love*.

Just two examples there, but there are almost limitless ways in which you can screw up grammar. There are a few obvious ways of improving it, though.

Reading a great deal is beneficial, of course, and writers never stop reading.

Plenty of good primers are available.

When you redraft, you will be using the spell/grammar-check tool in Word (although you should not rely on this alone): Word, as you will have noticed, often makes bizarre suggestions about grammar.

There are excellent online resources.

You ought to have a dictionary and a thesaurus on the bookshelf above your computer.

You will also find newspaper style guides useful; in the UK, the *Guardian, The Times* and the *Mirror* have all published guides on usage that were developed for their writers, and the same will be the case in other parts of the world.

Reading your work aloud will throw up many of the obvious flaws in your grammar (and your style), as will getting others to read and give feedback on your drafts.

Many books about grammar written by experts in the field are published every year. If your grammar is letting you down, you could do worse than study one or two of them. (See *Further Reading* at the end of the chapter.)

Good Choices

Another way you can improve your style is by making good choices. This has many applications, but here are just a few. You think a little longer and select stronger verbs. *Fred Astaire moved across the room* is not as effective as *Fred Astaire glided across the room.* You can duck clichés. *After winning, Claire was over the moon* is rather threadbare, but *After winning, Claire was so far over the moon she reached Mars* is a little less obvious. Choosing the active rather than the passive voice will make your sentences more dynamic, more direct. *That school trip to London will always be remembered by those of us who were there* goes round the houses to make its point. Much simpler and more potent is: *We will always remember that school trip to London.* The word *there* is often used in a superfluous way:

> There was something under the bed.
> Outside there was a door banging.

More alive would be:

> Something was under the bed.
> Outside a door was banging.

Oakley Hall calls this use of *There* a 'deadener of prose'.[10]

Try This: Develop Your Style 2

Write a further 500 words of the piece of fiction you began in the previous exercise. Now, with 1000 words under your belt, revise it in the light of what you've just been reading in the sections above:

■ Concrete Detail

■ Syntax

■ Dialogue

■ Grammar

and

■ Good Choices

Further Reading

Rachel Bladon, *The Usborne Guide to English Grammar* (Usborne, 2003).
  Written for children, but that means it's clear and easy to understand, which if your grammar or punctuation is holding you back – and it holds back a lot of people – is exactly what you want. Note that it's just 38 pages long.

The Elements of Style: http://www.bartleby.com/141/
  If you want to find time-honoured advice about improving your written expression, take a look at William Strunk and E.B. White's classic, *The Elements of Style*. You can buy it in book form, but the full text is available online, free of charge.

The Internet Grammar of English: http://www.ucl.ac.uk/internet-grammar/.
  Produced by the University of Central London and aimed at undergraduates, this free online resource has been recommended by *BBC Skillswise*, *Guardian Education* and the *Chicago Tribune*. It's also available as an App for Android and Apple mobile devices.

19 Memoir
Robert Graham

Everything we write exposes who we are, but, even more than other kinds of writing, the memoir strips us to the skin. As such, it isn't a form for everyone. The best memoir writing exposes the author in a raw state, for which not all of us are ready. A memoir also exposes the other people in your life, and not all of them are going to be enthusiastic about being shoved into the spotlight...

Where I teach, we call it memoir writing, but it's also known as life writing and autobiographical writing. Americans call the short memoir 'the non-fiction short story', which flags up the relationship between memoir and fiction writing. And that's the first thing I would say to you here: every skill you use in writing short stories will be equally helpful to you when you tackle the memoir form.

To illustrate this point, let's take a look at an extract from Augusten Burroughs's best-selling memoir, *Running with Scissors*. It concerns the years during which Augusten's mother handed him over to be brought up by her psychiatrist. The shrink in question, Dr Finch, is the one speaking at the start of the extract. He is in the throes of trying to provoke Deirdre, Augusten's mother, to anger, so that she may express some of her repressed rage.

'Deirdre, answer me', Finch demanded. 'Do you see how Hope's sneaking in here and invading my private space is wrong?'

After a moment of thinking about it, my mother said, 'Well, I can understand not liking one's space invaded. I can understand how it would be upsetting to have somebody messing with your things without asking.'

'Then confront her!' Finch directed.

I stood back, not wanting to get sucked in.

'Well, I ...'

'Deirdre, speak up! Tell Hope what you feel.'

> My mother looked at Hope as if to say, What can I do? Then she said, 'Hope, I don't think it's right for you to disturb your father's space without asking.'
>
> 'This is none of your business, Deirdre,' Hope said. Her eyes were squinty with anger.
>
> My mother took another drag from her cigarette and tried to leave again. 'I think I'll just get another cup of Sanke.'
>
> Finch grabbed her arm. 'Just a minute there, Deirdre. Are you going to let Hope walk all over you like that? Jesus Christ, Deirdre. Are you going to be Hope's doormat?' [1]

If you didn't know where this passage had come from, if you didn't know what it was, how would you label it? My guess is that you might think it was a piece of fiction. It looks like fiction: there are characters and they do things and say things and there is conflict between them. More implicitly, it functions like fiction, because Burroughs doesn't tell us what these characters are like, he *shows* us. (You'll notice there isn't a point here where the author explains anything to us.) In other words, this isn't a monologue, it isn't an essay, it isn't a piece of journalism. It's a scene, material that has been dramatised rather than recounted. The dialogue, too, functions like that fiction. As such, it's identical to the kind of writing you will find in any contemporary short story or novel.

Selection

Bear this in mind, too: an autobiography will concern at the least many years from a life, but a memoir is selective. As Judith Barrington says, 'autobiography is the story *of* a life; memoir is a story *from* a life'.[2] This is true whether you are writing a book-length memoir or one that's only 2000 words long. Whatever their length, memoirs tend to be about a particular aspect of the author's life. *And When Did You Last See Your Father?*, Blake Morrison's memoir, is about – no surprise – his father; and Anne Patchett's *Truth and Beauty* focuses exclusively on the author's friendship with the writer Lucy Grealy.

When it comes to writing a short memoir, the focus may be very narrow. Of the student memoirs I've marked in recent years, two spring to mind. One was about a year of not being happy as a Cambridge student; the other was about being bullied on one particular school bus journey. Now a year out of your life could easily be a book-length memoir, but there's no way one bus journey could be anything more than the length of a short story. It's that tightness of focus and that length which we are looking at here.

How do you go about selecting your focus? Perhaps the first criterion is that you will need a significant and interesting memory to work with – something that will prompt an emotional response from the reader. We often remember the best and the worst moments. It's possible that the memory of a difficult experience is more likely to prompt an emotional response from your reader; the great time you had on holiday in Dorset may not be so interesting to others.

Try This: Selecting Memories

Mull over your past – your childhood, perhaps, or something more recent – and make a short list of aspects of it that might form the source of an engaging memoir. When you have your list, label each item on it with the emotion – loss, shame, envy – you would attach to it. If you can't attach an emotion to it, you can eliminate the item from your list. Next, select one experience from the list and briefly explore it in writing

    (a) why you find this episode memorable
          and
    (b) why you felt what you did.

Accuracy

If you are writing a memoir, what you write should really have happened to you. You may well have heard of the fuss that arose when it emerged that James Frey's memoir *A Million Little Pieces* was not all based on his actual experience. (Which is not to say, as we are about to find out, that a memoir is a wholly accurate account of what happened.) Frey was accused of inventing some of his criminal record and fictionalising the account of a girlfriend's suicide. If you're thinking of writing an account of your time as a Hell's Angel and you have never been one, then don't. But is that the same thing as saying that a memoir needs to be literally accurate? Most commentators seem to argue that it is not, and if you think about it, what are the chances that the middle-aged Augusten Burroughs had a word-for-word recall of every conversation in his adolescence (or that Bob Dylan, below, writing in this century, remembered every conversation he had in the 1960s, 1970s and 1980s)? Zero. There are some things about an experience, including what was said, that you will not be able to bring to mind – because you cannot remember them. (And it's just as likely that anyone else who was there at the time will not be able to remember every aspect of the episode with total accuracy either.) When we write memoir what we are dealing with is emotional memory. If I were to write about the time, aged 16, when I crashed a car without a driver's licence, I would not be able to remember very much that was said that day or all of the events in the correct order – but it wouldn't matter, because I can remember with some power how the experience felt. I would therefore have what Lee Gutkind calls 'permission to lie'.[3] Let me just spell this out for you. I am not free to write that I crashed the car while making an emergency dash to hospital to save a friend's life, because that isn't what happened. However, I am free to write something that will re-create for the reader the emotional truth of an episode when, driving illegally, I crashed a car because I wasn't looking where I was going.

An understandable failure to remember what was said at a particular time of your life may lead to you invent, but that's not the only reason to take a flexible approach to the facts. In order to create a successful narrative, you may well have to alter the chronology of events. Equally, sometimes it may be necessary to write one scene which will stand in the place of many similar scenes that actually happened; writing a series of very similar scenes will do nothing for your reader engagement.

Whether you invent dialogue, compress the chronology, conflate scenes or in any other way diverge from a one hundred per cent accurate version of your experience, it's vital that you make it aim to achieve something I mentioned a few lines back: the emotional truth of what happened. It will not be the objective truth, of course; but it should be your truth. And, as with fiction, scriptwriting or poetry, if you manage to achieve something true, it will have an impact on your readers. In the following passage, A.M. Homes shows her hurt at her newly discovered biological father's inability to include her in his family:

> I am the ghost, the one who does not exist. When I look in the mirror, do I see my reflection?
> 'Have you figured out how to tell them?' I ask.
> 'No,' he says. 'I'm still having a little bit of trouble with that.' He makes it sound like something he's trying to fix himself, a car part that requires tinkering.[4]

Is this what was actually said? Is it one scene that represents a compression of several? We can't know. Does it re-create the emotional truth of the author's experience? I would very much think so.

Techniques

In the extract from *Running with Scissors*, we saw Augusten Burroughs writing very effectively in scenes. You've read our chapter on immediacy; you don't need me to tell you again that writing in scenes is crucial. The other key discourse in fiction writing is summary, and of course when writing memoir you will use it, too, as Dave Eggers does here in *A Heartbreaking Work of Staggering Genius*:

> They took my mother's stomach out about six months ago. At that point, there wasn't a lot left to remove ...[They] hoped they had removed the offending portion, and set her on a schedule of chemotherapy. But of course they didn't get it all.[5]

As in fiction, you will use summary to speed the narrative up, and immediacy to slow it down, and as in fiction, a good test for which to use is that if the information is dramatically important, use scene, and if less significant, summary.

I want to look at extracts from two very different memoirs now, each with distinct techniques to teach us about creating character.

The following passage is from Bob Dylan's *Chronicles Volume 1*, specifically from 'Oh Mercy', a lengthy chapter on a turning point in his career that coincided with the writing and recording of his 1989 album of the same name. A frustrated Dylan has abandoned the recording sessions in New Orleans and headed out into rural Louisiana with his wife on a Harley Davidson motorcycle. They come across an obscure roadside shack called King Tut's Museum.

> The place sold trinkets, newspapers, sweets, handcraft items, baskets made of swamp cane that were woven in the area – elaborate patterns. There were figurines and sham jewels, some items in display cases, umbrellas, slippers, blue voodoo beads and votive candles ...It was run by an old-timer named Sun Pie, one of the most singular characters you'd ever want to meet. The man was short and wiry like a panther, dark face but Slavic features, wore a narrow brimmed, flat-topped straw hat. On his bones was the raw skin of the earth ...Sun Pie was working on a high loft chair. It looked like it came out of a cathedral. It was disassembled in pieces, clamped up on the sides and glued. He was sandpapering an edge of a six-planed leg ...
>
> Sun Pie carefully selected a chisel, began scraping on the back post of the chair. There were lions' heads on the leg rails and intricate swirling designs in the black wood. He was working close in. The Dale and Grace song 'I'm Leaving It Up To You' was playing on the radio.[6]

This is a striking piece of writing because of the way Dylan, through vivid description, has conveyed the character of Sun Pie and his environment. In fact, the use of setting is so prominent that it's hard to work out where Sun Pie ends and the interior of his King Tut's Museum begins; the two are very nearly one. The author is a keen observer of his world, and he takes in impressive amounts of detail. Clearly, the ability to observe characters and situations closely is a potent skill for a writer to cultivate. Note, too that Dylan is a great one for lists; a couple of lists are used in the creation of setting, of the interior of the shack. For most readers, lists make for effective description – perhaps because they are a speedy, economic form of summary; perhaps because the nature of a list makes us want to go through what's on it.

Andrea Ashworth's *Once in a House on Fire* is about her childhood, and particularly the effect of her mother marrying an abusive man. Like any other character in a piece of prose, the stepfather is conveyed through action and dialogue. However, Ashworth uses a further effect to characterize the man, one that is striking: her choice of vocabulary when she writes about him. When the focus is on the stepfather, more often than not she selects words that have a negative connotation, words with an ugly sound. The photograph of her mother's marriage to him '*squatted* on the sideboard'; he used to '*lug* bulging sacks of *misshapen* Mojos home'; his boots '*scraped* on the doormat'; 'he *smacked* our cheeks with kisses'; he sat '*chomping*'; he 'slumped back on the settee'.[7]

Since all memoirs are about the past, and often this means a decade or more in the past, an essential technique is the use of the cultural signifier. If I scan through the memoirs open on my desk just now, I can find the following cultural signifiers: Band-Aid, Coke, Lego, Motown vinyl, the Moors murders, Murraymints, Vesta curry, Formica, Safeway, Sanke, Sterling Moss, a baobab tree, a Nintendo and a Granny Smith apple. Each one of these signifiers represents an intrinsic part of a particular culture or (more relevant for the re-creation of an era) a particular time. You won't find a baobab tree in Cheshire, and as far as I know, you can't find a Vesta curry in a modern shop. Signifiers such as these are like little gems embedded in your narrative which light up for the reader who recognizes them. If I write a memoir and tell you it is set in 1962, it may not register very much. But if I include signifiers that indicate the era – if a character is eating a packet of Spangles or a bar of Cadbury's Nut Crisp; if The Beatles' *Love Me Do* is playing on the radio, or *Z-Cars* is on TV – something of the ear begins to resonate.

Emotion

One of Natalie Goldberg's rules of writing practice is that one should always go for the jugular, which I take to mean tackling the things we find it most difficult to write about. This is perhaps especially so in memoir writing. Gutkind advises you to 'Tear yourself inside out. Unearth, dramatise, relive bad memories, frightening and life-shaping experiences.'[8] For some of us, this is difficult, but perhaps motivation may come from the suggestion that if it's painful to write, it will more than likely be a powerful read.

In your study of writing fiction, no doubt you will already have noticed that the more you try to make a powerful experience emotive, the less likely it is to be so. In this, as in so much else, less is more. Calum Kerr, in 'Stranger Than Faction', argues that 'any attempt to find words large enough, laden enough, or even simply long enough to convey something truly heartfelt, leads to melodrama, telling not showing, and, often but not exclusively, bad writing'.[9] Be warned.

In the following passage, A.M. Homes re-creates the moment when she received confirmation that the man she believes to be her biological father actually is:

> Norman waits for the ginger ale to arrive before he says anything.
> "The test says it's ninety-nine-point-nine percent likely that I'm your father." There is a pause. "So what are my responsibilities?"
> *I am not a slice of pie.*
> "So what are my responsibilities?"
> I say nothing.[10]

Would a response such as this from the father be hurtful in the circumstances? For sure. Does Homes say she was devastated, or that she felt like she had been kicked in the teeth? No. She doesn't even mention feeling hurt. But it's completely clear to the reader that this was a very painful moment. How does she convey that to us? By doing nothing but reporting what was said and leaving readers to work out for themselves how the experience would feel.

Try This: Staying On the Surface

From the previous exercise, you will have some notes on a particular experience. You will have explored why you find this episode memorable and why you felt the way you did. Now, using the brief extract from A.M. Homes's memoir, write the experience as a scene. Just as Homes does, stay on the surface, sticking to what characters say and what characters do. And remember that the dialogue may well be indirect: in the Homes extract, when the father says, 'What are my responsibilities?' he's really saying that he doesn't want to have any.

Further Reading

Alexandra Fuller, *Don't Let's Go to the Dogs Tonight* (London: Picador, 2002).
  War and more than one bereavement mar family life in this compelling account of growing up on a farm in Zimbabwe. If you want to learn how to write about painful experiences, this is a good starting point.
Blake Morrison, *And When Did You Last See Your Father?* (London: Granta, 1994).
  In the UK, the success of this book probably marked the start of the rise of the memoir in contemporary publishing. Using the focus of his father who is dying from cancer, Morrison moves backwards and forwards in time to examine this father–son relationship. It's very well written, and often highly emotive. The character of the father, warts and all, comes over strongly.

20 Flash Fiction
David Gaffney

In 2006, I published a book of flash fiction called *Sawn-Off Tales*. But until only a little while before that, I hadn't heard of flash fiction or micro-fiction or sudden fiction or short-short stories. Then, on poet Ian McMillan's recommendation, I parcelled up a manuscript made entirely of this stuff and sent it to Salt Publishing, a poetry specialist. Fifty-eight stories, each exactly 150 words long. The odds were entirely against me. No one wants to publish short stories, least of all by an unknown. And stories that took less time to read than to suppress a sneeze? I was chancing it, I knew.

I began to produce these ultra-short stories – sawn-off tales, as I call them – when I was commuting from Manchester to Liverpool: a 50-minute journey, often elongated by windscreen-wiper failure, fights on the train, or getting stuck behind the 'stopper'. But I had a book, as did most passengers. One day, while ruminating on the number of train journeys it took to read a novel, I began to wonder how long it would take to write one. I decided on 500 words a trip – there and back was 1000 words a day – taking just four months to reach a respectable novel length of 80 000 words.

So the next day I boarded the 8.12 at Manchester Piccadilly, rushed for a table seat, and, instead of whipping out my paperback, set up my laptop and began tapping away. But after a couple of weeks it was clear that the novel wasn't working. What I'd produced was a set of separate stories, each around 1000 words long. I was about to ditch the idea when I heard about a new website called The Phone Book, which needed 150-word stories to send out as text messages. All that was needed was a bit of editing.

Initially, as I hacked away at my overstuffed paragraphs, watching the sentences I once loved hit the floor, I worried. It felt destructive, wielding the axe to my carefully sculpted texts; like demolishing a building from the inside, without it falling down on top of you. Yet the results surprised me. The story could live much more cheaply than I'd realised, with little deterioration in lifestyle. Sure, it had been severely downsized, but it was all the better for it. There was more room to think, more space for the original idea to resonate, fewer unnecessary words to wade through. The story had become a nimble, nippy little thing that could turn on a sixpence and accelerate quickly away. And any tendencies to go all purple – 'If it sounds like writing, rewrite it', as Elmore Leonard said – were almost completely eliminated. Adjectives were anthrax.

It worked. By the time I got to Birchwood I had it down to 500 words, by Warrington to 300, at Widnes 200, and as the train drew in to Liverpool Lime Street there it was – 150 words, half a page of story; with a beginning, a middle and an end, with character development and descriptions, everything contained in a Polly Pocket world.

These stories, small as they were, had a huge appetite; little fat monsters that gobbled up ideas like chicken nuggets. The habit of reducing text could get out of hand too; I once took away the last two sentences of a story and realised I had reduced it to a blank page.

Luckily The Phone Book liked my stories and published them, and I continued to churn them out each day on the train, while the train guard announced the delays, the tea trolley rolled past, and a succession of passengers sat next to me, reading over my shoulder.

A week after sending the manuscript to Salt Publishing I got a call from Jen, their editor. They wanted to publish it, and quickly. All I needed was a quote for the cover, a photo for the cover, and we were off.

I don't commute that route any longer – my new job covers the whole north-west of England, involving train trips to Blackpool, Lancaster, east Lancashire, west Cumbria and Cheshire, so my stories have grown quite a bit longer. But last time I was on a train to Lime Street the guard's identity badge took me right back – because that's where I got the names for all of my characters.

How to Write Flash Fiction

1. *Start in the middle.*

You don't have time in this very short form to set scenes and build character.

2. *Don't use too many characters.*

You won't have time to describe your characters when you're writing ultra-short. Even a name may not be useful in a micro-story unless it conveys a lot of additional story information or saves you words elsewhere.

3. *Make sure the ending isn't at the end.*

In micro-fiction there's a danger that much of the engagement with the story takes place when the reader has stopped reading. To avoid this, place the denouement in the middle of the story, allowing us time, as the rest of the text spins out, to consider the situation along with the narrator, and ruminate on the decisions his characters have taken. If you're not careful, micro-stories can lean towards punchline-based or 'pull back to reveal' endings which have a one-note, gag-a-minute feel – the drum roll and cymbal crash. Avoid this by giving us almost all the information we need in the first few lines, using the next few paragraphs to take us on a journey below the surface.

4. *Sweat your title.*

Make it work for a living.

5. *Make your last line ring like a bell.*

The last line is not the ending – we had that in the middle, remember – but it should leave the reader with something which will continue to sound after the story has finished. It should not complete the story but rather take us into a new place; a place where we can continue to think about the ideas in the story and wonder what it all meant. A story that gives itself up in the last line is no story at all, and after reading a piece of good micro-fiction we should be struggling to understand it, and, in this way, will grow to love it as a beautiful enigma. And this is also another of the dangers of micro-fiction; micro-stories can be too rich and offer too much emotion in a powerful one-off injection, overwhelming the reader, flooding the mind. A few micro-shorts now and again will amaze and delight – one after another and you feel like you've been run over by a lorry full of fridges.

6. *Write long, then go short.*

Create a lump of stone from which you chip out your story sculpture. Stories can live much more cheaply than you realise, with little deterioration in lifestyle. But do beware: writing micro-fiction is for some like holidaying in a caravan – the grill may well fold out to become an extra bed, but you wouldn't sleep in a fold-out grill for the rest of your life.

A Sawn-Off Tale

Happy Place

He hated grocery shopping, hated the time it took. But he came up with a method. People bought the same things, more or less. So he would look for someone of his type, sneak up behind them and roll their fully laden trolley off to the checkout.

It made life interesting. Often there were things he would never have bought; once there was a fat orange pumpkin.

But today he was in trouble. He had been stealing mostly from women because he liked the sense of order to their selections, but his victim had spied him and was stomping over. There were women's products in the cart, so it was going to be difficult. He decided to pretend he knew her.

'Darling, I'll just get eggs.'

'We've got eggs,' the woman chirped. 'Listen, do you want to go out to the car? You look stressed. You can listen to your tape.'

This story is interesting for me as it ends with a reveal in the final line, which is a technique I usually try to avoid. However, the reveal is so strange that I think it acts as a key to open the whole of the rest of the story, which gives it a creepy, sad dimension.

In the original, longer version there would have been more descriptions of the man wandering about with his trolley, standing in the queue 'ooking at the contents of other people's trolleys and realising they were the same as his, then a description of his first attempt at stealing a trolley, and then getting good at it. After I had created what I believed was the full story, I distilled it down to its current form.

I think the story works because when you write about people behaving weirdly, it's usually from the point of view of the normal person, who can then calibrate the odd behaviour against their own. I'm fascinated with giving the point of view of the outsider – not rebel, exciting outsiders, just people on the edges of society, people with rich interior lives.

Ending with him listening to his tape adds a nice old-fashioned analogue feel to it, I think, and also implies that the couple haven't got much money.

The title took a long time coming. Originally it was called 'Happy Shopper', but then I tried to think about what was missing from the dialogue at the end. What was the tape? What was it about? I decided that the tape was meant to send him to his happy place when he was stressed, so it works as a double meaning for the first part. The supermarket has become a happy place for him owing to his new ingenious plan; then the happy place becomes a mysterious virtual land he has to imagine for himself, and probably doesn't really exist for him at all.

(This story first appeared, in a different form, in the *Guardian*, 14 May 2012.)

Try This: Write a Flash Fiction Story

Now it's your turn. Have a go at a 150-word story, then 100-word one, and finish with a 50-word polished gem. Here some suggestions for each one.

150-word

Include a mandarin orange, a book for children and a tanning studio.

100-word

Use this somewhere in your story: *It's not a word; it's just a collection of letters.*

50-word

Sprinkle these words in this order somewhere in your story: *therefore, but* and *Australia.*

Further Reading

If you enjoyed 'Happy Place', David's other collections will provide you with a feast of funny and often poignant flash fiction. For a list of titles, see Chapter 26, 'Taking Your Work out into the World'.

Also recommended is Dan Rhodes's very entertaining collection of 101 101-word stories, all about girlfriends (most of them ex-), *Anthropology* (Edinburgh: Canongate, 2010).

Finally, there are many, many online magazines to which you can submit your flash fiction, but here are a couple of good places to start:

Word Gumbo

This is a magazine run by Calum Kerr, director of the UK's National Flash Fiction Day. Obviously, it offers a warm welcome to flash exponents. http://www.gumbopress.co.uk/wordgumbo.html

Thumbnail Magazine

A quality literary magazine that publishes a fresh collection of flash every month. http://www.thumbnailmagazine.org/

RG

21 Scriptwriting: for Nervous Beginners

Helen Newall

> The fundamental premise of scriptwriting is that you are writing not to be read but to be made. This does not mean that the script is not read by producers, directors, and others who must decide whether to put resources into producing it. It means that the audience doesn't read the script.
>
> Anthony Friedman

Dramatic writing requires the craft skills of character making and narrative patterns dealt with in many other chapters in this book, but it differs fundamentally in that it concerns the creation of what is in effect a list of coded instructions, or a blueprint, for a work still to be completed rather than the finished work itself. Between writer and audience there are many more stages requiring others to read and interpret and add to what the writer has written before the audience experiences it. A scriptwriter's first readers are thus the team who may or may not decide to commission the work. And then, if it is in production, subsequent readers include the directors, designers and performers who will realise the finished thing. So before it is ever watched, a script should still be a very fine read (but as Friedman notes above, remember that the audience doesn't read the script). And it should use the narrative and layout conventions of the medium for which it is written. This is a huge signal to those first all-important readers that you know what you're doing and that, in a hugely competitive market, you might be worth a second glance.

So what are these conventions? There are no hard and fast rules, but studying the works of the masters in each field is the first place to begin. So if you don't already, go to the cinema, go to the theatre, watch television dramas and soaps, and tune into the drama slots on the radio. After all, would-be writers must immerse themselves in the medium of their choice: it makes sense that if you want to write a novel you should read as many novels as you can. But would-be dramatists have further work to do: they must shift from being the audience of films to being the reader of the scripts that precede them, because the more scripts you *read*, the more apparent the narrative conventions of each medium will become: film, for example, thrives on short, intercutting scenes, sometimes with no dialogue in them at all; whereas, in general, theatre might take longer to build its scenes because frequent scene changes can be more disruptive to the narrative flow (unless this is the effect the writer is seeking: there will always be exceptions which disprove the 'rules', because excellent writing can prove any rule wrong).

The second place to begin is with the gurus whose textbooks weigh down the shelves of many would-be dramatic writers (and frequently the professionals too), and often for good reason. The dramatic media are quite different from each other in the visual semiotics and techniques they employ, and these storytelling codes are so different that there isn't space here to detail them, so I advise you to use what follows as an overview, and then to make further studies of medium-specific texts, examples of which are given at the end of this chapter.

And finally something to know, before you venture any further, is that there is the concept of the 'calling-card script' or 'spec script'. When you submit something to an agent or a production company, it's likely that if it impresses, the script itself will not be produced; it acts merely as an example of what you can do. So while you may pour your heart and soul into it, that script may never get made; it is merely, if you get lucky, your entrance ticket to other projects and writing jobs. Harsh but true. So don't have just one brilliant idea, have lots.

Which Medium? Which Story?

Not all narratives are simultaneously suitable for screen, stage, radio and TV without adaptation. If, for example, your story is long and involved, crossing continents and spanning decades, and set in vast landscapes, with a cast of several principal characters, hundreds of extras, fires, storms and floods, then it's problematic if you want to write it for a theatre stage ... though not impossible, but admit it: it feels more suited to the expanses of a big cinema screen. Film is a visual medium and suits sweeping epic tales in sweeping epic landscapes. Think of the John Ford Westerns filmed in Monument Valley, or, more recently, *Life of Pi*, with its stunning hallucinogenic presentation of the ocean expanses. Put simply, landscapes look fantastic in Cinemascope.

Note also that films, with their bigger budgets, bigger screens and verisimilitude of presentation, give us the illusion of reality, and because of the edit, they can flit over the world in seconds without confusing the audience (hence the visual signifiers we often see: the London double-decker bus; the Eiffel Tower for Paris; the Statue of Liberty for New York: but confusion *is* possible, so don't be too blasé!). Television, however, can diminish landscapes, although the new widescreen HD formats might see this shift; nevertheless, it has, up until now, suited people-centred dramas; consider the soaps, with their familiar domestic settings of front rooms, launderettes, pubs, residential streets. But like film, television drama can cut rapidly from one location to another.

This swift cutting and intercutting can be more problematic for stage narratives because the stage is an art form dealing in presence; the audience and performers are together in real time. As such, hefty scene changes from one perfectly realised location to another can either be time-consuming, while assistant stage-managers move things around (which can disrupt a story flow), or costly (big moving sets are possible but beyond most modest theatre budgets). As such the stage has traditionally offered stories set in what Aristotle termed 'a unity of time and place', where the narrative unfolds in real time, that is to say, it flows at the same time as it takes to tell it. But the clever writer can subvert this. Note that it's a symbolic medium: it can successfully *suggest* location without needing to fully represent it. A wood in *Macbeth*, for example, can be implied with one tree branch, or even a lighting effect. Thus theatre's practical limitations become its magic, for it is as much about the imaginative collusion between performers and audience as the tales it tells.

And radio? The imaginative collusion is true here too. Radio is an underestimated medium for dramatic writers. But it is a wonderful place to learn about the power of words to incite an imaginative response in the audience. It seems, relying as it does on aural cues and the visual imagination of the listener, that radio can suggest any location and get away with it: they have the best and the cheapest sets on radio.

These are negotiable generalisations: with good writing, nothing is impossible. And while you should be aware of the best medium for your story, don't let the complexity of representation extinguish the story you want to write. Your job is to write the narrative, not the production: let the director and the designers solve the practicalities of *how* the story is told. But certainly, as with any other form of writing, make sure that you have selected a suitable recipient for your work. Melissa Hillman, artistic director of the Impact Theatre, Berkeley, California, cites in her blog, Bitter Gertrude, the following reason for rejecting a manuscript: 'It had technical requirements that were outside of the physical capabilities of our idiosyncratic space.' She adds: 'and, more to the point, it was poorly written'.[1] The first moral of this rejection story is save yourself, and the recipient of your work, a lot of time and effort, and do your homework! The second is that sending out only the very best writing is non-negotiable.

Try This: Compare and Contrast Stage, Screen and Radio as Media for Drama

Think about:

- Production budgets
- The numbers of characters in a narrative
- The numbers of people in a creative team
- The cost of a ticket
- The audiences: who are they?
- How captive are audiences? (How easy is it to leave?)
- Audience numbers
- Popularity of the medium
- Marketing
- Writer's status
- The medium's cultural status

The Small Screen

Television and film are often lumped together, but in reality they are two very different media for which to write, and television has in itself a vast range of different dramatic writing opportunities ranging from soaps to drama series, serials, period dramas, police procedurals, daytime soaps, children's TV, and one-off dramas with one or two parts... So while the film industry might seem the epitome of glamour and cultural importance, don't discount television drama as a place to find a voice. Many young writers dream of writing screenplays, but while it does produce amazing films, the film industry chases those all-important opening weekend box-office receipts: with so much money at stake, taking risks is rare, and as an untried and untested writer you are likely to be considered a risk too far. Television, however, saturates our lives with the soundtracks to our meals, but it eats up new writers with a voracious appetite and it does offer some very challenging and brilliant writing. Think of *The Sopranos*; Ronald E. Moore and David Eick's *Battlestar Galactica*; *Twin Peaks*; *Doctor Who*; *Homeland*; *Father Ted*; *Breaking Bad*; *The Wire*; *The Killing*... It's also likely that in your formative years, television lit something in your imagination and created the writer you are today: I was an avid reader in my youth, but certain scenes from television dramas seem indelibly etched in my mind's eye: *Children of the Stones*, *The Changes*, *Grange Hill* and *Tales of the Unexpected* made me want to be a writer. As William Smethurst says: 'Television is desperately short of writers';[2] the sheer amount of drama broadcast on a daily basis, not to mention the range of channels broadcasting, means that material is used up quickly. But beware: however desperate for writers it is, television still demands excellence. You must, in other words, start studying seriously the art and craft of television writing, because however familiar it feels, its conventions and requirements are complex, so be prepared to hone your skills. Visit online resources such as BBC Writersroom; read William Smethurst; read television scripts; take a course – the Arvon Foundation is an excellent place to start – but whatever you do, if you want to make it, take it seriously.

Radio Drama

It used to be the case that radio scripts were hard to come by, but these days they are readily available in the archives of the BBC Writersroom website. Here you can read scripts from radio series and comedies, as well as the famous afternoon plays, to get a feel for what is currently broadcast and what you might add to the airwaves. With a play broadcast almost every day, there's a high turnover of material, so, as with television, there are opportunities for new writers. If you listen to enough broadcasts, you'll find that sound effects enhance but do not overpower narratives, and that sonically rich environments are attractive to radio producers, so a comedy concerning a clumsy love affair set in a musical-instrument shop might go down well in this medium, whereas stage producers might worry about the expense of dressing the set and finding performers who can act and play tubas, banjos and flutes... Radio can deal magnificently with such things. You should also consider the times of day of broadcast and the audiences who might tune in. It is one thing to stage risky material in a theatre where someone chooses to buy a ticket: quite another to broadcast 'lively' material that someone easily offended might unwittingly tune into. So to increase your chance of success, know the type of material that is suitable for the slots before submitting. And don't knock the afternoon slot as insignificant. The Afternoon Play carries people down motorways, lifts their sickbed spirits, or takes them on flights of fancy as they iron piles of clothes. *Spoonface Steinberg* by Lee Hall, first broadcast in 1997, had lorry drivers weeping in lay-bys, and people parked up in car parks and arrived late for meetings because they had to hear the ending. Never underestimate the power of a beautiful story simply told.

Stage Writing

We are a television- and film-literate society: the dramas of these media permeate our lives and punctuate our cultural existences. Going to the theatre, however, seems more of an occasion. But if you have any pretensions about writing for the stage you have to start going to see theatre as regularly as you can. You can learn what works and what doesn't from texts, but there's nothing like experiencing a great play in full production for showing you what theatre can accomplish. And when you've written a play, there's nothing quite like seeing it in rehearsal and noting how certain bits work and certain bits don't. The living embodiment of your words in an actor's mouth can be exhilarating; but it can also be a dangerous exhilaration. The dialogue spoken on stage appears to be real, but it is heightened and lifted out of the mundane, however mundane it seems to be. There is a huge difference between a scene that has dramatic energy and a scene that is merely behaviour. The former can silence even the rustliest of sweet-wrapper rustlers; the latter mimics reality but goes nowhere, lacking as it does the dramatic tension of a finely crafted exchange. And no one can teach this; they can tell you about it but you have to find it for yourself. So by all means read plays, but go to the theatre as well and watch drama in action; and then compare this to the scenes and conversations you witness around you in everyday life (without, of course, being accused of stalking!).

Big Screen

Alex Epstein says that whilst television is a relationship, a movie is a one-night stand[3] (although the proliferation of sequels and prequels might now contradict this ...). Generally, however, you have a couple of hours to persuade an audience that a protagonist is worth worrying about, while demonstrating some extreme situation happening to this protagonist. This is not easy. Then we must consider the status of the writer. There may be a cast of thousands in front of the camera and a crew of thousands behind it. As the writer of the screenplay, you are small cog in a vast machine that must not fail. Theatre is a writer's medium. (How many theatre directors can you name? How many playwrights?) But film is very much a director's domain. You may have submitted a treatment and been asked to draft it out, only for it then to be given to someone else, and perhaps someone else after that for several other drafts. Hollywood is not for the fainthearted. But if you never pitch you'll never know, but make sure you've scrutinised what a studio or an agent accepts and what they don't accept. And make sure that your calling-card screenplay is the best it can be. And prepare for disappointment. But don't give up – unless the agencies tell you to!

The Writing Process

If you've never written a script and you're not yet sure which medium to write for, then the following might be useful. If however, you're not a stranger to scriptwriting now is the time to cut to the specialist texts.

Just as with fiction, or poetry, there is often a giddy, untidy mix of exploratory writing in journals or on the backs of envelopes or in the inside covers of library books; and planning that feels difficult; and drafting, and manic redrafting; and scribbling genius things down at midnight, and crossing them out again at dawn.

So begin by finding a story. Think of a narrative: a chain reaction of events – with a beginning, middle and end – that happens over a period of time to a character. Ha! More easily said than done, but take heart: just as with short stories and novels, it takes time; stories rarely descend fully formed in a flash of lightning to the accompaniment of the Hallelujah Chorus (however hard we all wish they did!). Instead, you pace about the room, or round the block: you mull over possibilities; you play the 'what-if' game: what if a man has a dog he hates?

What if he tries to get rid of the dog, but the dog loves the man so it keeps coming back? What if, one day, it doesn't come back, and the man misses the bad breath and the dog hairs and the whining, and sets out on a quest to find the dog and bring it home?

These 'what-if' doodlings in your head, in your journal, on the backs of toilet doors may either lead you somewhere, or they may turn out to be dead ends: in the case of the former, fantastic! And as for the latter: well ... fantastic! The trick is to keep coming up with ideas: they're not dead in the water until you've satisfied yourself that they don't work. Perhaps they simply don't inspire you at this particular moment, but don't discount them; they may be the stepping stone to another, better idea. A thrifty writer never throws anything away; ideas, like elastic bands, might just come in useful one day ... and if they don't, you can flick them at your scriptwriting tutors.

The joy of the 'what-if' structure is that the story is already active; it is already a chain reaction of events: perhaps not a particularly brilliant one, but it is from the outset more than the phrase, 'I think I'll write about a man and his loyal dog.' Wanting to write *about* something, whether it be an emotion, a woman who has a secret, a town that is about to suffer a natural disaster, is a long way from *the chain reaction of events told over a period of time*, which is the essence of most scripts.

When scribbling down potential 'what-if' stories, use the third person and the present tense: this allows you to put yourself into the position of the audience, or camera, receiving the story. While with prose we can creep inside a character's head and admire the interior first-person view, stories told on stage and screen tend to be external affairs, unless voice-over is used, and some scriptwriting gurus strongly advise avoiding voice-overs if at all possible. Radio drama is a different kettle of fish as far as interior monologues are concerned, and you'll hear them quite often, but it's still best to use the third person as you plan, until you start trying out your character's voice.

Try This: An Extended Exercise

Jot down as many 'what-if' chains that you can and see where they lead. Working with a partner is great because you can take turns to add sentences and bounce ideas off each other, helping each other to keep the chain going without veering off into the surreal (although, come to think of it, why not?).

- What if a man finds a dog?
- What if the man hates the dog and the dog loves the man?
- What if the man tries to get rid of the dog?
- What if the dog keeps coming back?
- What if, one day, the dog doesn't come back?
- What if the man then sets out to find the dog because he realises he quite likes it after all?

And so on. Take turns to add a sentence to the list. Don't let your internal editor cramp your style. If ideas feel silly, enjoy the silliness. This is a game, after all: the point is to keep the sentences flowing because you might just find, among the silt, a golden nugget: experienced writers know that it's not *what* you say, but the *way* that you say it that counts. The most innocuous idea might be priceless for a writer who believes in it, and sees its potential. You can also play the 'but' game:

- A woman has a house.
- But the house is haunted.
- But a girl comes to stay and at first the woman feels better.
- But the girl is quiet and strange.
- Etc., etc.

So, now, in your journal you have a paragraph or three of what-ifs and buts. Now you need to fashion them into a rough paragraph story by crafting 'what-ifs?' and 'buts' into a flow of definite actions.

> What if a man finds a dog he hates?
> What if he tries to get rid of the dog?

> becomes:

> A man finds a dog he hates, and feeds it and looks after it and takes it for walks, until he decides to get rid of the dog...

Eventually you'll end up with a rough chain of sequential events, which might loosely be described as a treatment. So which medium do you think suits the narrative? Now translate the treatment into a series of visual scenes or units of action.

A man is walking down a road when he finds a mongrel tied to a lamppost. There is no one about. He grimaces but unties the dog. The dog wags its tail and licks his hand. Etc., etc.

Nothing to it? Ha! Prepare to bite your pencil: this can be a very frustrating time. It may take days or weeks, but it's worth spending time and energy on these early phases: although you're not yet writing the working script, this is a vital part of the process. You need to decide how much of this material you need to tell the story. Not everything is required. How short or sparse can the story be and still make sense?

And now you must decide which medium your story is best suited for. Only then you can start moving into layout, working out scenes by defining the visual action and crafting dialogue (if there is any – watch *The Artist*). More specific texts can deal with conventions of dialogue particular to screen, stage and radio scripts, but it is worth mentioning here that often less is more: so after you've written what needs to be said, edit. We tend to speak in the same way that water runs downhill, taking the easiest route. So, 'No, I will not throw a stick so that you can chase it, you horrible smelly dog' is more likely to be 'Get lost!' because the former in inferred in the latter.

Laying It Out

And finally: a word on layout. Beware that when you start to format the work, you're using working layout as opposed to published script layout: they can differ considerably. As I said earlier, using the correct layout is a good hint to a reader (who might produce your work) that you know what you're doing. But finessing layout can be something that gets in the way of creative flow, so I often lay out roughly and then set it properly as part of the proof-reading redrafting process.

Experiment

As you watch more and more plays and listen to radio dramas and read scripts and screenplays, you'll get a feel for the 'vocabulary' of a medium. This doesn't mean that you should always write what you've seen or heard. Try writing what you'd like to watch. Read your work aloud. Get friends to read it out. Enter it for rehearsed reading events. Push the possibilities, and have fun. And, if nothing else, doing this may improve your fiction writing; readers like visual and dramatic narratives!

Further Reading

The small screen

Alex Epstein (2006) *Crafty TV Writing: Thinking Inside the Box* (East Peckham: Owl Books).
Nicholas Gibbs (2012) *Teach Yourself Writing Television Drama: Get Your Scripts Commissioned* (London: Teach Yourself, Hodder Education).
William Smethurst (2009) *How to Write for Television* (Oxford: How To Books).

Radio drama

Tim Crook (1999) *Radio Drama: Theory and Practice* (London: Routledge).
Shaun MacLoughlin (2001) *Writing for Radio* (2nd edn) (Oxford: How To Books).
Vincent McInerney (2001) *Writing For Radio* (Manchester: Manchester University Press).

Stage writing

David Edgar (2009) *How Plays Work* (London: Nick Hern Books).
Laos Egri (1960) *The Art of Dramatic Writing* (New York: Simon & Schuster).
Steve Waters (2010) *The Secret Life of Plays* (London: Nick Hern Books).

The big screen

Linda Aronson (2010) *The 21st-Century Screenplay: A Comprehensive Guide to Writing Tomorrow's Films* (London: Allen & Unwin).
Syd Field (2007) *The Screenwriter's Workbook* (London: Delta).
Robert McKee (1997) *Story: Substance, Structure, Style, and the Principles of Screenwriting* (London: Regan Books).

Useful Resources

Radios 3, 4 and 4Extra regularly broadcast plays. They are generally available on BBC iPlayer if you miss the scheduled broadcast time.

Your local repertory theatre may run a writers' group or a playwrights' development scheme. And don't forget that new writers aren't always young writers.

If you search online for screenplays, you'll find plenty of sites offering free access and downloads. Beware, however, that some of these sites may be less than legal!

Seek out www.bbc.co.uk/writersroom/ for resources, script libraries, layouts, advice, news and the all-important portal to submit work to the BBC.

Many writers, industry insiders and production companies have blogs and/ or Twitter feeds. Try blogs such as Melissa Hillman's *Bitter Gertrude*; or *Theatre Blog with Lyn Gardner*; or www.theatrevoice.com.

22 Poetry

Robert Sheppard and
Scott Thurston

Moon in June

Writing poetry, or beginning to write poetry seriously, seems to throw up unique problems. We're often faced with students who are either filled with dread at the prospect of writing a poem, or ones who feel quite confident about what is required, but know very little about it. It's sometimes easier to encourage the first group than it is to redirect the second. In fact, both groups are often labouring under the same illusions. Perhaps you, too, are prevented from achieving a breakthrough because of your notions about what poetry is.

One of the biggest blocks is the notion that poetry has to be full of sententious thoughts, mediated through a voluminous and unusual vocabulary, that there is a necessary special language, even code, in which poetry is written, a poetic diction that it falls to the clever reader to locate. I'm not saying that some poetry isn't difficult (or that difficulty isn't part of the fun), but that similes, metaphors, imagery or symbolism need not be necessary complications.

Secondly, it is often assumed that poetry can only be poetry if it rhymes and if it is in metre. Plenty of poetry doesn't rhyme. It's actually a very simple device. Metre, however, is complicated. This is the pattern of the syllables in the line. There are hundreds of such patterns, but the most common is the iambic beat, which alternates weak stresses with strong ones. Metrical theory is a fascinating subject, but it can operate as a block to new writers. The dedication to rhyme and metre often produces weak writing, where the rhymes carry the poem along, the limited available words distorting the meaning of the poem: if there's a moon in it, it'll have to be in June! All too often the result is a piece of verse that swings between rhymes like telegraph wires between poles. The name of this is doggerel.

The third misapprehension is that poetry must always be personal, the exposure of some traumatic emotional wound or of the ecstasies of love, for example. Doubtless, these have been subjects for poetry, but they needn't be yours! If you're a student writer, or belong to a writing group, you'll either have two responses to this. Either you will be horrified at the thought of having to commit continual acts of literary self-revelation, or you will revel in it, seeking to shock or impress your audience. Neither is fair; neither is productive.

Let's try something else.

Poetic Hygiene

First, think small. Many poems are short anyway, but this is not the result of exhaustion, but of condensation *in* the act of writing, and in editing after. One of the shortest types of poem is the Japanese haiku. Probably the most famous haiku is the near-untranslatable one by the seventeenth-century Zen Buddhist monk, Basho. Our version goes like this:

> An ancient pond, yes –
> The frog there, leaping into
> Its own rippled splash.

Formally, the poem consists of three lines, with the simple syllable count of 5–7–5. Try writing in this form. Don't think poetry. Think description: describe the moment of arriving in the space you are now in. It'll get you used to the form.

There are a couple of other 'rules' to help you. At the end of the first, or at the end of the second line, there is a slight pause, a change of theme, an articulation, a hinge. It might be marked by a punctuation mark: a full stop, a semicolon or a comma. Or you might like to omit formal punctuation altogether and use a dash or a space. We call this the 'turn'.

In the traditional haiku there is always a recognisable word (called a *dai*) which tells you what season the poem was written in. (For example, the frog in Basho's haiku suggests it was written in spring.) Our next two haiku demonstrate variations of 'turn' and *dai*. What is the effect of the different position of the turn?

> September morning,
> blackbird runs along the edge
> of a shadow.

> The garden in spring.
> Through the stiff white covering – daffodil dances.

Basho believed that a poet learns about 'a pine tree from a pine tree, about a bamboo stalk from a bamboo stalk', and contemporary Japanese haiku writers have followed this by adopting the technique of 'on-the-spot composition'.[1] The writer, preferably standing before the object, enters 'into the object, sharing its delicate life and feeling'.[2] Haiku should try to 'contain feelings that have come from the object', in the words of one of Basho's disciples.[3] In other words, haiku are all about what's out there, immediately in front of you, not about what's inside you. Slip a small notepad into your pocket and step outside into the world whose moments will offer you numerous potential haiku. The trick is to keep on writing them. Perhaps haiku writing, with its immediacy, will become a habitual part of using your writer's journal, even if you don't focus on poetry. As an exercise, try writing them in your head.

Try This: Haiku

1. Write a list of 10 *dai* for the season. You are not in Japan watching frogs and bamboo. What do you associate with the season?
2. Paying attention to the form, write up to 10 haiku, using one *dai* per poem.
3. Think about each word and describe some aspect of the season.
4. Remember to use the articulation of the 'turn'. If it's just one long sentence, it lacks tension.
5. Pick out the most successful, the most surprising. Why does it work?

The haiku was a great influence on a group of poets called the Imagists in the early twentieth century, and some of the things their leader, Ezra Pound, said about this 'school' of poetry are relevant today. He proposed a haiku-like 'direct treatment of the "thing", whether subjective or objective'.[4] This involves the use of the 'Image', which Pound defined as 'that which presents an intellectual and emotional complex in an instant of time'.[5] It gives 'that sense of sudden liberation', the instantaneous sense of surprise, feelings evoked by objects, that you get with the very best haiku, where the focus is objective (that is, in the object seen not in the self observing).[6]

Pound added: 'Use absolutely no word that does not contribute to the presentation.'[7] This is good advice for any kind of writing, of course, but Pound's lessons in poetic hygiene had in mind the kind of wordy pseudo-poetry we dismissed in our opening. But he is also agreeing with another useful saying (although it was an architect who first said it): 'Less is More'. Pound's demands were specific: 'Use no superfluous word, no adjective, which does not reveal something.'[8] The poet Basil Bunting went further: 'Fear adjectives; they bleed nouns.'[9] That is, in poetry adjectives seldom act as 'intensifiers', as linguists call them; they actually 'dull the image', as Pound said of a cliché, like 'dim lands of peace'.[10] According to Pound, this 'mixes an abstraction with the concrete'. As William Carlos Williams puts it: 'No ideas but in things.'[11] This is a particular way of expressing a more general creative writing maxim: 'Show, don't tell.'

Pound's most famous Imagist poem is called 'In a Station of the Metro', which is a kind of haiku, though it only two lines long (but originally was over fifty lines long, and itself a miniature testimony to his monumental editing skills). Have a look at this poem and many other Imagist poems in Peter Jones's *Imagist Poetry*, and see how they did (and didn't) stick to Pound's 'rules' (which are also reprinted there in full).[12] Our poem is modelled upon Pound's:

IN A CITY SQUARE

The pushing of this person through the crowd;
A figure on a sharp, high prow.

The word 'image' is often used loosely in discussions of poetry, almost to the point of meaninglessness, but I want you to think about it quite literally as things we can see (at least in these exercises). I want you to forget everything about figurative language you've been taught, and to think for a moment only of similes: those markers of similarity marked by the word 'like' (or 'as'), and only of ones you can see. 'His teeth were stained like a Victorian urinal' may not be very nice, but you can see it! 'His teeth were as loose as a call girl's morals!' is very funny, but you can't see it! This is the sort of simile I want you to avoid; it is one of Pound's abstractions. Notice how in our poem the word 'like' could have been added. We have used the line break as a sort of hinge, a kind of 'turn'.

Try This: From Simile to Image

1. Decide on a visual image for exploration.
   We suggest: images of teeth, good, bad or decaying; an image of a crowd: at a railway station like Pound, or at a café table in our version, or a

concert or football match; an image of a single person in movement: a dancer in full flight, or an athlete in action, or somebody moving inelegantly.

2. Write a short first line that states the subject, as in 'A Pavement Café in Warsaw'.

3. List as many possible second lines you can. If it helps, use the word 'like' or 'as'.

4. Select the most effective, the one with the greatest surprise.

5. Delete the word 'like' or 'as'. Place at the end of line 1 the most appropriate punctuation mark. We've followed Pound in using a semicolon, but we could have used a colon for a more direct sense of equation between the object and the image.

We have yet to pay attention to another of Pound's injunctions, which was: 'As regarding rhythm: compose in sequence of the musical phrase, not in sequence of a metronome.'[13] A metronome is a device for measuring equally spaced beats, very useful for learning to play a musical instrument, but too regular to use in a real performance. Pound explained: 'Don't chop your stuff into separate iambs', by which he meant a strict, repetitive metre.[14] He was advocating what is sometimes called 'free verse', although this has never been a satisfactory term. A common misconception is that free verse has no rhythm. All language has rhythm, but not all language is in a regular metre. 'Free is properly a synonym for "nonmetrical" and it follows that the prosody of free verse is rhythmic organisation by other than numerical modes', or by counting syllables, writes Charles O. Hartman.[15]

The chief problem for any writer in this form is how and where to break the line (and stanza). Pound has some solid advice about what is often called enjambment, that is, the act of breaking a line while continuing the sense: 'Don't make each line stop dead at the end, and then begin every next line with a heave.'[16] Look again at lines 2 and 3 of our 'September' haiku. The demon of beginners in non-metrical verse is that they (unconsciously) arrange their lines as phrases because that is where a 'break' appears to be (a worse habit is to put a comma at the end of each line). 'Let the beginning of the next line catch the rise of the rhythm wave, unless you want a definite longish pause.'[17] This question of line is strictly a question of judgement. Pound's Metro poem, and our Café poem, both have a deliberately irregular pattern of heavy syllables in line 2, which slows the poems down. As Bunting said: 'Vary rhythm enough to stir the emotion you want but not so as to lose impetus.'[18] One sound guideline from Pound is to remind the poet that 'your rhythmic structure should not destroy the shape of your words, or their natural sound, or their meaning'.[19] You need not distort your ordinary voice. The best way is to try this out for yourself before we suggest some more technical ways of doing this. We often tell students to 'get a feel for the line'. Different people perhaps have personal rhythms.

Pound is clear about rhyme in these freer structures, where it is not necessary: 'A rhyme must have in it some slight element of surprise if it is to give pleasure.'[20] Notice how in our example (like Pound's) there is a half-rhyme at the end of both lines, but it is neither intrusive nor mandatory.

Try This: Imagist Poem

1. Study this section so far and go outside or sit at a window with a view and write freely.
2. Try putting feeling into a description of a landscape.
3. Try to evoke an emotion in the piece without naming it. Your ideas must be completely articulated by *things*.
4. See if you can develop several images in one poem.
5. Let the poem flow. Try to think in lines as you go. Avoid end-stopped lines except where necessary. Experiment with verse breaks.

In revision:

1. Check the poem for abstractions and consider replacements.
2. Check that you haven't written the piece in lines that are phrases, and relineate until you are happy with the 'flow'.
3. Change any clangy rhymes or remove altogether. (If you are a habitual 'rhymester', practise doing without this prop.)

Small Machines of Words

William Carlos Williams famously defined a poem as 'a small (or large) machine made of words'.[21] A poem is not often thought of as a machine, with parts that can be built up to make a whole. While any poem should work *as a whole*, it may be useful in the writing of poems to think about how its mechanisms may be isolated, and even pulled to bits and reassembled. When a group of poets around Williams developed Imagism further, they called it Objectivism, not because they were being objective towards the world, or writing about objects, like the haiku writers, but because they thought of writing poetry as the making of these machine-like objects. We are going to pretend that there are only three parts to the poetry machine: line, line break and enjambment. The line break will be thought of as a hinge.

We don't often think enough about line. But it is the basic component of a poem. Think what a line break does to the flow of language that would otherwise be 'prose'. Derek Attridge writes:

> Free verse is the introduction into the continuous flow of prose language, which has breaks determined entirely by syntax and sense, of another kind of break, shown on the page by the start of a new line, and often indicated in a reading of the poem by a slight pause.[22]

This means that where the line breaks, the point of enjambment, becomes crucial. Take a piece of prose – your own from your journal, perhaps – and put it into different arrangements of lines: experiment with the 'break' described above. 'Enjambment', Giorgio Agamben writes, 'reveals a mismatch, a disconnection between the metrical and syntactic elements, between sounding rhythm and meaning, such that… poetry lives… only in their inner disagreement.'[23] We prefer to speak of tension between the parts of the poem, instead of disagreement. It is clear that there is a tension between the sentence and the line-lengths it trails along and breaks. In writing your small machine, you will be able to play off line length against sentence (or syntax), and punctuation against enjambment.

THE SNIPER, WASHINGTON
The observer –
spotted with crooked
elbow

the sights parallel
with a loaded
rifle image –

camouflaged. The
cuff exposed, the
mobile hovers

above the head
a dis-
connected thought

Williams was a master of this kind of enjambment:

> in all its kinds and degrees: phrases and clauses splay, leap or crawl across line and stanza breaks, in deliberate violation of natural pauses and syntactic boundaries. Some poems play frequently enjambed lines against end-stopped stanzas; others build up successively stronger enjambments in order to emphasize one big stop.[24]

Try experimenting in the light of this inspired description. A good way to help you practise these skills is by using photographs, as we have in 'The Sniper, Washington'. Daily newspapers often have excellent quality images to work from; unlike the world itself they are often dramatic, but they are also static, Imagist and Objectivist in their own way. Also try paintings as in our next poem, in homage to Williams's late poem *Pictures from Brueghel*:

LADY WRITING A LETTER, WITH HER MAID (Vermeer)
A thought
Approaches her cap:
A slender leg.

The discarded implements
Complement the marbled floor;
Implicate a visitor

Just departed.
The maid watches
Him go.

Her lady
Addresses
The page.

However visual and imagistic the contents of these poems are, there is a different kind of visualising required: to read the text with the eye. The line and stanza breaks are visual shapes as well as (possibly) representing a pause in sound. Williams may have invented new forms of typography and lineation inspired by his use of the typewriter, the word processor of his time. Text is a visual entity (a process accelerated with our use of white space and computer screens, hypertext and cyberpoetics), and there is hardly a language to talk of this, but it is our hunch that writers have always been aware of it, and that, if a poem is a machine, then the three gears of listening, looking and meaning must work together (and in tension). An easy way of remembering this is to think: sound, shape and sense.

Try This: Objectivist Poem

1. Obtain some newspaper photographs.
2. Select one that impresses you.
3. Write a poem, thinking hard about line, syntax and enjambment.
4. Never use words like 'in the photograph'. Just be there, capturing what you see.
5. Revise in the light of this. Check the flow of the lines. Is it smooth or jagged? Which is appropriate to the object or image captured?
6. Reading for the ear: read your poem out loud. How does it sound? Experiment with ways of reading it. Test out Attridge's remark about a slight pause between lines and stanzas.
7. Reading for the eye: look at the poem as a shape upon the page. Does it look right? Does it feel right, for you?
8. How do sound, shape and sense work together (or in tension with one another) in your poem? Does this suggest how you might redraft it?

Then Try This: Write an Objectivist Sequence

Late in life Williams was incapacitated by a stroke. During this time he wrote his book *Pictures from Brueghel*, relying on a book of the artist's pictures. He was writing on an early electric typewriter, and this encouraged him to experiment with dropping punctuation completely (as we nearly have in our 'The Sniper, Washington').

1. Select a book of paintings by any representational painter (other than Brueghel: go and read Williams's sequence instead). We picked Vermeer, who often painted scenes of ordinary life that would have appealed to Williams.
2. Repeat the objectivist method in terms of form and focus
3. Optionally, experiment with removing punctuation.

All these things will sensitise you to line and will enable you to experiment with appropriate ways of maintaining the tension between line and sentence, form and content, as well as between sound, shape and sense. All of these exercises may be adapted (just think of all the images you might use, from your own snapshots through to the dozen images on a calendar). Part of the reason to concentrate on short poems is the lesson of concision in writing and editing. Basil Bunting's advice to young poets was 'Cut out every word you dare', which represents editing and redrafting as a daring enterprise.[25] But he adds: 'Do it again, a week later, and again.'[26] Go on. It's a good preparation, whether you end up exploring the texts we recommend below, or whether your taste leads you back to traditional poetic forms.

Further Reading

J. Rothenberg and P. Joris (eds) (1995, 1998) *Poems for the Millennium*. 2 vols, Berkeley: University of California Press.

We teach from the second volume, *From Post-War to Millennium*, but the first contains the works of Pound, Williams and Bunting. Each poet's work is accompanied by excerpts from his or her poetics, or philosophy of composition, which gives an insight into both general attitudes and questions of technique. A generous international cross-section of work, and a useful source book for poets.

H. Smith (2005) *The Writing Experiment: Strategies for Innovative Creative Writing*. Sydney: Allen & Unwin.

This book, published in Australia, is a different kind of creative writing book, in keeping with the focus of our exercises here. It covers prose and narrative as well as poetry, but is focused upon a language-centred approach rather than expressing yourself or using traditional forms, although it suggests new ways of writing about life-experience.

23 Poetry for People Who Don't Like Poetry

Heather Leach

Walk into a seminar room and ask a normal-looking bunch of students whether they like poetry. Watch their reactions. Many people will screw up their faces as if they'd smelt something disgusting; a few will grimace awkwardly and waggle their hands in an awkward 'maybe, maybe not' gesture. After a few moments one or two brave individuals – three at the most – will raise a finger, looking round the room to make sure they're not alone.

These days poetry is apparently not very popular. I say apparently, because if you were to continue the experiment and take each one of the members of the seminar out of the group and ask them about their experiences of *writing* poetry, you'd find that quite a lot of them would confess (and confess is the appropriate word here) that they'd actually jotted down the odd poem or two: an interesting contradiction, my dear Watson.

One of the problems is that Poetry is a word burdened with a big P: a word that needs to be pronounced in a special, rather reverent, voice. Poetry, as it has been handed down to many of us, through school English literature – or 'litterachooer', as Tony Harrison called it[1] – is often experienced as serious and difficult to understand, needing translation and explanation by an expert, usually a teacher. This is a bit like having a joke explained: by the time you've got the point you've lost the point, if you see what I mean. I am not going to argue that all poetry should be easy to understand but I do think that for many of us, this high-literature approach to poetry is not the place to begin. However, before I talk about alternatives, I have a confession to make.

I am not a poet, or at least only a poet with a small p. (But there is another chapter in this book written by real poets.) Here are my poetic credentials. I began writing rhyming verse when I was 12 or 13 and filled a few notebooks, going on to read some of my efforts to friends and family. There are two memories associated with this period: one good, one excruciatingly bad.

The good one was being asked by a girl in my class to write a poem for her father's birthday card (fame at last!). The bad one was reading a poem aloud to my mother and grandma. I can't remember all of this poem but, for reasons, which will become clear, the last two lines are burned into my memory. Here they are:

> And dances like the daffodil
> While silver fishes leap at will.

After I'd finished reading there was a long silence. Then Grandma said, 'Who's Will?', before going back to her newspaper. My mother said, 'Haven't I heard the bit about the daffodil before?' I was mortified: a laughable double meaning and a crude copy in only 11 words.

Some time later, during my cooler teenage years, I stopped writing poetry. It was obvious that I could never be a real poet and anyway, who cared about poetry when there was rock and roll? I threw away the notebooks, embarrassed by the evidence.

You're Already a Poet, But You Don't Know It

As adults we may be cynical about our childish and adolescent poetic efforts when comparing them with the 'real stuff', but that would be to miss some key points. In my daffodil line I was certainly plagiarising Wordsworth, but this was because I had learned some of the pleasures of pattern and alliteration and wanted to use them for myself. We all learn by copying to begin with, and we all write emotional stuff which sometimes goes over the top. The only difference between adolescent poets and real ones is that the real ones don't give up. You may have written poems when you were younger. You may still be writing them but keeping them secret. Some of these poems may be song lyrics and many may explore deep emotions: love, anger, frustration, despair. A large number probably also draw on existing poems and songs as models. By the time we are adults most of us have heard and unconsciously learned poetic styles, methods and patterns from hundreds, if not thousands of poetry-with-a-small-p examples. We all know a lot more about poetry than we think we do. Here are a few examples.

Happy Valentine, Deepest Sorrow

One popular outlet for poetry is the greetings card. You know the kind:

Here's a card just made for you
With lots of love so rich and true
I wish you all the joy and love
That dum de dum de dum de dove

Quite a few people would deny that this stuff is real poetry at all, and I have to admit it isn't my cup of tea. But it does have pattern and rhythm and it can provide a template for beginners to build on. The other place for popular rhyme is the newspaper obituary. These also often follow a well-worn format, but some people rewrite and adapt the verses to fit their own circumstances, which makes them more moving and original. It is striking that many people feel that the deepest emotions are best expressed in poetic forms.

Song Lyrics

If you love contemporary popular music, you probably know the words of many songs. As they also rely on the music, song lyrics are not exactly the same as poems, which are meant to be read or spoken. But many poems have been made into songs, and many songs are powerful poems. There are huge variations. Some lyrics are as simple and as compelling as a chant: The Beatles' *Hey Jude* is a good example. Others are wilder and more complex. Look at and listen to some of Bob Dylan's 1960s lyrics. Try *A Hard Rain's A-Gonna Fall* from *The Freewheelin' Bob Dylan*. 'Riot Van' by the Arctic Monkeys has a punk in-your-face bluntness that fits the subject. *All* use poetic forms: repetition, sound patterns, line scanning and rhythm, end-rhymes, half- and almost-rhymes.[2]

Riddles

All children, if they get the chance, love wordplay. Many of the first poems we learn are nursery rhymes – *Jack and Jill, Baa Baa Black Sheep* – although these days we're more likely to get them from television – Postman Pat, Bob the Builder, and so on. See how many you can remember and, if you can cope with the embarrassment, recite or sing them aloud, preferably in a group, in order to recapture the sheer pleasure of playing with word and sound. You could have a go at writing an alternative grown-up version of one of your favourite nursery rhymes or jingles, using the same patterns and musicality. Although you may need to pick your audience carefully, as many of my students have produced rhymes that are far too rude to reprint.

There are also many riddle poems, and children and poets invent new ones all the time. A riddle poem is a puzzle. Try this one:

> It's the beginning of eternity
> The end of time and space
> It's the start of every end,
> And the end of every place.

(Anon)

The poem 'You're' by Sylvia Plath,[3] is also a riddle poem, using a list of original images to describe something strange but very familiar. Have a go at working out what the subjects of these riddle poems are.

Making Poetry Belong to You

Poems are shorter than novels, so if you have a demanding day job and just the odd hour to spend, poetry may be your ideal medium. If you write a poem a week, you'll soon have a collection. They're also ideal for sharing with others. If you've got the bottle, try an open-mic event, or dedicate a poem to friends or family for a special occasion. But even if your poetry is never shared with anyone else, it can be the place where you laugh at the ridiculousness of life, work out what you really believe, vent your rage, open your heart and make silver fishes leap at will.

Try This: Write Your Own Valentine's Card

In this witty example from his poem *Valentine*,[4] John Fuller focuses on the bits of his lover's body that often don't get a mention. He uses a simple rhyme but subverts it with his two-word punchline.

> I like your eyes, I like their fringes.
> The way they focus gives me twinges.
> Your upper arms drive me berserk.
> I like the way your elbows work.
> On hinges ...

If you read the whole poem, you'll see that Fuller does mention the naughty bits, but in a subtle and subversive way.

Choose someone, real or fantasy, to dedicate your Valentine to and have a go at writing your own, trying to make it specific and personal by avoiding all the familiar clichés.

Try This: Write a Song Lyric

Choose a song lyric you like. First play it, sing it or read it and listen to the patterns and rhythms. Then write it down and examine the ways it produces its effects. Next write your own, using some of the same techniques. You could also use the examples above (Beatles, Dylan, Arctic Monkeys) as models. Choose an unusual subject to write about: sport, food, clothes, dogs, money, computers or television, for example. If you write about a 'poetic' subject (love, nature, strong emotions, etc.) try to find fresh words or patterns.

Try This: Riddle Poem

Write a riddle poem for a common object.

■ First decide on the object.

■ Then list as many descriptions of the object as you can. Try to think metaphorically, the way Plath does, e.g. if your object was a spoon you could describe it as: lip-sipper/sip-lipper/soup-slurper/the way lovers sleep/silver bowl on silver arm/fork's mate, etc. Keep going. The best ones often come when you have reached the limits of rational thought.

■ Then choose 5 or 6 of the best and shape them into lines.

■ Next, try to make these lines work together as patterns and sound. If rhymes develop, use them, but don't force the material into awkward shapes to make a rhyme.

■ Try it out on other people. If they guess it too easily, make it harder. If nobody gets it, make it slightly easier.

Further Reading/Websites

Laura Barber (ed.) (2010) *Penguin Poems for Love*. London: Penguin.
Riddle-Poems, and How to Make Them at Eric Redmond's site:
   http://www.catb.org/esr/riddle-poems.html (accessed 6 September 2012).
   Excellent resource, with many examples of riddle poems from the Anglo-Saxon to the present day, plus ideas on how to make your own.

24 Digital Writing
Heather Leach and
Helen Newall

Let me tell you a short story, not short enough to fit in a tweet or a text, but brief enough to qualify as flash fiction.

> Girl dreams of becoming a writer. Writes in spare time for many years and gets a few things published in small magazines. One morning she wakes with a brilliant idea for a novel. Imagines her words in print. Her name on the cover.
> Just at that moment a virtual angel appears.
>
> *'Fear not,'* he says. *'I bring you good news. The future is digital. Paper books are done for. Print publishers will go to the wall and there shall be only texts and screens and kindles and apps. Rejoice! Rejoice!'*
> *'Hang on a minute...'* says the girl.
> But the angel has gone already, disappeared into the digital cloud.
> End of story?

In the few short years since the first edition of *The Road to Somewhere* the internet has continued to expand exponentially. Those of us who live in the wealthy regions of the world can now access cyberspace (the Net, the interweb, GoogleCloud, or whatever cool new name it will be called by the time you read this) through fast broadband, wireless, 3G or 4G, using smartphones, iPads, e-books, laptops and Macs; we connect with each other through ever-changing applications: Facebook, Twitter, YouTube, Skype, LinkedIn, etc. To people born since 1990, this probably feels normal; just the background hum of everyday life. To those who remember a world before the net, it often feels like a roller coaster, a thrilling but terrifying ride, taking us who knows where?

So how should writers respond to the digital revolution? Should we fear it or welcome it? There are a number of people who argue (some with dread and some with delight) that the internet may soon send the printed hard-copy book the way of the papyrus scroll and the illuminated manuscript. Traditional bookshops, publishers and libraries are all having to scramble to survive, and many won't make it unless they adapt and change. Writers, too, can't afford to keep their heads down and hope it all goes away. It can be hard, however, to know how to respond.

It may be challenging and sometimes downright terrifying, but there are plenty of reasons to be cheerful. Jay David Bolter, author of *Writing Space* and one of the world's leading thinkers in relation to books and new media, is optimistic: he believes that 'electronic technology offers us a new kind of book and new ways to read and write'.[1] In 1991 (ancient history in digital terms), Bolter was arguing that online writing and publishing would tend to turn readers into writers, and his predictions have so far been right on the money, as can be seen by the enormous proliferation of personal websites: Facebook, blogs, etc. And, far from the digital revolution meaning the death of the book, the rise of online shopping, plus e-readers, iPads and smartphones, has made it much easier to access books, ideas, stories, and writers and that access can be instantaneous.

It's useful to remember that narratives, plays, poetry and song have been part of human existence from the very beginning and have successfully negotiated a number of revolutions already, from an oral to a written culture, from parchment to print. Stories, imagination, drama and poetry will surely survive the digital shift; it's just us humans that need to adapt.

Another positive, although not everybody will agree, is that it has become much easier for writers to publish their own work and to have direct access to a world of readers. Until recently, the only way you could get your work published was by going through a series of gates and barriers (agents, slush piles, publisher's commercial departments, etc.), and although this process, at its best, means that for the most part, bad writing doesn't get through, it also means that a lot of good writing doesn't get through either.[2] Publishers have to try to make a profit and unknown, experimental, quirky, uncommercial writers may not get a look-in. The internet offers these writers a platform and a means to connect with people who might not otherwise ever encounter their work.

Some people argue that there is a lot of bad writing online, that the gates and barriers stopped rubbish getting through. But there are a lot of bad cricketers, cooks and violinists out there too, and nobody suggests that they should give up batting, baking and scraping. Most internet writing is of this amateurish kind; people are doing it because they love it, expressing themselves, having a go. But there's room in cyberspace for all kinds of writers.

Of course, for us 'serious' writers, this isn't quite the same as finding a prestigious publisher who will turn our novels/scripts into critically acclaimed bestsellers/films, but one medium does not necessarily rule out the other: it's not digital *or* print, but print *and* digital, and one may very well lead to the other. The first challenge is to get your stuff written and posted, and after that to find online readers. If you're talented, hard-working and persistent, the rest might follow. So, the internet is brilliant, if not essential for writers, but it has its dangers ...

A Warning to the Curious

Let's not forget, in all this enthusiasm, that the internet is a wild and largely unpoliced landscape. While it's true that it's studded with strange and lovely bits of stuff of which writers of past generations would be envious, it can also be a wasteland of information deserts, truculent trolls and fact factories. It's therefore only as good as the quality of sites you visit and how you use what you find.

The Internet and Research

First issue: the internet is information. And writers need information. And some people live under the illusion that all the information they'll ever need is on the internet. As mentioned above, herein lies the problem with the new democracy of online publishing: since anyone can now bypass the gatekeepers (agents, editors, publishers), and publish anything, anything gets published, thus the information you find might not be as excellent or accurate as it could be. So: don't fall into the trap of believing that everything online, or in print for that matter, is reliable. Wikipedia, for example, is a collaboratively created encyclopaedia and is notorious for its 'fact wars': some entries are constantly edited, sometimes by well-meaning users, and sometimes by malicious pranksters.

Even if entries are accurate, they are often a good beginner's overview of a subject, but they're generally not comprehensive or authoritative enough to offer enough detail for the historical novel you're researching, or for that matter, that university assessment essay you're writing. So, unless you know the source is a strong one then be wary of 'facts' you find on the internet. The same is of course true of material in print, but here the books and journals you find in bookshops and libraries will generally have gone through the gatekeeping process of peer review and quality control. For a wealth of advice put into a search engine the following phrase: *how to tell if an internet source is reliable.*

The Internet, Your Bank Balance and Your Local High Street

Second issue: snaking through this internet landscape is the mighty Amazon, its rainforests teeming with hitherto undiscovered chirping gadgets and brightly plumaged books you didn't know you needed until you browsed (for an hour or six ...).

Amazon is a magnificent resource: I've discovered many hitherto unknown and now much-loved books in its forests, but I also have shelves of useful unread ones. (Note to self: never ever reactivate one click-ordering.) But then, when I go to my local bookshop to promote my work to local readers, it's shut down. I'm also guilty of forgetting that the time to read the books that pop so easily through the letterbox does not come free with them. The slow pace of library borrowing limits is less bruising on the bank balance. Maybe just as there's a slow food movement, maybe there should be one for slow book acquisition! So stop looking for more useful books and get on with writing your own! Buying books is a displacement activity.

The Internet and Time

The final issue to bring to your attention lies with the internet as an attention-seeker. It's instant access to everything we ever thought we wanted. It's a siren calling to the weary, seasick writer, gripping a storm-tossed desk, drifting on the waves of a recalcitrant first draft. Its song is full of the incessant chatter of an outside existence beyond this lonely sea. Click online and all the world is here: our friends, our enemies; more information, more viewpoints, more news; not to mention our deepest desires, whether these are fluffy and innocent as kittens, or found on a site you'd rather your mother didn't know you visited ... Writer beware! This siren is a time vampire; an endless labyrinth of connections; a cornucopia of useful displacement activities, something that Auntie warns you about in the Help section of this book.

It's not just a problem for the inexperienced and unpublished: Zadie Smith famously used software to block internet access while she wrote her novel *NW*. And Jonathan Frantzen has spoken of supergluing up the Ethernet port of his computer.[3] Will Self eschews the word processor altogether and favours the good old typewriter, and J.K. Rowling and Jon McGregor, the slow pleasures of paper and pen.[4]

So: advice (to myself as much as to you); switch off the Wifi router; try some lovely thick cream paper and an ink pen. If you usually stare into the white glare of a screen, then this might be as good as a weekend away to revitalise your internet-shattered attention span. That said; what follows is a compendium of ways that writers might engage with the internet (for the moments when your internet blocking software lets you back online).

Facebook

Facebook has tended to be less about posting the work itself and more about promoting it and the people involved. Whilst it began as a social network, it is increasingly populated with pages belonging to businesses, writers, films, performance events, novels. These presences can be brief: a new writing performance event soon comes and goes and its page disappears rapidly down the timelines. But a professional presence as a writer doesn't if you keep updating with posts about your ongoing work. So, get news of readings and writing events out there, or promote your writers' circle. But put the work in: don't set up a page and expect instant success: you have to work hard at it.

Twitter

The world of Twitter is awash with flirting, debates, gossip, trolls and inconsequential updates about breakfasts and trains. But there are also long strands of comments, connected with hashtags (that's a # for those of you who, like me, need these things explaining), posted by people comparing notes about television shows as they're broadcast: some people no longer chat with those on the sofa next to them, but with strangers in distant cities as well. All comments with a common hashtag are collated in a Twitter search, meaning you can join the flow of a discussion (or online rantathon – there are lots of those).

In the midst of all this Twitter noise, there is also *Twitter Fiction*. As each Twitter post is restricted to 140 characters, such fiction is even flasher than flash fiction. Some people also tweet beautiful *Twitter Poetry*, which, in its 140-character brevity, has the aura of haiku. And if you think 140 characters is not enough for something worthwhile, consider Ernest Hemingway's short story of six words, or 32 characters:

For sale: baby shoes, never worn.

Twitter is also an interesting way to connect with other writers. With a little searching, you'll find people tweeting advice, or posts about their writing experiences, frustrations and triumphs. Twitter can be a timewaster but it can also be a line into the *Zeitgeist* of what's going on: who's looking for writers, who's looking for readers, and who's just looking for attention. Twitter even has guidance for authors: have a look at https://dev.twitter.com/media/authors.

Brave New World

It now seems a bit dated to be examining digital sites through a print medium alone (nudge to publisher), but it probably won't be long before you'll be able to open a book exactly like this one but with clickable interactive pages.[5] I don't know about you, but I've occasionally found myself pressing my finger onto a word on a page as if my finger were a cursor and the page a screen. Sad.

In the meantime, here's a caveat: any list of websites and microsites is, of course, a dip into the vast, ever-changing digital jungle of the internet: there are millions of other sites and Twitter users miniblogging away out there besides the ones offered here, and we can't guarantee that all these sites will still be active when you read this. Such is the ephemerality of the web: some will be extinct and others will have evolved into existence before this is printed (books take sooo long to get out there!). Some of the sites below may excite you, inspire you, offend you or bore you, and no doubt you'll find others even better those listed here. Such is cyberspace! So, welcome to the jungle. Here are just a few of the bewildering proliferations of experiments, online publications, writing communities, blogs, websites and twitterati that are part of the *Zeitgeist*. Grab a virtual machete and go and explore: for there are new species out there waiting to be discovered!

Online Writing

It is undoubtedly true that the online possibilities are immense for the writer. You could make a website operate as a narrative repository (see Geoff Ryman's *253*), or you could download an app and create an e-book. This is self-publishing for the internet-savvy. And the same caveats exist: just because it's in digital print doesn't mean it will get read. But for those willing to learn new software to get published online there's iBooks Author, LiberWriter, eBookBurn or Smashwords.

There is a shift among some writers to get back to the loveliness of the book as an object. The pleasures of Chris Ware's *Building Stories* would be diminished in an online version. And the series *Sabine and Griffin* by Nick Bantock is much more beautiful in the hand than online, consisting as it does of images, text and envelopes you open to find letters, postcards and notes ... This is the Ahlbergs' *The Jolly Postman* for adults, and it's a gorgeous experience. However, the possibilities of what the online format can achieve are exciting. I advocate a world where what follows does not replace the paper book, but exists alongside it.

Geoff Ryman: 253 – A Novel for the Internet: www.ryman-novel.com

An award-winning site, structured in blocks based on the coaches of a London Tube train. Its characters are the passengers, and you can click on each person in any order you choose, but there's an underlying story and plenty of small stories, with witty and thoughtful subplots and digressions. There are no bells and whistles, no pictures or multimedia, just text that reads interactively. There is a printed version, and you might want to compare the two. Any writer with reasonable computer competence could produce something like this. You don't need specialist skills.

These Waves of Girls: www.yorku.ca/caitlin/waves/

Made by Caitlin Fisher, this prize-winning hypermedia novella includes image and text, personal stories of sex and love, plus an eerie soundtrack. Although technically and creatively raw, this site gives an example of how hypertext fiction that can be made using everyday computer skills.

www.nickbantock.com and www.griffinandsabire.com
@NickBantock

Have a look at the online version of this if you're unsure about purchasing this on paper. This is beautiful to look at, the love story works quite well, and it even has W.B. Yeats reciting his own poem. There is some interactivity and the animated visuals, while enjoyable, are often unconnected to the storyline. Bantock is a good writer but a better visual artist and animator: the visuals are stunning and inventive. However, everybody who has seen it loves it, and as an inspirational example of a creative word/image/interactive project, this is one of the best.

Jeff Noon: www.cobralingus.com@jeffnoon

Noon applies techniques from dance music to the production of words: he 'samples' and 'remixes'. The idea of transferring a method or technique from one art form to another has been tried often before, with mixed results, but this site is worth a visit and you might be inspired.

British Electronic Poetry Centre: www.soton.ac.uk/~bepc

A great reference guide to poetry, with access to poems, performances and debate.

Electronic Poetry Center: www.epc.buffalo.edu/

A fantastic online library of poetry and epoetry. Prepare to lose hours browsing.

Twitter Poetry and Prose

@badbadpoet,@DeadEndFiction@welloverthought,@3hundredand65, @MiniatureNovels @VeryShortStory, and the Twitter collective @ echovirus12

Authors' Websites and Blogs

Many authors' websites are marketing sites intended to promote the writer's career, which is fair enough. But there are author sites that have added value for writers.

Dan Powell Fiction: http://danpowellfiction.com/

A minimal, smart-looking site which includes reviews, interviews with writers, pieces about doing a writing MA and developing work. Powell's short stories have won prizes and been published in magazines and anthologies. He promotes his own writing in a low-key way and he's also generous to other writers. The site is interactively linked with Twitter and Facebook plus his other, more literary website, providing a good model of how to use similar content in different ways and on different applications to reach a wider audience. (See also our interview with Elizabeth Baines in Chapter 26 for a similar model.)

Jacqueline Wilson: www.jacquelinewilson.co.uk/

Aimed at children, this site offers competitions, games, forums and stories, plus guidance on illustration and discussion about some of the serious issues in her books. Illustrator Nick Sharratt's colourful graphics are also used on the site to appeal to a young audience. Pictures, cartoons, graphics and photographs can all enliven your website, but unless they are your own work beware of copyright issues.

Jeanette Winterson: www.jeanettewinterson.com/index.asp

Includes articles, poems, writing tips, interviews, readings and biography as well as information and extracts from her books.

A.L. Kennedy: www.a-l-kennedy.co.uk/

Includes a useful area for writers. You have to register to access part of the site, but it only takes a moment and it's worth it for ideas, insight and encouragement.

Authors on Twitter

@MargaretAtwood, @valmcdermid, @jeffnoon, @ANNELAMOTT, screen writer Danny Stack on @ScriptwritingUK, @barrylyga, @megcabot; @agnieszkasshoes, @AliceHof, @Cbarzak, @chuck-palahniuk, @paulocoelho, @neilhimself (Neil Gaiman)

Resources

These are sites where you can find excellent resources, tips and tricks. Having surveyed quite a few of them for this chapter it's clear that you could waste a serious amount of time that might be better spent writing, so beware of spending too much time finding out how to write and not enough time actually doing any! That said, have a look at the following.

Writers Online: www.writers-online.co.uk/

A UK-based site, created from *Writing Magazine* and *Writers' News*. Although this site has some commercial elements, advertisements for subscriptions to the magazines, etc., it also includes links to agents, publishers, features and opportunities to post your work and enter competitions. Up-to-date and well-managed.

The Poetry Portal: www.poetry-portal.com/

A huge archive of poets and poetry and all things connected.

Poetry Magic: www.poetrymagic.co.uk/experimental.html

Useful advice and examples of how to develop your work for the Net.

Writers' Digest: www.writersdigest.com@WritersDigest

The huge site of the venerable American writers' magazine, *Writers' Digest*. They annually post *101 Best Web Sites for Writers*, and if that doesn't satisfy your lust for more, go back to the parent site and explore a raft of material on writer's craft.

National Association of Writers in Education: www.nawe.co.uk@ NaweWriters

Shedloads of resources relating to creative writing – and not just-relevant to those working in an education context. They are, they say, 'the one organization supporting the development of creative writing of all genres and in all educational settings throughout the UK'.

The Association of Writers and Writing Programs: www.awpwriter.org@awpwriter

Especially good for writers' conferences and finding postgraduate programmes in the USA. The AWP supports 'over 24,000 writers at over 370 member colleges and universities and 125 writers' conferences and centres'.

Varuna: www.varuna.com.au@Varunawriters

A wealth of writing experience with an Australian focus.

www.irdp.co.uk

Sadly, this is now an archive rather than an active site, but it still hosts everything you ever needed to know about radio drama. Now go and listen to some!

www.booktrust.org.uk@Booktrust

Full of information about the book world given in videos, reviews, listings and web links to sites like booktrusted.com – a resource for those writing for children.

NaNoWriMo: www.nanowrimo@NaNoWriMo

November is National Novel Writing Month, and this site aims to be with you every word of the way.

Daily Writing Tips: www.dailywritingtips.com@writing_tips

A site offering insights into report writing, the use of the comma, book reviews... You can subscribe to their daily posts via an RSS feed or by email.

Resources on Twitter

@Quotes4Writers, @shewritesdotcom, @JaneFriedman, @bbcwritersroom, @ElectricLit, @NWPlaywrights, @Mini_stories, @ShortStoryWeek, @ fuelyourwriting, @virtualwriters, @AdviceToWriters, @goodreads, @ poetswritersinc, @kiwiwriters, @AdviceToWriters, @99fiction

Writers' Communities

There are numerous sites where you can interact with other writers, showcase your work and give and get feedback. There should be no charge, although you may have to register. It is said that agents and publishers also access the most reputable of these sites to search for talent. The difficulty is to know which are the most reputable. So ask yourself:

- Who set up the site? What are their credentials/background?

- Is it managed, monitored and up to date?

- Do people give feedback to others as well as posting their own work?

- Where is the site based? (the UK, the USA?) Does this matter to you?

That said, try:

figment: write yourself in. http://figment.com/

Mainly aimed at and used by teenagers and young adults, *figment* covers 'sonnets to mysteries, from sci-fi stories to cell phone novels... you can find it all here'. It has an excellent pedigree and the site is well managed and active with links to writing competitions, publishers, established authors and writing opportunities.

Authonomy Writing Community: www.authonomy.com/

A UK-based site for writers, readers and publishers, set up by editors at HarperCollins and offering guidance on writing and getting published, articles and forums plus the chance to have your work read by a publisher. *authonomy* claims to be *the* place to improve your writing, find a literary agent or even get a publishing contract. It sounds great, but keep in mind that there are thousands of books uploaded onto the site. Up to date, well managed and informative.

Writersroom: www.bbc.co.uk/writersroom/ @bbcwritersroom

This is packed with brilliant writers' resources and is an essential destination for anyone wanting to learn about writing for television, radio and film. Essential for script layout information. This is also now the submission portal to the BBC for unsolicited new writing.

Getting Published/Performed

www.publishing-services.co.uk

An annotated catalogue of excellent websites and a brilliant resource. Pick and choose.

www.writers.net

Especially useful for research that may lead to you finding an agent.

Publishers on Twitter: @Riverhead Books, @holdfirepress, @commapress, @littlebrown, @BloomsburyBooks, @CinnamonJan

Magazines, journals: @GrantaMag, @fourthwallmag, @parisreview, @Mslexia

Agents: Carole Blake @caroleagent, @MBAAgents, @cjlitagency, @UpstartCrowLit

Promoting Your Work Online

First of all, read the interview with Elizabeth Baines in Chapter 26, 'Taking Your Work out into the World'. Next, visit Salt Publishing's extensive website and their blog within it, which are both packed with essential advice. (Salt Publishing can make a strong claim to being the UK's leading independent publisher. An indication of their success – much of which is down to skilful use of social media – is that at the time of writing, one of their latest novels, Alison Moore's *The Lighthouse*, has been shortlisted for the Man Booker Prize.)

Here are three areas where you can benefit from of Salt's wisdom:

How to do a virtual book tour

The aim of this is to generate word-of-mouth online. It is advised that over a period of a month or two you find ten blogs who will host a brief interview with you.
http://blog.saltpublishing.com/about-virtual-book-tours/

100 words of advice

Salt's director, Chris Hamilton-Emery, offers 100 words of advice on each of the following:

- Be your own agent: know the list you are submitting to
- Discoverability: for publishers, authors and readers, the Web provides collisions
- Why selling points matter
- The gatekeeper's three question
- Publicity is the art of remembering your choices.

http://blog.saltpublishing.com/category/100-words-of-advice/

Miscellaneous

Although now a decade old, Steve Raiter's website offers a comprehensive list of some of the best graphic novels:
http://my.voyager.net/~sraiteri/graphicnovels.htm.

Tim Guest's article on web-based graphic novels is a portal to many intriguing websites.
http://www.guardian.co.uk/online/story/0,3605,544266,00.html

Fun and games for writers and wordsmiths:
www.philobiblon.com/isitabook

Final Thoughts

You should have a look at a current copy of *The Writers' and Artists' Yearbook*. Amongst the listings and other excellent sections every writer needs to know about, they have an excellent section about digital resources, which in my 2012 edition is called 'Writers and Artists Online'. Since the internet is not going anywhere soon, this section is here to stay; just make sure you're consulting as recent a copy of the *Yearbook* as you can. Now all you need to do is set up a blog, or open a Twitter account and start experimenting.

III
GOING WHERE?

25 Writing as Self-Invention

Julie Armstrong

Why do people want to write? It can, after all, be a frustrating activity, and a very lonely job, as Stephen King notes in *On Writing*. However, whether one is a published writer or not, writing is rewarding, and if not a compulsion, a way of life.

The Autobiography in Writing

Writing is self-expression. When we write, we preserve emotions, thoughts, experiences, relationships and memories: writing captures the importance they had, just as photographs can capture *defining* moments. Writing enables us to mourn our losses and celebrate our joys. All writing is autobiographical in that the fictional worlds you create come from you: undoubtedly, the trace elements of your unique experiences are in your narratives, waiting to be found by someone who knows what they're looking for. And what autobiography is ever totally and utterly as it happened? Writing gives you a second chance: you can take revenge; you can refashion the dialogue as you wish you'd said it. Rebuilding and rewriting events from our lives, however much they are framed as things that happen to our characters, helps us make sense of them. Writing is thus a way of discovering who you are, and working through the parts of your life that trouble you. Alice Sebold has done both in her memoir, *Lucky*, and the companion novel *The Lovely Bones*.[1] In other words, if you want it to be, it can be a form of therapy, psychoanalysis even.

Writing is often seen as a search for some kind of truth. Maybe life doesn't seem 'true' until it is written down and encapsulated in a form. Whatever your views, if you want to write, writing has to be essential to your well-being as an individual. If not, why do it?

So what *exactly* is it that makes us want to write?

As well as being a craft and an art form, writing is an intellectual and philosophical pursuit. As a student of writing you will be a thinker: you'll observe life, reflect upon it, then explore your findings and experiences through creative writing. Why? What is it that makes *you* want to write? Why do you choose to express yourself in this way? Why words, and not paint, dance, music?

Why Express Yourself through Language?

Jot down some thoughts and ideas in response to the following questions:

- Why do *you* express yourself through language?
- How do you see the world?
- What is the use of reading? And writing?

Writing can offer a different way of looking at things and the world: it is often about asking and answering questions; you should take some time to ponder the reasons for your wanting to engage in the process of writing.

What follows is a list of questions for you, the answers to which will give you insight into your motivation for writing. Don't worry if you can't answer some of them straight away: mull them over. The answers will form over time.

- *When did you first start writing?*
Some writers have written for as long as they can remember. During childhood, they may have simply scribbled in notebooks or kept a diary. A diary can be a place where we take refuge, as Anne Frank did. Other writers take it up out of the blue. There's no advantage in either position (readers can't tell that you've always wanted to be a writer!).

- *What was your first piece of writing about? What inspired you to write it?*
Your first piece of writing – and by this I mean a longer work, something you've spent time crafting – may well have been autobiographical, or it may have been an escape world you created, in the same way that a child has an imaginary friend.

■ *What is your favoured form? Why?*
There are no rules: you don't have to stick at writing just poetry, or fiction, or scripts. And you can write in any genre you choose, be it science fiction, magic realism, romance or thriller, whatever. However, the chances are you'll find yourself gravitating towards a particular form and genre. Experiment and discover what is best for you.

■ *What themes recur in your work?*
There are often repetitive themes across the body of a writer's work: these will reflect the ideas and subjects that fascinate the writer. They will also reflect a world-view, of which the writer herself may be unaware. When you've finished a piece of work, sit down and ask yourself: what's it all about? How does this compare with other pieces I've written?

■ *Do you have to write?*
If the answer is no, forget it. Writing has to have relevance in your life. Writing *is* a life. Yes, it's a slog, fraught with disappointments, but it's also fulfilling and fun. It can also be a means of escape: while he was writing during his lunch hour, Stephen King was transcending the workplace and his boss!

■ *Do you look at the world differently when you write?*
Of course, it's personal, but I suggest it's like putting on a pair of glasses: some things are blurred; others are in sharp focus. The world takes on a new perspective.

Answering such questions helps you become a more self-aware writer. Having read this chapter you might also want to read Chapter 9, 'Reflection'.

A Journey of Self-discovery

It is worth contemplating the notion that writing is a journey of self-discovery, one in which we construct through language a sense of self. Writing is empowering, it can enable us to *save* our lives. Through writing we explore our identities, confirm and affirm them, and find a sense of control over our lives (however illusory that sense might be). It enables us to make sense of the world, and our role in it. Through the act of writing we solve problems, record, order, process and express our experiences and communicate these to others, the reader being the 'other'. We learn what it means to be human.

Other Worlds, Other Selves

As we've mentioned elsewhere in this book, if you don't read you'll find it very hard to be a good writer: reading is an excellent focus for a writer's craft. Ask yourself this: do you read to be entertained, or to be given something to think about? Perhaps both? And what do you like to read? Fantasy, horror, crime? Of course the list of genres is endless, but in each case, when you read, you enter other worlds, and so it is when you write: the virtual reality of the imagination, of writing, is one where writers and readers step out of real time and space into other dimensions, other worlds. Adam Thorpe speaks of taking the reader into his own universe, a universe that he likens to a wild garden or the forest.[2] When we make up other worlds, we can briefly forget this one. How liberating!

In postmodern times there isn't a single 'truth' or viewpoint: we are free to discover other selves and to create other realities. As writers, we have ultimate freedom to construct worlds outside and beyond our environment, beyond our experiences and cultural history. The only limitation is our imagination.

The Best Time to Be a Writer

Take time now to reflect upon your writing process. The process of writing is a *personal* journey, a different journey for every writer, but one of the most fascinating journeys you can make. We all have a time when our imagination is most fertile, a time when our creative juices flow unhindered. For some writers this may be at night, for others very early in the morning. These are quiet times, when we're more in touch with our unconscious, when we can inhabit the 'secret' place of our imagination and explore our secret lives, our lives beyond our 'real' lives. It's just a question of dipping into our creative drive.

Try This: Fictional Worlds

Think of a world you experienced vividly when reading a book: you may have read the book years ago, and intricate plot details may have faded, but your memory of the world might still be as fresh as the day it was imprinted into your imagination. Describe it.

Self-Invention

In an ideal world, what kind of person would you like to be? What attributes would you like to have? For example: I'd like to be able to fly. Now write for 10 minutes without stopping. Now put this character into a predicament and write them trying to work themselves free. You have the rough beginnings of a piece of writing. Take it further. Take it any direction you choose. Write with it for half an hour.

Further Reading

Natalie Goldberg (2005) *Writing Down the Bones* (New York: Shambhala).
  A marvellous book that should be on every writer's bookshelf.
Michèle Roberts (1998) *Food, Sex and God: Inspiration and Writing* (London: Virago).
  Roberts articulates wonderfully the private process of constructing identity and reinvention of the self through language.
Ralf L. Wahlstrom (2006) *The Tao Of Writing* (Avon, MA: Adams Media Publications).
  An engaging book which investigates writers' inner worlds, enabling them to tap into secret parts of themselves, which can be expressed through their writing.

26 Taking Your Work Out into the World

Robert Graham and Heather Leach

The Writer in the Digital Age

Elizabeth Baines is a prize-winning author of novels, short stories and stage and radio plays. Her stories have been widely published in magazines and anthologies, and her collection, *Balancing on the Edge of the World*, was published by Salt in 2007. Her latest novel, *Too Many Magpies,* which came out in 2009, was described by one Amazon reviewer as 'an appealing, bewitching read, one that feels slightly dangerous and a little bit thrilling'. As well as being an occasional actor, she somehow also manages to find time to maintain a lively and creative presence on digital media. Her blog, Fictionbitch, covers the contemporary book world both on- and offline – see her October 2012 post, which reports on a fascinating debate on the impact of the internet on publishing. She has her own author's website and blog – with the strap line 'How To Be A Writer Without Ending Up Sozzled, Behind Bars or Insane', and links all of these with Facebook and Twitter accounts.

Of course, although these digital sites help to advertise her work, they are also much more than that, offering a rich insight into the life of a working writer, links with literary events and debates, book reviews, and a celebration of writers, books and ideas in today's fast-changing world.

In this email interview, we asked Elizabeth to talk about how she promotes her writing, what works best, and how she finds a balance between the creative and commercial aspects of being a writer.

Elizabeth, you're a seasoned and successful author, you've been promoting your writing for some time, and are skilled and creative in the use of digital media, but some writers find self-promotion a challenge. Is this something you've developed over time, and has it been a challenge for you too?

I'd say that at this time when it's taken for granted that authors should be active in promotion, the elephant in the room is the fact that the personalities and inclinations of many authors make it difficult for them, and that this is indeed the reason they write in the first place, retreating to the private communication of the page. This was certainly why I started writing. I guess no one would suspect that of me now, and one thing that helped – and which goes on helping – is my experience as an actor: it helps, I find, to operate a kind of Jekyll and Hyde position, pulling the cloak of proactive author over my introverted writing self. Not that it's ever easy. I was brought up also not to blow my own trumpet: self-promotion still goes against the grain for me, and I have a revulsion against the cult of personality that now surrounds literature. When I first engaged with digital media, as a blogger, I was motivated by this very idea, that writing should stand up for itself, separate from the identity of the author, and my critical blog, Fictionbitch, which I started in 2006, was initially anonymous. However, Fictionbitch brought me such attention that I quickly realised the power of digital media for writers, and (against my grain!) started my author blog specifically to promote my own work.

What do you think are the best ways that a writer can support and market their work? Agents/readings/festivals/competitions/short fiction/small magazines/ digital media, etc.?

All of these things are important, but the internet, I'd say, is pivotal. It's clearly created a total revolution in the matter of author/book promotion. In the past you were entirely dependent on your publisher for promotion – all invitations for readings, to write articles, etc., ensued from your publisher's promotion, and if your publisher didn't bother much, which often happened, your book was in trouble – and now the internet has put power of promotion in author's hands. I'd say that all the invitations I've had in recent years, and a good proportion of the sales of my books, have been due to this digital exposure. If you have a good internet presence you're more likely to get an agent (and a publisher) and, once you're published, more likely to get invited to read and do other related things. If you do a reading you can advertise it on the internet beforehand and write about it afterwards, increasing your profile. You can do the same if you win a competition or get published in a small magazine. Networking is also important: meetings with other writers and literary professionals can lead to commissions, and the internet is now crucial here. Add to all this the fact that publishers now expect and even require digital engagement by authors, and there really isn't much choice but to bite the bullet.

How much time do you devote to marketing your work in relation to the amount of time you spend at work on your writing? Has this changed with the expansion of digital media? How do you protect your writing time to cope with this?

I'm still working on the balance. The internet, as everyone knows, is a huge gobbler of time. When I first took it up so enthusiastically I wasn't writing very much, and once I started writing again in earnest I found it a challenge. For me it's not simply a matter of time but also of attention and headspace. As David Foster Wallace put it, when you're immersed in a writing project 'you're terrified to spend any time on anything other than working on it because if you look away for a second you'll lose it'. In addition, as I indicate above, promotion and writing for me are different ways of thinking and of *being*: to be involved in promotion is to be extrovert, realist, even hard-headed, whereas writing for me needs a mentality more dreamily in touch with my unconscious. Switching from one to the other in the same day feels painfully like twisting my head right round on my neck, and quite frankly is not always possible. An extra problem is that resistance has now grown up to author 'spamming', especially on Twitter, and authors are now advised to woo readers by engaging with their followers and friends on other subjects, rather than simply promote their books – more hours in the day to spend not actually writing, and more of other people's random thoughts to scatter your writing brain! The solution I've come up with (so far) is spending certain periods, the periods when I have new work out, exclusively on promotion, and at other times working really hard not to let the internet interfere with my writing by restricting it to an hour a day, and then, once I'm too immersed in the writing to care about anything else, forcing myself onto the internet once a day!

Elizabeth Baines, interviewed by Heather Leach,
November 2012

Weblinks

www.elizabethbaines.com
http://elizabethbaines.blogspot.com
http://fictionbitch.blogspot.com

Latest publications

Balancing at the Edge of the World (2007)
Too Many Magpies (2009)
The Birth Machine (2010)
All published by Salt Publishing (http://www.amazon.co.uk/Elizabeth-Baines/).

The Commissioned Writer

David Gaffney is a flash-fiction specialist who shows what you can achieve if you are a little more imaginative about how you reach an audience with your fiction. His work has appeared in a wide range of anthologies, print and web magazines and in conventional, printed book form (see below). This might make him appear to conform to the traditional role of the writer – but that's where the resemblance between Gaffney and most fiction writers ends.

David's job with the Arts Council has probably done as much as anything to shape his writing career. Coming from that background has inspired him to find funding for taking literature down avenues other than print or online publication. (Although he clearly manages to do that as well.) Visual artists certainly operate in a similar way, and poets, too, and playwrights are often commissioned for community projects, but amongst fiction writers, the way David has created literary projects that perhaps have more in common with Live Art, and the way he as found funding for them, may be unique.

Looking at David's track record ought to inspire any writer to do things differently. Here are just a few of his commissioned projects. (You can find more examples at his website.)

Spoilt Victorian Child

A commission for Manchester Art Gallery of six text pieces in response to the Art Treasures of the UK Exhibition (2007).

Destroy PowerPoint

A series of stories in PowerPoint format launched at Edinburgh Festival (2009).

Buildings Crying Out

A story for Lancaster Litfest 2009 using lost cat posters.

The Poole Confessions

Stories told from a confessional box at Poole Literature Festival (2010).

Sawn-off Opera

A collaboration with composer Ailís Ní Ríain: mini-operas that have been performed at, for example, Liverpool's Philharmonic Hall, Manchester's Royal Exchange Theatre and London's Tête à Tête opera festival. *Sawn-off Opera* was also broadcast by BBC Radio 3 (2010).

You are very much a writer who performs his work. What made you move away from the conventional author tour?

I set out writing novels which somehow morphed into flash fiction, and then I was asked to do a few live readings and I was struck by how dull I might be, standing on a stage on my own with no acting skills, reading words off a sheet of paper. So I was always looking for ways to spice up the experience, to take the attention away from a dusty author with his head down in a folded bit of A4. I began to get to know about all the peripheral activities around the publication of books – festivals, live appearances, commissions, participatory and community work and began to realise that there was more to writing than producing text for printed books. I realised that more people might see a piece of text in an art gallery, for example, than on the pages of a slim volume in the little-visited short-story section of Waterstones. Through my work for the arts council I also became more aware of developments in contemporary visual arts, public art, live art, performance and music, and I began to see how literature could be enhanced by linking up with other platforms and formats. So while producing a strong short story in a printed form is still my ultimate goal, I discovered a love of playing with different ways of translating short stories for audiences. This means I am always trying to come up with writing projects that flex with the culture and push at boundaries. Different artistic formats can converge into exciting new products no one has ever seen before; an example might be the recent project (not one of mine) linking car satellite-navigation systems with stories about certain places, and emerging iPhone apps that use augmented reality to relate fictions about cities as we wander about and point the device at buildings. This way of working can mean coming up with really meaningful art form collaborations. I performed my PowerPoint stories project with live free improvised music; I collaborate with comic-book artists, and have produced mini-operas and sound installations. All art forms are fair game for collaboration. Having said all of this, I value very highly a good-quality printed product – something to hold and enjoy – which is why I enjoy the innovative design and graphic work of McSweeney's printed books, for example, and also the work of graphic novelists like Daniel Clowes. In this world of transient digital ephemera people still want things they can touch and own and hold on to. And it's not all about digital, which is the mistake some people make when trying to force freshness onto a writing project. New developments need to be more than can be simply reproducing printed stories on websites.

You've been very successful at finding channels for your fiction beyond print or online publication – and gaining funding to do that. What prompted you to head in this direction?

I have found that venues promoters and festivals like projects that stand out from the crowd of other literature events and are eye-catching to the media. So when I produced my stories in a PowerPoint format, I was able to speak about it on Radio 4 and write about it in the *Guardian*, which all helps. My project for Poole Literature Festival set in a confessional box got some interesting press, as did Station Stories, a site-specific live literature promenade event using digital technology and live improvised electronic sound in which six writers took an audience, linked to the writer's microphones by headsets using wireless technology, on a tour of [Manchester] Piccadilly Station and read specially commissioned stories inspired by the station. Other projects I've delivered, and in some cases am still involved in, include *Les Malheureux*, an ongoing experiment with live text and live music and visuals in which micro-fictions are performed to specially composed musical pieces against a backdrop of an original slide show; *Preston 3twenty*, a two-decade-long multi-art form and multi-platform new writing project in which 60 writers produce a three-stranded portmanteau tale of Preston covering the period from 1972 to 2072; and *Errata Slips*, a micro-commission for Cornerhouse Manchester in which I used the standard erratum-slip format to explore ideas around truth and authenticity by adding false information to real magazines in the Cornerhouse bookshop. All of this sort of work takes literature to new audiences and encourages participant artists to push at the boundaries of presentation and format.

Is there a knack to gaining funding?

I try to make sure what I am doing fits with the needs of arts funders like the Arts Council, whose main aim is to grow and build new audiences for high-quality work. So keeping in mind the twin issues of high-quality and expanding audiences, projects can be designed which hopefully do both, and satisfy the needs of lots of funders. For example a local-authority funder will wish to see engagement with as many people from their hard-to-reach communities as they can get, and as well as this, if your literature project can reduce crime, boost the economy, improve health and clean chewing gum off the pavements, you are laughing.

If any readers of this book wanted to emulate what you have done, where would you recommend them to start?

I would say develop strong working relationships with artists from other art forms, with people who can manage projects, and with digital designers. Small teams of people who work together regularly can really get things done quickly and well. Every project needs a visual element, a digital element and good project manager/producer. I see collaborative, cross-art-form work growing. Most people get their fiction fix from the screen – TV and film. The literary fiction audience comes from a very narrow demographic and the way we understand and receive stories has changed. Audiences have become sophisticated in the way they read and understand texts. They pick up subtle nuances and complexity very quickly, and writers of fiction have to keep up with this. The fictional worlds of *The Wire*, *Mad Men*, *Breaking Bad*, are densely packed with information, often obtuse and obscure and sometimes difficult to understand, and it is all thrown at the 'reader' in a rapid-fire, unforgiving way. Us book writers at the back have to keep up with this.

David Gaffney, interviewed by Robert Graham,
December 2012

Weblinks

www.davidgaffney.org/

Latest publications

Sawn-off Tales (2006)
Aromabingo (2007)
Never Never (2008)
The Half-life Of Songs (2010)
More Sawn-off Tales (2013)
All published by Salt Publishing, except *Never Never,* which is published by Tindal Street Press (http://www.amazon.co.uk/David-Gaffney/).

The student writer

James Harker, who graduated from MMU Cheshire in 2012 with a First in Creative Writing, has also just won Edge Hill University's £1000 Jo Powell Memorial Writing Competition – prize for writing crime fiction.

During James's third year with us, 2011–12, he won a place on the Young Writers' Programme at the Everyman Theatre in Liverpool.

He impressed so much during that scheme that he was recently awarded a salaried place on the Liverpool 'Writer on Attachment' scheme run at the Everyman.

James also won a Guardian Student Media award in 2010.

1. *How have you managed to do so well so quickly?*
Well, I've actually been at this quite a while. I wrote freelance articles for local papers in my teens (highlight: covering a rivalry between Meatloaf tribute act 'Maltloaf' and the owner of a local concert-hall) and I spent several years out of school, cleaning up baby-sick at Mothercare and writing angry lyrics for a punk band called 'Dead Elvis', before I even heard of Creative Writing as a degree.

At university, I was stupid enough to send my short stories to magazines and anthologies immediately (I still have my first, and in many ways most-crushing, rejection letter: from the Salisbury-based sci-fi magazine *Jupiter*). Small opportunities gradually led to bigger ones and, by the time of my graduation, I'd already edited (and been sacked from) the uni's student magazine, won a mildly prestigious journalism award, spent a month in London humiliating myself in front of very clever people at the *Guardian*, and survived one complete nervous breakdown.

Ultimately, I was lucky to live so close to the Liverpool Everyman Theatre (and its fantastic dramaturge Lindsay Rodden, who saw through the obvious flaws in an awful script I'd sent her – about bomber pilots in occupied 1940s France – and gave me a writing job). I think my small success has been about three parts luck and maybe one part obstinate determination. A quick warning about my definition of 'success', however: I may have a cool-sounding writing job, but I'm a long way from rivalling my old Mothercare salary (though my hands are a lot less sticky these days).

2. *How did a Creative Writing degree prepare you to become a professional writer?*

It gave me three years in which reading great literature was not only a hobby but an obligation (I came to uni reading Robert Sheckley sci-fi novels; I left obsessed with Louis Celine and Heinrich Böll). It was also a great place to toughen myself to criticism. I think the hardest part of my professional writing life has been dealing with failure (a month wasted on a huge commission for the *Guardian* which was later binned by the editor; the embarrassed-audience laughter which met my first short play). Without experience in the lion pit of creative writing seminars, I'd've probably run home crying years ago.

3. *What's the difference between students who persevere with their writing after graduation and those who don't?*

Meaningful writing involves months of research and self-examination: peering into the ugliest corners of society and your own soul, then painstakingly turning these revelations into story, into narrative, into *entertainment*. To persevere with writing you have to realise that a good portion of your life will be spent sitting on your arse in a dark room, alienating your family, struggling against your own stupidity, struggling against your own innate limitations and endlessly, endlessly repeating the same thoughts, the same clumsy processes in the hope of producing one (*even one*) truly illuminating sentence. And those are just the good days.

Perseverance requires a genuine love of literature and a deep-rooted masochistic streak. Without these: you're probably toast.

James Harker, interviewed by Robert Graham,
November 2012

27 Getting Published
John Singleton

First: Write the Book

The hard yards: write a *good* book; one that excites you, not your mum, not your kids, not the vicar, not your imagined reader. *You* are the first, last, and most important reader of your work. Nothing else matters.

You, however, are not the only reader of your work. There are people out there who will have a say in what and how you write – if you want to get published and read. They form the market – agents and readers and distributors and editors and publishers and reviewers and librarians and booksellers and teachers. And though all these interested parties will impinge on your choice of material and approach, they shouldn't control what you write or how you write.

Taking too much notice of the market by trying to write what you think the market wants is a recipe for failure. Another novel about the serial dating of three or four typical 25-year-old city-somethings will probably produce a dull, typical and unsurprising write-by-numbers book. Find what works for you and stick with it. If it's familiar fictional territory you must enter, give it your own spin. Do something different. Surprise the reader. It's *your* voice we want to hear, not an imitation; a real voice, not an echo. If you want to write popular family drama, go for it. If you want to write gritty fiction about the chemical generation, do so. But do it your way, not the Irvine Welsh way.

On the other hand, taking too little notice of the market may leave you isolated and unpublished. What it comes down to is this: everyone has to work out for themselves how to balance market demand and personal aspirations as a writer. My view is this: yes, keep a weather eye on the market, but first get that book done. It's a good book that will impress an agent or a publisher, not some clever pitch and market-savvy narrative. Leave it up to the professionals for guidance on adjusting to market conditions.

And here is another crucial point. Having a book accepted for publication is only the beginning of a long evolutionary process. You will inevitably be asked to revise it, maybe a number of times. Revisions may well be driven by market considerations, but editors and agents have made these decisions for you, and you will follow their advice to the letter because you're not going to pass up a chance to be published, are you?

Six months after acceptance, many letters and phone calls later, the text is finally agreed and the book goes into production. You've kept your artistic integrity; others have adjusted and helped you fine-tune the product for an eager readership out there.

As with all advice, this lot comes with conditions and small print. Here's some of it: your book may be great, but the market still has to want it. Like all markets, publishing is subject to the whims of change. Take the non-fiction sector. At the time of writing social history is the going thing. Hocus-pocus is out. This includes all those books with titles like *The Mysteries of the Pyramids* and *Blood Gilt: Human Sacrifice and the Ancient Aztecs*. Books with single titles like *Cod*, *Salt*, *Spice* and *Diamond* are also out. But in the mid-lit field of quality readable historical fiction things are on the up. Books like *The Girl with the Pearl Earring* and *Tulip* have been big hits, and anything set in eighteenth-century Japan will be snapped up.

In popular fiction, chick-lit is out; the old hands like Freya North, Jill Mansell and Marian Keyes have carved up the territory anyway. Because the Bridget Jones experience is currently out of literary favour, so too, for the time being, is the diary as a popular narrative form. And don't try to be a second Joanna Trollope. First, remember your writing isn't homage to other writers; it's about your voice sounding loud and thrilled. Second, you won't succeed as a Trollope clone because no publisher wants Aga-sagas any more. But, if you are sensitive to the market and consider trends in demographics, you will notice that more and more readers are active into their eighties. So, you might want to consider saga-sex as your subject!

But sex is one subject where you do need a bit of protection. Write about underage sex and no one will publish your work. And don't make your protagonist a sexually predatory librarian. Librarians sit on book selection panels and award committees: it doesn't pay to upset them. Publishers tend not to be keen on religious themes either. They don't like vicars in children's stories. God and Satan are out everywhere:

mention the devil, and editors will exorcise your manuscript. Teenage necrophilia is definitely off limits. Restriction, if not censorship, is alive and well in every fiction executive's office.

Research Your Market

Research is common-sense, but worth spelling out. And you must be dedicated. If you're not prepared to research, don't expect to be published. You do research because it's the first step to maximising your chance of getting published.

The first thing you might find out is that recent changes in the market are not helping writers. Large companies are buying up small independents and forming huge conglomerates. When profit is the bottom line, risk, innovation and adventure disappear from the market. In other words conglomerates could be less likely to risk money on an unknown writer, especially as most of the market (editors and agents) are desperately looking for the next mega-seller.

In the big organisation it is harder to create that crucial personal touch and the nurturing environment that good editors in attentive publishing houses manage. The upside, however, is that the profits from highly successful enterprises like the *Harry Potter* series mean that the publisher can afford to develop new products and new imprints, and even put money aside to invest in new writers.

Before...

First, there is what I call before-writing research, the useful enquiry you can do *before* you write. I'm assuming you are writing fiction. You're doing the first bit of research by reading this chapter. Next, check on the bookshop shelves. See what's happening in crime fiction – women and forensics and pathology are the in thing – but for how long?

Maybe you want to consider another angle. Thinking of writing a children's novel? How long will it be? At 100 000 words your story may prove too expensive. A publisher may be reluctant to put up the money for a first-time writer and a 300-page teenage novel, unless your name's Philip Pullman. What age ranges do publishers divide the kid-lit market into? Are you aiming for the 7–9-year-olds? Or the 11–13s? What's the average length for each category? What sort of book is getting published here? Do kids' books divide along genre lines like adult ones do? Are there crime novels for children? Sci-fi? Horror? If so, do they interest you? Read a few. See what the standards are like. Are you after character development and psychological reality, or a fast-paced narrative where plot is king? Is it social realism you want, or a good escapist read? All this is before-writing research and will help clarify your fictional aims and add a touch of market realism to your grand ideas.

Select your readership. Browse in Waterstones and sample-read over cups of cappuccino. You'll be surprised how bad some published work is, and how much better you could do. Read magazines like *The Bookseller*, *Publishing News* and *The Rights Report* for trends and insider knowledge. These trade publications offer you an inside glimpse of market workings. For instance, you might see what a particular agent is interested in from reports of their recent acquisitions and deals. If it looks from these accounts that they could be interested in your kind of work, give them a ring. In this game you've got to push yourself and sell yourself. Shrinking violets needn't apply!

But, remember it's different if you're just browsing the market for ideas on *what* to write. I'm talking about a situation in which you already have an idea for a book and I'm suggesting how you can save yourself a lot of time and heartache by using research to make sure your work fits into the requirements of the market.

... And After

The other kind of research is the after-writing kind. By this I mean sussing out, not the products out there, but the main players – primarily agents and publishers. Here you are an outsider and dependent on a few expert guides on how the market drivers work. Apart from the trade journals mentioned above, the two best guides and essential reading for new writers are *The Writers' and Artists' Yearbook* and *The Writer's Handbook*. Both list all UK and some overseas book and magazine publishers, all literary agents, and both offer sound advice on presentation of manuscripts and proposals.[1]

Agents...

These days more and more publishers are refusing unsolicited manuscripts, so start with agents, not publishers. These days, publishing houses are relying on agents to do their initial sifting out of the good from the bad, the unpublishable from the publishable. Even publishers who do read new material often employ freelance readers to go through their 'slush' pile (unsolicited manuscripts) and depend on them for recommendations.

So, a good agent is the key to getting published. It follows therefore that these days, it's harder to get an agent than it is to get a publisher, and you want a *good* agent, one who will know your work, and know which publisher is best for you. What an agent does is promote you, enthuse others – editors, publicity and marketing people – about your work, advise what will and won't sell, keep your publisher in line and, if you're really lucky, do some sharp editing of your manuscript and advise on changes.

Not-so-good agents will not set up an initial meeting, will not offer market or editorial advice, will hand over everything to publishers (if they get one for your work), will not keep an eye on progress, will not talk and report back often over the phone enthused and optimistic, will never take you out to lunch, will not discuss future projects. Remember a good agent wants you for life, wants to build up a good working and personal relationship with you, wants to map out your future writing with you.

A good agent is a networker who keeps their finger on the market pulse, who has contacts not just in the UK, but in Europe and the USA through their associated agents and sub-agents, and who knows everyone in the trade. And, more importantly, knows what's happening inside publishing houses. She might find out on the grapevine that one publisher is looking to develop a new list in children's books and wants writers who can turn in socially real, hard-edged material.

Now how could any writer know about this critical information? It takes a good agent, ear to the ground, to know this and seize the opportunity on your behalf. Thus, what you are getting for your money (you pay an agent 10 per cent of royalties as a fee) is an unrivalled knowledge of the market and a powerful advocate for your work.

A good agent knows how to wheel and deal; she is someone with commercial savvy; she can talk to BBC film producers or French sub-agents on your behalf at the Frankfurt Book Fair or the Bologna International Children's Book Fair; she is someone who is familiar with contractual arrangements and she can check through the 20-page contract a publisher is offering you and advise on its appropriateness, etc., and she controls the translation rights and subsidiary rights, and manages film options, and how advance royalties are paid. This sort of advice is critical nowadays. Contracts are getting more and more restrictive. Good advice about the legal aspects of publishing also comes from *The Society of Authors*, the writers' union. Other brilliant sources of information are listed below.

...And How to Get One

Convinced you need an agent? Here's how to get one.

First, I repeat, *write a good book*. If it's good, it will get taken up by an agent and it will get published.

Next, go through the agents listed in one of the guides mentioned above. The entries will tell you what kinds of genre they deal in; make a list of the ones most suited to your work. Obviously, if you've written a historical novel, don't send it to an agent specialising in biographies and technical subjects. Be realistic. And eliminate from your shopping list agents who state, 'no unsolicited manuscripts'. This means they have a full client list and are not taking on new ones.

Having made your list, ring each one up to ask whether they are still taking on new clients. Check their submission requirements. This is usually: 2/3 chapters (typed, double-spaced, A4 one-sided), a synopsis, and a covering letter explaining who you are, a bit of background, target readership for your work (especially if non-fiction), and where you think your work fits into the market. Enclose a stamped envelope and address it to a named person. If the guide doesn't give the name of the editor you want, phone and find out, especially if you have an old guide. In this business, people change jobs often. Getting the right person gives a good first impression.

The submission letter should convince the agent they are dealing with someone who knows what they're about, has done their research and has a commercial proposition. For non-fiction works you really need a proposal: this includes an extended summary of the book, with main argument, chapter headings if possible, a statement of market appeal, a rationale for the book in commercial terms, and three sample chapters. Keep a copy of your submission. Agents and publishers always run a disclaimer that they are not responsible for loss or damage to the work.

If you've not heard from an agent within three weeks, call and make polite enquiries. Polite, because that's the way you are: why antagonise people who may be able to help you? A middle-sized agency may get up to 100–200 manuscripts a week, and it's tough turning that amount of reading round quickly.

The Marketing Buzz

So, you've got an agent and the agent has come up trumps: the book is with the publishing house. Home and dry? Not quite.

An unhelpful trend is the increasing power of marketing and publicity teams within big publishing houses. Again, this is two-edged. If your work is taken up by a big house, they will have the resources to push your work with wholesalers, reviewers and booksellers prior to launch, and to market you strongly after launch. What publicity departments aim to do is create a 'buzz' about a book, talk it up within the company so everyone inside is gunning for the book. They want everyone on side to push it with distributors, librarians and award committees so that a wave of expectancy rises with publication date and the book becomes a bestseller. A good agent will also try and create a buzz when selling a book to publishers, talking it up over the phone, over lunch, etc. And once a book is sold, agent and publisher work together to promote it.

On the other hand, if a book is slow to sell, it is Marketing who decide to remainder it, just as it is Marketing and Publicity who decide whether to promote a book strongly or ignore it in the first place. Your publishing editor has no say in these critical decisions, however much he or she believes in the book.

Perhaps most telling is the growing management habit of appointing marketing people as editors in their publishing houses. What happens to literary quality then, and to real editorial guidance and advice so essential to new writers on the brink of being published?

But you can help the marketing department. Make suggestions. Listen to theirs. And keep smiling. Do the readings. Sign the copies. And smile.

Alternative Forms of Publication

Community publishing

Co-operatives set up within a community centre, Adult Education class or arts centre offer opportunities for group publishing, especially collections of shorter works such as poetry and short stories. Research is the answer here. Check in local libraries for information.

Small presses

They publish poetry and short-story collections/anthologies as well as works of fiction. See the ipg website listed below for details.

Arts projects

Regional Arts Boards, through their literary officers, *promote* writing through a wide variety of schemes, which include publishing ventures. Contact the local Board for details or website.

Self-publishing

Not to be confused with vanity publishing, where a company offers you a flattering assessment of your work and thereby persuades you to part with a lot of money in exchange for publishing your book. Self-publishing is about taking advantage of desktop publishing technology and producing your own book with the help of a local printer. See *Self-Publishing: Not So Difficult After All* (25 St Benedict's Close, Church Lane, London SW17 9NX).

Electronic publishing

The internet offers a different kind of outlet, changing all the time. Just set up a web page and fill it with a few biographical notes and the text of your book? Easy!

Blogging, ebooks, smartphone stories – you name it, writers are trying them all. By the time you read this, everything could be different. Also see Chapter 24, 'Digital Writing'.

Facts and reassuring figures

The good news is this: according to the Publishers Association, UK publishers sold an estimated 739 million books in 2010, and the numbers are not going down. Surely one of those could be yours. And my tip for the top? Children's books. There's a big surge of interest amongst publishers and readers, especially for cross-readership works, ones that are read by kids and grown-ups. Books by Philip Pullman, J.K. Rowling and Mark Haddon fit into this category. At the time of writing, 70 per cent of the Harry Potter readership is adult!

And finally...

Now write the book.

Further Reading

Bingham, Harry (2010) *The Writers' and Artists' Yearbook Guide to Getting Published*. London: A&C Black.
Offers a contemporary inside view of the publishing industry.
The Writers' and Artists' Yearbook. London: A&C Black.
A companion to the above. The essential market tool. Many useful articles on aspects of writing and publishing as well as exhaustive lists of agents and publishers, national and international.

28 How Not Being Published Can Change Your Life

Heather Leach

Not Thinking about Elephants

Here's a story. You wake up one morning and make your way slowly and carefully down to the place where they give you some coffee. You're nursing a headache: let's not go into the reasons why. You look out of the window and see whatever's out there: grass, street, traffic; the usual. Somebody, a friend, sits down opposite you and tells you to cheer up. You don't cheer up. They say, this so-called friend, 'OK. Well, just don't think about elephants', and then they get up and go away, whistling. Loudly. You stare at the tabletop and try to forget what they just said. You look out of the window and see, mixed in with the grass, street, traffic, the faint but unmistakable outline of an elephant. You shut your eyes. No, you think to yourself, I don't want to think of an … . But the word insinuates itself into your mind: the more you tell yourself not to think of an elephant, the stronger the thought-elephant becomes. Test this for yourself – with a little variation. Today, as you go about your normal business, try not to think about a giraffe. Try hard.

Writers are often told not to think about publication: just to get on and write their book, story, poem, script: to do their very best to forget about money, fame, the admiration of friends and foes, critical and commercial success. Love of words, language, story: that's the real point, we are told, it's what we tell ourselves. Art, inventiveness, creativity is what it's all about, not all that crass and greedy ambition. There's truth and value in this, of course there is, but, in my experience, for most writers, not thinking about publication just isn't possible, and the more you try not to think about it, the bigger the thought grows.

Look Away Now

John Singleton's wise and witty Chapter 27, 'Getting Published', gives a sound practical guide to the publishing world. As he rightly asserts, if you have writing talent, if you try hard and keep at it, then you have a fair chance of publication in some form or other. Chapter 24, 'Digital Writing', explores some of the opportunities for online publication. But in *this* chapter, I want to explore some of the more edgy and ambiguous sides of the drive to be published. There's a lot of good news to come, but I'll begin with the bad news, so if you don't want to hear it, look away now:

- Most writers don't make much money.
- Most writers don't make any money.
- Most writers don't gain commercial success.
- Most writers don't gain critical success.
- Most writers don't get published at all.

There are lots of different reasons for this: the writing isn't good enough; the writer gives up too soon; they're not writing for the right markets; the writing is really good but nobody wants to pay for it; the writer hasn't got a famous dad; they don't live next door to a publisher; they didn't go to the right school. These are just a few reasons, but there are plenty more. You can't do anything about a lot of them, so it's probably best not to waste energy worrying about them. (I say probably, because I have to admit to not always taking my own advice. I do get hot under the collar about versions of *my dad/brother/mother's auntie just happens to be a big publisher but it's never made any difference to me* ... I try to keep it under control.) But you can make a difference to one or two of them:

- Buy more books by unknown writers. This is another version of reading as a writer. If you don't want to read other people's new writing, first novels, and so on, how can you expect other people to want to read yours?

■ Write better. Obviously.

■ Keep on trucking. If you have any reason at all to believe that you have writing ability and that you have something to say, then keep going. Don't give up in face of rejection.

That word: *rejection*. It's painful, awkward, humiliating. It has echoes of being the only kid in the playground who doesn't get picked, of being dumped by a lover, of not getting the job. And yet, despite the unpleasantness of the word and the experience, the majority of writers who send their work off for publication have to get used to being rejected. All those jokes about rejection letters being used to paper the walls are just pitiful denial. We hear famous stories about writers who didn't get recognised to begin with: Charlotte Brontë, William Golding; J.K.Rowling. People who sent off their books to publisher after publisher, each one of whom foolishly rejected it until the final … well, you know how it goes. We think that could be me … one day it will happen, preferably before I'm dead. And it's true, it might. But, then again, it might not.

Perhaps you don't want to think about this. Let's face it, *I* don't want to think about it and I'm writing it. After all, I'm a writer too. And not rich or famous either. Yet. But this is a book for writers who want to *think about* writing, as well as simply to *be* writers. We need to find a meaningful and realistic way to deal with ambition and rejection and that means, I believe, looking at them hard.

I sometimes think that the writer's ambition for publication is like doing the lottery. You know that the likelihood of getting your work accepted is low and that there are so many other punters that your little story may get lost in the machine. But the dream itself is so compelling that you forget all that cold and scary realism and take your chance. You need to have a bit of the gambler in you to have a chance of making it as a writer: after all, if you're not in it you can't win it. But if the gambling becomes compulsive, if you think about publication as your be-all and end-all then you're probably on a serious loser. You have to care about it but not too much. You have to think about it without thinking about it. Like the elephant. No one said being a writer would be easy.

OK. Let's wind this one up. So it's hard to get published and most writers don't make it. So publishing is a buyer's market. So not many people read books by unknown writers and even fewer buy them. So what? That's the bad news. End of. If you're keen I won't have put you off. You've looked the Gorgon in the face and she hasn't turned you to stone. There's plenty of good news.

The Internet!

A writer's paradise. Freedom. No agents. No publishers to convince. Just you and the world. Write what you like. Join the millions of writers already online. Same issues though – you still have to write well, find readers who like what you write, and if you want to earn money ... that's another story altogether. See Chapter 24, 'Digital Writing' for more discussion and ideas.

Write for Yourself: You're Worth It!

You are your own first reader. This is the way many of us begin: writing a diary or poetry about our lives, thoughts and feelings, and there is no reason why you can't continue. You don't need to show anybody else what you've written, and you can allow yourself to be honest and direct in a way you couldn't be if other people were to read it. There are plenty of people who will knock this kind of writing, complaining that it isn't real writing: just therapy; an overflow of emotion or ego; too individual and personal etc., etc. Ignore them. Writing belongs to you: do what you like with it. Writing for yourself is a way of deepening and strengthening your own ideas and sense of self; it can help you to understand the way your mind works; the way you relate to others; the way you change through time.

Writing doesn't have to be a stepping stone on the way to somewhere else; it can be an end in itself: a way of making yourself up as you go along. Even with this kind of writing, I think you should set yourself some expectations and challenges, otherwise you will lose momentum and the writing self you make up won't be as interesting as it could be. My checklist would be:

- Be as honest with yourself as you dare.

- Use the writing to learn: ask questions; be curious.

- Describe and comment on what you observe and experience, including other people as well as your inner world.

- Keep trying to find the best words, the most accurate description.

- Read other people's diaries: Samuel Pepys's diary is probably the most celebrated; still a good read and a good example of honesty, observation and lively writing.

Write for Your Family and Friends

'Every family needs a writer.' I can't remember who said this, but it makes a lot of sense. Writers observe. They witness events: births and deaths; divorces and love stories; funerals and holidays. They describe people, houses, animals; they notice the things other people miss; they analyse and interpret; they keep a record; they pass on stories from one generation to the next. The sad thing is that most of the stories passed on in this way are written by established and published writers. Most family history and experience soon get lost: people die and the stories they told get forgotten. Photographs and films usually show a happy but superficial world, but they lack an individual viewpoint, interpretation and creative narrative. A lot of people who would not consider themselves writers already write a little: speeches at weddings; eulogies at funerals; letters and the like, but there is a lot of scope to extend this, to make writing a part of a family's record, its story of itself.

Make Up Stories for the Children You Know

Think about what different age groups like. Try them out and choose the most popular. Read, give or send them to the children. Ask the children to comment on them; what they like and dislike. Ask them to be really honest. Write them down and develop them further. You could collect these stories into books.

When you're away from people, instead of, or as well as, normal letters or emails, keep a continuous written record of your experience in episodes. Edit and rewrite as you would any other piece of writing and then send or give them in chapters to people.

Be the Recorder for a Special Event

Pick out what goes on at the margins as well as the centre. Use your writerly abilities: storytelling; detailed observation and description; listening carefully to voices and getting them down accurately; scene-setting; truth-telling. You could interview people during or after the event, and use their perspective to add to your account. Add your own viewpoint and interpretation – this is real writing, not tape-recording. Write it up afterwards and lay it in an article, blog or Facebook page. Include an introduction explaining the way it was done and why it's important to be accurate and honest. Send or give copies to key people and ask for feedback.

Write a Description of Family Members/Friends

Describe them in detail: looks, character, strengths. Include stories about them; things that have happened to them; the way they've developed and changed. Don't be cruel or hurtful but try to be accurate and particular. Miss out people you don't like. Collaborate with the photographer in the group and produce an album or exhibition: words alongside pictures.

Write Your Autobiography

Writing can be more subtle and more powerful than the spoken word – use it to communicate, to tell your own story.

Write Other People's Biographies

There are lots of people out there with really good stories to tell but without the skill or confidence to write them. Ask questions, find out about people and offer to write their stories. Tell them it will be collaborative, with both your names on the final product.

I can already hear some readers going *aaaargh*! at these suggestions. It's true there are problems with this kind of writing. One of the biggest is bad writing. If you are determined to upset nobody, to tell only sweet stories, to avoid controversy, and to present yourself and everybody else in a shining and golden light, you will almost certainly produce bland and boring stuff. Those embarrassing round robins which people send at Christmas are often written in this kind of style, which is why they come in for so much stick. Many family histories and autobiographies are not very exciting and dynamic because they are written in syrupy-hindsight language. And the sins are multifarious: piety, self-congratulation, humourlessness, perfect lives with no mistakes, sex or swearing. They all equal tedious reading. Don't go there. Write the best you can, even if the audience is only yourself or one or two others.

Another problem is that you might annoy people: you could hurt feelings; you could lose friends and relations, although in some cases, let's face it, that could be a good thing. You will need to be thoughtful about whom you show your writing to and how you present it. But this is true of commercially published work too. Many so-called *fictional* stories, scripts and novels are thinly disguised autobiographies: many an angst-ridden poem is based on the real-life marriage and break-up of actual people. Think of Sylvia Plath and Ted Hughes for starters. It's in your control how much you tell and how much you keep quiet: writing is not a court of law; you may want to tell the truth but not the whole truth. If you really can't bear to let anyone see what you've written, then write for people not yet born: speak to them directly, imagine them finding your words, show them this world, the times we live in.

Read/Perform Your Work at a Poetry Slam or Pub Writers' Event

Some venues have a slot for anyone willing to stand up and try out their work on the half-drunk audience. You probably need to be half-drunk yourself, but it can be a great thrill to be up there with your adrenaline buzzing and those beer glasses flying.

Start Your Own Magazine – Print or Digital

These days you don't need much equipment, just a computer, an online presence, maybe a printer. Advertise for writers to submit their work: produce as many as you can afford and distribute them as widely as possible.

But it May Happen ...

You may not want to try any of these. You may consider them small beer compared to the 'real' thing and want to wait until *it* happens for you. Fine. You might just write that great book or script, and it's funny, clever, beautiful, popular – everything you wish it to be. Accepted by a publisher and actually paid for, your work recognised by the public, admired by the critics. Of course, it could happen. There is absolutely no reason why not. It has already happened to thousands of writers. Believe it and work for it. But while you're waiting, I think it helps if you can reflect on and reframe the ways you think about being a writer.

Think Hard about Why You Were Attracted to Writing in the First Place

I've included a questionnaire at the end of this chapter that you can use to reflect on your beginnings as a writer. The point of this exercise is to help you revisit the freshness of your early ambitions. You may have wanted to emulate a writer you liked or to put down on paper something you couldn't put into speech. You may have written something for a school project, which turned out to be good. There are all kinds of reasons writers start, but only rarely are they based on the desire for fame or loads of money. Most of us begin because we like it, sometimes with the added perk that other people (teachers/parents/friends) also like it. All writers need readers, but you don't have to wait for the big publishing break to find them. Of course, most of us change as we grow older: we become a little more cynical, greedy and egotistic. The world's a tough place. But from time to time it helps to revisit those beginnings, to rediscover that original spark and to make it burn again.

Remembering Why You're a Writer

Remember the first piece of creative writing that no one made you do: the piece you wrote just for yourself.

- Did you show the first writing you ever did to anyone? If not, why not?

- Who did you write for: was there someone you wanted to show it to but didn't? Who were your first readers?

- Were you praised for your writing? Or did you get negative responses? Give details.

- Who are you writing for *now*?

Not Waiting but Writing

Remember the bad news at the beginning of this chapter and don't wait too long. Think about all the other things people do: cycling, playing football, making music, painting, pig breeding, dancing. The pig breeder may sometimes dream of one day being recognised as the best pig breeder in Britain, Europe, the world: there may be big prizes to be won, and there are almost certainly the pig breeder's equivalent of the Booker Prize. But does the pig breeder stay sulkily and artistically at home waiting to be recognised before he or she lets anybody look at his or her half-grown piglets? You know the answer already. That pig breeder is out there with all the other hopeful pig breeders, *living* pig breeding, because that's what you do with life, you live it now. If your work lies unread in a pile on your desk or locked in a cupboard then it still isn't quite real. All writers need readers, so get out there and find them. Think laterally and creatively about ways to get your own and other people's work out there into a public space. *Live* writing. Oink!

Further Reading

R. Lathem (ed.) (2003) *The Diary of Samuel Pepys: A Selection*. London: Penguin.

D. Morley and K. Worpole (eds) (1982) *The Republic of Letters: Working-Class Writing and Local Publishing*. Syracuse, NY: Syracuse University Press, 2010.
 A hotchpotch of information, ideas, writing and resources for writers beyond the metropolitan and mainstream. A bit outdated, but still useful.

T. Olson (1980) *Silences*. London: Virago.
 A creative work in itself, the book explores the history and politics of many writers' blocks and silences.

IV
HELP

29 Paragraphing and Punctuation

Robert Graham

This chapter is designed to help you if you are in any way uncertain about some of the basics of written expression. Sometimes I may well end up teaching my grandmother how to suck eggs, but my guess is you won't read this part of *The Road* unless you are in the dark about some aspect or other of paragraphing and punctuation.

Paragraphing

In writing, you could be said to be working at four levels: word, sentence, paragraph and chapter. The last three are ways of organising information that a reader may access. As you will see in Chapter 11, 'Layout for Fiction and Memoir', the intelligent use of white space makes your writing inviting to the reader. So too will skilful use of the paragraph.

Not just in fiction, but in any kind of prose writing, a paragraph will often have a structure. The opening sentence of a paragraph may be a succinct introduction. The middle sentences are where you place the content that the paragraph is there to transmit. The last sentence may well be a conclusion; or a transition to the next paragraph; or both. (For better, more detailed help with paragraph construction, try Frank L. Cioffi's *The Imaginative Argument* – specifically the chapter called 'Paragraph Design'.[1])

In general, as I suggest in 'Layout for Fiction and Memoir', go easy on paragraph length. Further suggestions about writing or revising paragraphs might include the following:

■ The beginning of your section or story or chapter is more likely to engage your reader if you use short paragraphs and short sentences.

- A new speaker needs a new paragraph. (This is not by any means the case in every piece of fiction you will read, but why not make things easier for the reader to follow? If you want to keep them in the dark about anything it ought to be plot-related; if they are confused about who's speaking they may just get fed up and find something else to read.)

- If the focus in fiction shifts from one person to another, take a new paragraph. (Why? See previous bullet point.)

Of course, creative paragraphing decisions like these won't cut much mustard if your use of paragraphing and related layout is technically wrong. Here's a checklist for making sure you avoid some of the pitfalls.

- Make sure the first line of a story is not indented.

- Thereafter, every first line of each paragraph should be indented – except the first line of a new scene or section.

- When you go to a new scene/section, leave one line's-worth of space.

- Do not leave one line's-worth of space after paragraphs – only to indicate a break between scenes.

Punctuation

Many great fiction writers of the past had an imperfect grasp of punctuation, grammar or spelling. Scott Fitzgerald couldn't spell. Presumably the editors at Scribner's sorted that out for him. An editor today might well provide similar support for an Anne Tyler or an Ian McEwan, but it's a safe bet that they won't for you or me. When it comes to mid-list and tyro authors, editors expect manuscripts to arrive perfect, not only in terms of narrative, but also with every 'i' dotted and every 't' crossed. So...

Speech marks in dialogue

Like everything else in life, punctuating direct speech is easy when you know how. For many of you, what I'm about to say will be glaringly obvious and you will have known it since the age of 9, but the fact is that year in, year out I come across a substantial number of students who get the punctuation of direct speech wrong.

Here are a few pointers, based on the elements that tend to get confused. (Please note that the guidelines on single speech marks are contemporary conventions.)

1. Put the dialogue (that which is directly spoken) inside *single* speech marks:
   Wrong: "Given a choice, I prefer white chocolate."
   Right: 'Given a choice, I prefer white chocolate.'
   Double speech marks are used for quotations within dialogue.

2. Place any punctuation of the dialogue *inside* (not outside) the speech marks:
   Wrong: 'Given a choice, I prefer white chocolate', Kirstin said.
   Right: 'Given a choice, I prefer white chocolate,' Kirstin said.

3. Consider the speech tag a part of the same sentence which includes it and the dialogue:
   Wrong: 'Given a choice, I prefer white chocolate.' She said.
   Right: 'Given a choice, I prefer white chocolate,' she said.

The apostrophe

Plenty of learning writers fail to understand how the apostrophe works. The apostrophe has two functions:

1. To indicate possession.

2. To indicate abbreviation: that a letter or letters have been omitted.

Apostrophes to indicate possession

The car's steering wheel = The steering wheel of the car

's = singular possessive

The cars' steering wheel = The steering wheel of more than one car

s' = plural possessive

Being the English language, the way apostrophes to indicate possession work is not the same 100 per cent of the time. Something that belongs to *it* is the exception:

The dog has lost its collar.

its = singular possessive

There's no apostrophe on the *its*, because that would confuse the issue: *it's* is always the abbreviated form of *it is* or *it has*. Which brings us on to the second function of the apostrophe.

Another intricacy of apostrophe use is when you need to use a noun ending in *s*, for example, *stylus*. Usually this would be punctuated like this:

The stylus' point

However, when it comes to a name at least, you do have another option. The robe belonging to Jesus is usually:

Jesus' robe

But you might also see *Jesus's robe*. However, we're in punctuation-geek territory here, so let's move on.

Apostrophes to indicate abbreviation

Straightforward: the apostrophe here indicates that one or more letters have been omitted.

It is > It's
He cannot > He can't
She will not > She won't
It is not > It isn't
They would not > They wouldn't

If you've gone through the British education system's regularly rejigged National Curriculum, the theory is that you already know all of that. If you haven't, or if you don't, as far as the apostrophe goes, the above should be enough to get you by.

The colon (:)

A colon goes before an example of something:

Martha was especially passionate about Australian film directors: Peter Weir, Gillian Armstrong, Baz Luhrmann.

Sometimes a colon may precede a list:

The bowl was overflowing fresh fruit: apples, bananas, mangoes, mandarins and cherries.

And sometimes a colon may introduce an idea:

John and Yoko say: war is over (if you want it).

The semicolon (;)

A semicolon is more emphatic than a comma, but less emphatic than a full stop (or 'period' if you're in, for instance, the USA). A semicolon may separate the main part of a sentence from a clause, which qualifies it in some way. For example:

Belfast has a thriving restaurant scene, with a range of international cuisines; you're almost spoilt for choice.

It may also be used to separate out items in a list that consists of phrases:

Driving involves many skills: changing gear; steering the car round corners and pedestrians; and not crashing.

So the one lesson to take away from this section and the last is:

Don't use a semicolon before you present an example of something; doing so will upset me. A lot.

Punctuation Checklist

When you are revising work at the technical level, you will, I hope, be in the habit of beginning by using your word-processing program's spellchecker. Remember, however, that it won't find every mistake – and it will sometimes tell you to do the wrong thing, so read each suggestion carefully before hitting the change button.

Having tested your spelling and grammar against the software, you might consider using the advice on punctuation above to track the work for common technical errors that may turn up in early drafts. Beyond that, there are a few other aspects of punctuation to consider when you are revising your work:

■ Check that each sentence really is a sentence (and not two).

- If you have a whole sentence in brackets, the punctuation goes inside the brackets. *(Gualchos is in Spain.)* But otherwise not. *We had a great holiday in Gualchos (which is in Spain).*

- Mum and Dad – better with a capital initial letter.

- Questions always need a question mark, don't they?

- Don't overuse exclamation marks. One will do! But not at the end of *every* sentence! (And remember what Scott Fitzgerald said – using exclamation marks is like making a joke and then laughing at it yourself.)

Further Reading

Angela Burt and William Vandyck (2001) *English Repair Kit* (London: Hodder).
   A quick and accessible fix to problems with written expression, which includes three of their earlier books: *Spelling Repair Kit*, *Punctuation Repair Kit* and *Grammar Repair Kit*. It's out of print at the time of writing, but you can easily find used copies through Amazon. (And check the Further Reading section at the end of Chapter 18, 'Style'.)

30 Agony Aunt

Dear Auntie,
Where do ideas come from?

Ideas are a tricky little kettle of fish. Some writers lay traps for them and surprise them at dawn. Others go hunting at night with sharpened pencils and alcohol. But ideas are not always on the run: sometimes, they chase you, and they can ambush you at surprising moments. They hide in atmospheric pieces of music, in beautiful pictures, and childhood memories. They can be particularly troublesome at night, when they have been known to disturb the sleep of unwary writers. To protect yourself from such nocturnal encounters, always keep a pen and notebook by your bed: this almost certainly guarantees that no ideas will ever come to you at night.

No More Ideas

Dear Auntie,
I can't write any more. All my best ideas have gone into the first project and I know I'll never have any others! I've read there are a finite number of stories. Surely they've all been used up by now. Why am I a writer? Why am I doing this? No one will read anything I write. I have nothing new to say. I'm nothing. AaaAAAaAaaargh!!

(*Writer tempestuously screws up paper, aims at bin, throws and misses.*)

The blank page can be a very frightening place. It's wide open and so full of possibility it can paralyse even the best writers: when you could say anything, it's sometimes difficult to say anything at all. This is called writer's block, and it's a disturbing condition that afflicts most writers at some point in their careers. Don't be embarrassed; we've all been there, apologising to our keyboards, muttering things like, 'This has never happened to me before.' And take heart that it can strike at any phase of any project: sometimes writers begin with ease, fearless of the blank page, but get blocked mid-way through and can't finish a work. Sometimes problems stem not from a lack of ideas, but from the stern internal editor rejecting ideas before you've had chance to explore them. Understand that ideas are like seeds; if you throw them away too soon, they don't get a chance to germinate, and while you may find they sprout into thin, weedy, useless little things, they might not; they might just put out strong, fresh roots and shoots and flourish and grow into mighty oaks. Remember also that the blank page can be defeated with doodles. Scrawl random words over it and play with them, putting them into sentences. Have fun and ideas may start sneaking up on you before you know it.

Writing at different stages of a project can be different. So if things are slow, it might not necessarily be a bad thing. Relax. Allow yourself to daydream. If lazing in a hot bubble-bath with a glass of wine does it for you, then lock the bathroom door and laze and drift and drink, pen and paper nearby. Or perhaps you get ideas looking at paintings or photographs; so, go to an art gallery, go the library and browse through the coffee-table photography books you've been meaning to look at for ages. Or even, dare I suggest it, read other people's writing. Choose an author whose work you admire, whose work first made you want to be a writer. Capture the desire again. Or try doodling with a pencil if you usually type: try typing if you usually write by hand. Put on music. Because they are written to follow a narrative, film soundtracks can be very effective for evoking new images and stories.

If you're still stuck, try a new angle. Change the point of view; make a third-person narrator into a first-person narrator; or try shifting a paragraph into the present tense to see this helps you find the flow with this project again. Maybe you've worked too hard on the story: perhaps it's as simple as taking time out to watch films, read poetry, listen to new music. Let your subconscious simmer for a few days. But don't forget that a walk round the block can help, but only if you then go back to the desk! When you return to the work, the fog may have cleared.

Having nothing new to say is a common fear, for there are finite combinations of story structures. But you are a unique person. You must find your angle on your story. No one will ever tell it quite the way that you tell it: take comfort; lots of tales are retellings.

In the end, writing is hard. So, you could either give up now, or come to terms with the fact that it's not always about inspiration so much as perspiration, and then roll up your sleeves and get on with it. No one promised it would be easy: there are few rose gardens out there, but when you find them, they smell very sweet indeed.

The Trouble with Adjectives ...

Dear Auntie,
I love adjectives – lots and lots of them. Why do they have such a bad reputation?

In controlled numbers, adjectives are harmless little things, and may even be beneficial to your text, but occasionally they proliferate and all balance is lost; the outrageous, rampant result is a gruesome and vile pest infestation. Always keep adjectives under control by only using those you need. Detox your work every so often, and you'll find that your paragraphs are neater, and your sentences clearer. In severe cases, an astonishing condition called Purple Prose results. It is not incurable, but can be painful to deal with. To treat: rinse work well. Shaking it firmly will then loosen unnecessary adjectives. But if all else fails, it may be kinder in the end to put the gorgeous golden garlanded text down and start again with a fresh piece of paper.

Dialogue

Dear Auntie,
Do scriptwriters just do the dialogue, or do they write the stage directions as well?

No, writers do not just do the dialogue. At the outset, when wrestling with an embryonic script, dialogue is often the last thing on your mind: not many scriptwriters I know sit down thinking, today I think I'll write a play, and, flexing their fingers, type at the top of the page ...

ACT ONE: SCENE ONE

... and having typed, sit, fingers drumming, waiting for inspiration to strike. A script is much more than what characters say: if in doubt, watch a film with the sound turned down and it's likely that you'll still be able to follow some of the story, because a large percentage of the narrative information is carried in images and visual action. This is what you have to find: the action, both visual and verbal, that carries and fleshes out the abstract summaries of your story. Now read the script-writing chapter! And then watch *The Artist*.

Scaffolding

Dear Auntie,
I've got plenty of ideas, but I can't seem to organise
them. What's the best structure to use?

Hey! There's no magical one-size-fits-all structure: the best structure for any piece of writing is the one that enables you to finish it: because form and narrative are often intertwined, different narratives need different structures. If you're not sure what I mean, go away and watch *Donnie Darko, Memento* or *Run, Lola, Run*,[1] or read Kurt Vonnegut's novel *Slaughterhouse-Five*, or Martin Amis's *Time's Arrow*.[2] In each case the structure *is* the story. These structures almost certainly didn't arrive fully formed with the first idea; their writers worked at them, and remember that this is often the difficult bit that feels like squeezing stones to get blood. (See Chapter 2, 'Creativity', for more on this.)

So, if you frequently find inspiration fails after you've raced easily through the first three paragraphs, or in the case of a novel, the opening chapters, before grinding to an ignominious halt, you need to scaffold your work with some planning. Writing on into the narrative interior is often only possible when an appropriate structure is assembled.

There is, you see, the raw material where the order of events follows the usual yesterday–today–tomorrow trajectory of a protagonist's existence. This raw material is what the Russian Formalists Victor Shklovsky and Vladimir Propp called the *fabula*. And then there's the best order in which to reveal these events or *fabula*, which might be tomorrow–today–yesterday, a concept which Shklovsky and Propp called the *sujet*, or the way the story is organised. The best structure is, therefore, the one that can accommodate the work, allowing it to continue to completion. Sadly, no one can tell you what that best structure might be. You have to find it for yourself. If you haven't already done so, read Chapter 16, 'Plot'. And start noticing in prose and films the difference between *fabula* and *sujet*. Does the narrative use a simple linear structure? Or flashbacks? Once you start looking, the structural possibilites for your raw material start to be very interesting indeed.

Size Matters ...

Dear Auntie,
My story just keeps getting bigger and bigger! Every time I work on it, I get another brilliant idea that must go in. My word limit is 3000 words but I think think this is turning into a novel...

When writing a first work, whether it be a short story, a play or even a novel, writers often find themselves fighting a strong impulse to stick everything in: it's very tempting in the first rush of ideas to want to include them all. Besides that there's the vanity of creativity: many a writer has set out believing that their work will be the final say on a particular theme, and they research everything and anything to put in it because they want their first work to be tremendous: not only will it present a new angle, it will present every angle. It will be everything. It will be all-encompassing. It will be universal ... . But if anyone ever did manage to pull this trick off and put the entire world into a piece of writing, there'd be nothing left to say in the next piece of writing. Be aware that it can become a bit of a displacement activity to keep searching out more great ideas rather than working with the ones you've already got. So, be content to leave out some of your ideas; you can always use them in another piece. If you're writing to a tight deadline, then have a cut-off point at which you stop working in new ideas, and work solely with the ones you've already got.

The other thing to consider is that in the big, bad professional world of writing, word limits must be adhered to. If an editor needs 3000 words, then only 3000 words will do, the issue being print space. You cannot think that another 500 won't hurt. So be professional. If you're over the limit, stop driving! Be savage and edit. In all probability the work will be more powerful for it, because in the end, too many ideas can be as bad as too few.

It's Finished!

Dear Auntie,
It's finished. What now?

There are many ways to deliver your work to the wide world. *The Writers' and Artists' Handbook* has lists of small presses and magazines which accept unsolicited material. *Writers News* and *Mslexia* regularly give details of competitions and small-press magazines seeking new work. If you've completed a script, have a look at the BBC's webpages: www.bbc.co.uk/writersroom/. There's a growing community of webzines publishing new work. And you could, of course, publish it yourself, either in print or online.

If you want to send work out to magazines then have the courtesy to read them first. This will help in three ways: you'll get a sharper idea of what their editors are looking for; you'll understand better what kind of a writer you are by finding work you either like or dislike; and finally, small-press magazines need new writers and new *readers* to survive.

There may be little or no financial reward for publication, and entering competitions will almost certainly involve entrance fees, and there can never be any guarantees that you'll get into print or win a competition: writing doesn't operate on a merit system; 'I've entered one hundred competitions, it's definitely my turn to win' …. But writers who succeed are often those who didn't give up at the first, second or forty-third hurdle, and these hurdles may be the size of several novels and a hundred or so short stories sent out fruitlessly.

If this sounds bleak, then take heart. You should write for the love of it; after all, writing purely to get rich and famous is a precarious journey, beginning in blood and sweat and often ending in tears. Admittedly, some writers do strike it lucky with their first attempt, and some writers are people who make their own luck. Be one of those latter people; get yourself into the right place at the right time by sending out your work! Make sure it's good. Make sure it's properly presented. Make sure it's what the editor is looking for. But most of all: make sure you send it out!

Almost Famous

Dear Auntie,
I'm a brilliant writer, but no one's discovered me yet. Why is it that only my mother thinks I'm any good?

And have you sent off any work yet?

Er … not exactly …

Bad news for writers: no one's going to come knocking on your door, and discover you for a grateful world, and publish all the novels gathering dust under your bed. Think about it: if you don't send out your stuff, how will they know which door to knock on?

Is it because you fear failure?

Maybe ...

I've seen this happen so many times. Does this sound familiar? You've taken the advice in the books, started early; you've not waited for inspiration, but written yourself into being inspired; you've paddled valiantly against the rip tide of the bad days; you've surfed the magnificent rolling waves of the good days, and now – oh, momentous day – the thing is finished. What a feeling. You have conquered. You are a champion. And then, through the rose-tinted binoculars of desperate hopefulness, you see the distant shoreline of publication and instant success, and the leaves on the trees are fluttering like cheques.

But then the ominous music starts. Fins slice the water. The sharks of doubt begin to circle! So you spell-check everything again. You reread the manuscript and realise everything is terrible; you'll have to rewrite it; you'll just change that word; you'll check over that tricky section; and change that word back again. And when you finally read it all through you find that it's not terrible anymore: it's worse than terrible! It needs totally rewriting. It needs screwing up. It needs burning. You can't possibly send it off to anyone in this state ... .

And so, dear writer, you don't finish it, let alone getting to the point of sending it out anywhere. The fear it might fail prevents you from letting go, because – take a deep breath – if you don't send it out it can't fail ... .

But neither can it succeed.
Take a risk. Finish it. Then send it out.

Diversionary Tactics

Dear Auntie,
I love writing. I'm good at it. I get excellent feedback but I can't ever seem to get round to doing any.

Some people really are too busy to write: some people aren't, they just tell themselves they are: and some people make time for writing.

These people are lucky; the desire to write niggles them. It gets under their skin and they obsess over it like addicted gamblers rattling the dice for one last throw. Meanwhile, their washing-up festers for months, their carpets decay, their cats leave home to seek refuge and food.

Which one of the three are you?

Now answer this: you are about to start writing when you notice the carpet is covered with flecks of cotton wool, which your cat (prior to leaving to home) has carefully shredded.

Which of these do you do?

1. Sigh, and follow the trail back to the cat, feed the cat, de-flea the cat, de-flea yourself, de-flea the furniture, because, after all, a tidy room makes for a tidy mind and you can't possibly start writing until everything is in order, then abandon the day's writing because there's no time anymore.

2. Check Facebook. Write a few witty posts. Play Farmville.

3. Realise this cotton-wool incident has great potential for showing character, and write a new section about cotton wool and cats and fleas knowing it won't fit in your story anywhere but, what the heck; it feels good writing it.

4. Tidy the cupboard under the sink (or any other cupboard you haven't opened for over twelve months).

5. Feel that everything is spoiled, you can't possibly write now the cotton-wool incident has annoyed you, and anyway, you've got to go to the bank and that'll only leave four hours before you have to pick up the kids and you can't possibly write anything decent in only four hours....

6. My own personal favourite: Google 'cotton wool'. Make notes about cotton wool, email a friend about how you're writing a novel about cotton wool, sharpen all your pencils, check Facebook again, look at the time and realise you've left the kids waiting at the school gate....

7. All of the above.

Hmmmm! Well, these are displacement activities: things that writers do to avoid writing. The thing is, when you start actually writing you can wonder why on earth you spent so much time not writing because it feels so wonderful; yet the next day, it's just as hard as ever to get round to switching on the computer.

There's no real answer to this other than identifying what you do that might be displacing your writing activity; knowing your enemy is, after all, a good way to avoid being ambushed. Set yourself a time by which you must have started up the computer, or opened your notebook. Have breaks, but don't let them turn into five-hour coffee mornings.

There are other more deadly forms of displacement: maybe you spend hours browsing through Amazon.co.uk buying craft-of-writing books. Maybe you spend your evenings driving between various writers' circles. Maybe you research your story so well you deserve a higher degree in its subject matter and still you keep on researching, reading, making copious notes in your journal, never moving beyond acquiring the material and onto the slog of working with what you've got.... All of these are displacement activities disguised as useful writing activities. Craft of writing books are great, so are writers' circles, so is research, but if these activities make you too busy to write then adjust the time you devote to them.

The deadliest bit of displacement of them all, however, is Never Finishing, because if you finish, you might send it off somewhere, and it might get rejected and you will have failed: much nicer to be perpetually in the process of writing where you paddle about endlessly, the possibility of success still swimming with you. This is the deadly zone where you can still hope that the story might get published, or performed... when it's ready. But if you stay here, it will never be ready.

It's hard to stop fiddling, but resist temptation; put the manuscript away for a while; let it mature like a full-bodied red wine. When you look at it again with fresh eyes, you might see glaring errors and plot inaccuracies which you should fix, but if all you find is your own vague sense of dissatisfaction then perhaps what needs fixing is not the writing but your self-confidence: this is the time to let others read it; get some peer-group appraisal or feedback from a writing tutor, or an agent or even an editor who, if you're lucky, might accept it, or if you're even luckier still, will explain why he or she is rejecting it. Remember that rejection doesn't always mean failure; it can mean the right story has hit the desk at the wrong time. Editors and agents are often too busy to send out anything other than a standard letter saying thanks, but no thanks.

In the event of you finding your story to be absolutely perfect and brilliant and wonderful, then start redrafting immediately: I'm not sure I know of any writers who ever think their work is absolutely one hundred percent perfect. Now stop reading this and write something. Immediately. Unless you have writer's block…

Auntie's Favourite Fiction
Anything that makes you want to write.

Auntie's Favourite Films
Any film in which the writing is respected.

Auntie's Favourite Advice
Don't get it right; get it written.

V
GOING FURTHER

A Writer's Bookshelf

Writers' Companions

Becoming a Writer, Dorothea Brande (Pan, 1996)[1]
Bird by Bird – Some Instructions on Writing and Life, Anne Lamott (Anchor Books, 1995)
Everything You Need to Know about Creative Writing: But Knowing Isn't Everything, Heather Leach and Robert Graham (Continuum, 2007)[2]
On Writing, Stephen King (New English Library, 2000)
Reading Like a Writer: A Guide for People Who Love Books and for Those Who Want to Write Them, Francine Prose (Union Books, 2012)

Writing Fiction

The Art of Fiction: Notes on Craft for Young Writers, John Gardner (Vintage Books (USA), 1991)
How Fiction Works, James Wood (Vintage, 2009)
How to Write Fiction (And Think about It), Robert Graham (Palgrave Macmillan, 2007)
Short Circuit: A Guide to the Art of the Short Story, Vanessa Gebbie (Salt Publishing, 2009)
The Writing Book: A Practical Guide for Fiction Writers, Kate Grenville (Allen & Unwin, 2011)
Writing Fiction: A Guide to Narrative Craft, Janet Burroway (HarperCollins, 1992)

Scriptwriting

The Definitive Guide to Screenwriting, Syd Field (Ebury Press, 2003)

How Plays Work, David Edgar (Nick Hern Books, 2009)
How to Write for Television, William Smethurst (How To Books, 2009)
The Sound of One Hand Clapping, Sheila Yeger (Amber Press, 1990)
Story: Substance, Structure, Style, and the Principles of Screenwriting, Robert McKee (HarperCollins, 1997)
The 21st-Century Screenplay: A Comprehensive Guide to Writing Tomorrow's Films, Linda Aronson (Allen & Unwin, 2010)
Writing For Radio, Vincent McInerney (Manchester University Press, 2001)

Writing Poetry

Getting Into Poetry, Paul Hyland (Bloodaxe, 1993)
The Ode Less Travelled: Unlocking the Poet Within, Stephen Fry (Arrow, 2007)
Poetry in the Making: A Handbook for Writing and Teaching, Ted Hughes (Faber, 2008)
Poetry Writing: The Expert Guide, Fiona Sampson (Robert Hale, 2009)
The Practice of Poetry: Writing Exercises From Poets Who Teach, ed. Robin Behn and Chase Twichell (Quill, 1992)
Writing Poems, Peter Sansom (Bloodaxe (Poetry Handbooks), 1993)

Anthologies

Fiction

The Best British Short Stories 2011 (and annually thereafter), ed. Nicholas Royle (Salt Publishing, 2011)
The Granta Book of the American Short Story (Vols 1 and 2), ed. Richard Ford (Granta, 2008)
The Story and Its Writer, Ann Charters (Bedford Books of St. Martin's Press, 1995)[3]

Scriptwriting

BBC iPlayer (the BBC's complete radio and television drama output, available to play online for a week after broadcast)
Radio Times (UK TV and radio listings magazine). Your guide to a conceptual visual and aural anthology!

Poetry

Poems for the Millennium, Volume 2: From Postwar to Millennium, ed. Jerome
  Rothenburg (University of California Press, 1998)[4]

Basics

Eats, Shoots and Leaves: The Zero Tolerance Approach to Punctuation, Lynn Truss
  (Profile Books, 2003)
*English Repair Kit: Spelling Repair Kit/Punctuation Repair Kit/Grammar Repair
  Kit*, Angela Burt and William Vandyck (Hodder, 2001)

Style

The Elements of Style, ed. William I. Strunk and E.B. White (Allyn & Bacon,
  1999)[5]
The Guardian Style Guide, http://www.guardian.co.uk/styleguide[6]
The Oxford Guide to Style, ed. Robert Ritter (Oxford University Press, 2002)

Writers' and Readers' Festivals

In the past twenty years there has been a huge increase in the number of festivals for writers and readers. Some last for a fortnight, others only for a weekend; some are huge international events, some are small and local; but all offer an inspirational feast for lovers of language, ideas, debate and literature.

You can go along to hear Hilary Mantel talk about how she turns research into fiction, or join a debate about nanotechnology led by a Nobel scientist. You can go on a walking tour of Ian Rankin's Edinburgh, hear poetry performed by local poets on street corners and in cafés, meet other readers and writers and, of course, buy books. Even if you can't attend the event you can access the websites and, in some cases, watch videoed readings and debates.

Festivals can be good for writers, as many festivals commission new writing, set up blogs, websites and area-based projects which offer opportunities to contribute and showcase new work and discover local talent.

We've shortlisted of some of the more established festivals below, three in the UK, three in North America, and three Down Under. There are many more. We hope to see you there one day – maybe on a platform, reading from your book?

UK

Visit the one-stop shop for many festivals at
http://www.literaryfestivals.co.uk.

Hay Festival

http://www.hayfestival.com

For ten days in May this festival hosts an enormous programme of 'readings, debates and conversations with poets and scientists, novelists and historians, artists and gardeners, comedians and musicians, film makers and politicians'. There is no charge for entrance to the main site, but you need to buy tickets for specific events. Book well in advance for popular gigs. There's lots of free stuff, and it's all free for students if you apply from early May. Hay-on-Wye's lovely setting in the Brecon Beacons prompted Bill Clinton to call this festival 'the Woodstock of the mind'. There are also many spin-off festivals throughout the world.

Manchester Literature Festival

http://www.manchesterliteraturefestival.co.uk

This packed 15-day event in October takes place throughout the city centre, and includes many internationally renowned authors as well as brilliant and aspiring local talent. Alongside the programme of readings, performances and debate there are also specially commissioned projects: the Manchester Sermon in the Cathedral, Manchester Letters, the Dickens walking tour and Poems of the City. There are lots of great venues, including the Victorian Neo-Gothic town hall, galleries, libraries, the Anthony Burgess Foundation, the Midland Hotel, the National Football Museum and the street. All events are ticketed but there are good concessions, and some are free.

Edinburgh International Book Festival

http://www.edbookfest.co.uk

Taking place in August in the beautiful Charlotte Square Gardens alongside the main arts festival, the book programme hosts 800 authors in 750 events. There's an extensive children's programme and families are welcome. Novelists, poets, scientists, philosophers, sportsmen, illustrators, graphic artists, historians, musicians, biographers, environmentalists, economists, Nobel- and Booker Prize-winners meet their readers for entertainment, debate and inspiration.

Entrance to the gardens is free, with plenty to see and do without paying a penny, although you will need to book and pay for ticketed events.

The USA and Canada

PEN World Voices Festival, New York

http://www.pen.org/page.php/prmID/2231

This New York event is hosted by the American branch of the international literary and human rights organisation PEN, founded in 1921. There is a strong focus on open and free access for writers and readers and there are good online resources for writers. The 2012 festival highlights feature a video of Salman Rushdie speaking about the need for freedom to write, and Jennifer Egan on making up your own rules when writing dialogue.

Litquake, San Francisco

http://www.litquake.org/

San Francisco's annual October event includes *Art of Fiction* sessions and *LitCrawl*, which is described as 'a mob scene of literary mayhem' – free readings, pop-up performances and workshops in pubs, bars, bookshops, etc. – dozens of authors reading from their work and thousands of literati tramping the streets.

International Festival of Authors, Toronto

http://internationalfestivalofauthors.wordpress.com/

Most events take place in and around the Harbourfront Centre every year in October. See the festival blog for many useful postings on the writer's art and craft.

Australia and New Zealand

Sydney Writers' festival

http://www.swf.org.au

Held annually in May, this huge festival host over 300 events, half of them free, in venues which stretch from Walsh Bay to the Blue

Mountains. Visit the website to see online recordings of highlights of last year's festival.

Brisbane Writers' Festival

http://www.brisbanewritersfestival.com.au

The festival is held in September, but there are also ongoing events all year round, many throughout Queensland, including an ongoing Twitter story: *Many Writers, One Story*.

Words Down Under: Auckland Writers' and Readers' Festival

http://www.writersfestival.co.nz

This is held every year in May in and around this beautiful North Island city. It includes many international writers but also focuses on encouraging and supporting New Zealand and Pacific area writers.

Notes

I Becoming a Writer

1 Stephen King (2000), *On Writing* (London: Hodder & Stoughton), p. 147.

2 Creativity

2 J. Rogers, 'Teaching the Craft of Writing', in R. Miles and M. Monteith (eds.) (1992), *Teaching Creative Writing* (Buckingham: Open University Press), p. 108.
3 George Orwell, 'Politics and the English Language' (1946), *Collected Essays. Vol IV: In Front of Your Nose 1945–1950* (London: Secker & Warburg), pp. 127–40, p. 138.
4 Susan Greenfield (2000), *Brain Story* (London: BBC Worldwide), p. 161.
5 *Ibid.*, p. 182.
6 Betty Edwards (2012), *Drawing on the Right Side of the Brain* (London, Tarcher), p xi.
7 Guy Claxton (1997), *Hare Brain, Tortoise Mind* (London: Fourth Estate), p. 93.
8 *Ibid.*, p. 14.

3 Journals and Notebooks

1 Quoted in Julia Bell and Paul Magrs (eds) (2001), *The Creative Writing Coursebook* (London: Macmillan), pp. 11–12.
2 Hallie and Whit Burnett (1975), *Fiction Writer's Handbook* (New York: Harper Perennial), p. 86.
3 Dorothea Brande (1934), *Becoming a Writer* (New York: Harcourt, Brace).
4 Janet Burroway (1992), *Writing Fiction: A Guide to Narrative Craft* (New York: HarperCollins), p. 4.
5 Virginia Woolf (1953), *A Writer's Diary* (New York: Harcourt, Brace), cited in Joyce Carol Oates (ed.), *Telling Stories: An Anthology for Writers* (New York: W.W. Norton, 1998), p. 253.
6 From the journals of Sylvia Plath, quoted in Mark Robert Waldman (ed.) (2001), *The Spirit of Writing: Classic and Contemporary Essays Celebrating the Writing Life* (New York: J.P. Tarcher/Putnam), p. 28.
7 Tristine Rainer (1986), *The New Diary: How to Use a Journal for Self-Guidance and Expanded Creativity* (London: Angus & Robertson).
8 Jennifer Moon (1999), *Learning Journals* (London: Kogan Page), pp. 121–2.

9   Bell and Magrs, *The Creative Writing Coursebook*, p. 7.

10 *Ibid.*, p. 13.

11 Quoted in Caroline Sharp (2000), *The Writer's Workbook* (New York: St. Martin's Press), p. 10.

12 Burnett, *Fiction Writer's Handbook*, p. 86.

13 Bell and Magrs, *The Creative Writing Coursebook*, p. 10.

4 The Necessity of Mess

1   Robert Graves (2003), *The Collected Poems* (London: Penguin).

5 Visions and Dreams

1   Maura Dooley (ed.) (2000), *How Novelists Work* (London: Seren), p. 38.

2   Dorothea Brande (1934), *Becoming a Writer* (New York: Harcourt, Brace).

3   Stephen King (2000), *On Writing* (London: Hodder & Stoughton), p. 139.

4   Brande, *Becoming a Writer*, pp. 72–3.

5   Steven Soderbergh (2013), *Solaris*, Twentieth Century Fox.

6   Larry and Andy Wachowski (1999), *The Matrix*, Warner Bros.

7   Sigmund Freud, trans. Helen M. Downey (1993), *Delusion and Dream in Wilhelm Jensen's Gradiva* (Los Angeles: Sun & Moon).

7 Reading As a Writer

1   Jonathan Franzen (2000), *How to Be Alone* (London: Fourth Estate).

2   Francine Prose (2012) *Reading Like a Writer: A Guide for People Who Love Books and for Those Who Want to Write Them* (London: Union Books), p. 3.

3   Hilary Mantel, *Wolf Hall* (2009) (London: Fourth Estate), p. 3.

4   David Crystal (2005), *The Cambridge Encyclopedia of the English Language* (Cambridge: Cambridge University Press), p. 186.

5   Alfred Lord Tennyson (1851), 'The Eagle', at http://www.poetryfoundation.org/poem/174589 (accessed July 2013).

6   In Paul Keegan (ed.) (2005), T. Hughes, *Collected Poems 1957–1967* (London: Faber).

8 Writing Together

1   Quoted by Matthew Wright in 'Novel career goals' (*Guardian*, 18 December 2007), http://www.guardian.co.uk/education/2007/dec/18/highereducation.choosinga-degree (accessed 4 September 2012).

2   Stephen King (2000), *On Writing* (London: Hodder & Stoughton), p. 283.
3   Read Charlie Brooker's riff on deadlines at http://www.guardian.co.uk/commen-tisfree/ 2010/aug/16/charlie-brooker-writing-deadlines (accessed 5 September 2012).

9   Reflection: Looking Your Words in the Face

1   See also Heather's Chapter 28 in this book, 'How Not Being Published Can Change Your Life'.
2   Quoted in Will Blythe (ed.) (1998), *Why I Write: Thoughts on the Craft of Fiction* (London: Little, Brown), p. 33.
3   Quoted in Bonnie Lyons and Bill Oliver (eds) (1998), *Passion and Craft: Conversations With Notable Writers* (Urbana and Chicago: University of Illinois Press), p. 28.
4   Quoted in Paul Allen (ed.) (2001), *Art Not Chance: Nine Artists' Diaries* (London: Calouste Gulbenkian Foundation), p. 28.
5   Quoted in Carole Burns (ed.) (2008) *Off the Page: Writers Talk About Beginnings, Endings and Everything In Between* (New York: W.W. Norton), p. 88.

10   Revision: Cut It Out, Put It In

1   Quoted in George Plimpton (ed.) (1992), *The Writer's Chapbook* (London: Penguin), p. 128.
2   *Ibid.*
3   Bernard Malamud, in *ibid.*, p. 133.
4   I have no reference for this, although one probably exists somewhere. I heard Frank Conroy use the 'Things You Make Them Carry' anecdote when I visited one of his classes at the Iowa Writer's Workshop in September 2001.
5   Jane Smiley, 'What Stories Teach Their Writers: The Purpose and Practice of Revision', in Julie Checkoway (ed.) (1999), *Creating Fiction: Instruction and insights from teachers of the Associated Writing Programs* (Cincinnati: Story Press), p. 249.
6   Janet Burroway (1992), *Writing Fiction, A Guide To Narrative Craft* (New York: HarperCollins), p. 335.
7   From Kay Dick (ed.) (1972), *Writers At Work: Interviews from the "Paris Review"* (London: Penguin), pp. 175–96.
8   Thomas McCormack (1988), *The Fiction Editor, The Novel, and the Novelist* (New York: St. Martin's Press), pp. 16–17.
9   *Ibid.*, p. 17.
10   *Ibid.*
11   Smiley, 'What Stories Teach Their Writers', p. 251.

11   Layout for Fiction and Memoir

1   Mike Sharples (1999), *How We Write* (London: Routledge), p. 139.
2   *Ibid.*, p. 140.
3   John Haffenden (ed.) (1985), 'Fay Weldon', in *Novelists in Interview* (London: Methuen), pp. 305–20.
4   William Golding (1964), *The Spire* (London: Faber & Faber), p. 54.
5   Melissa Bank (2000), *The Girls' Guide to Hunting and Fishing* (London: Penguin), p. 57.

12   Characterisation

1   'The Art of Fiction', collected in Morris Shapira (ed.) (1963), *Henry James: Selected Literary Criticism* (Harmondsworth: Penguin), p. 131.
2   René Wellek and Austin Warren (1966), *Theory of Literature* (London: Jonathan Cape), p. 33.
3   Will Ferguson (2001), *Happiness* (Edinburgh: Canongate), p. 41.
4   Maggie O'Farrell (2002), *My Lover's Lover* (London: Review), p. 3.
5   *Ibid.*, p. 9.
6   Jane Rogers, in Moira Monteith and Robert Miles (eds) (1992), *Teaching Creative Writing* (London: Open University Press), p. 114.
7   Michael Frayn (2002), *Spies* (London: Faber & Faber), p. 12.
8   Robert Scholes and Robert Kellogg (1966), *The Nature of Narrative* (Oxford: Oxford University Press), p. 161.
9   David Lodge (1988), *Nice Work* (London: Penguin), p. 73.
10 David Park (2002), *The Big Snow* (London: Bloomsbury), p. 151.
11 *Ibid.*, p. 202.
12 Rob Watson (1999), *Extracts from a Work in Progress: Writing Life*, www.nawe. co.uk/forum.html.

13   Point of View

1   Quoted in Anne Lamott (1995), *Bird by Bird – Some Instructions on Writing and Life* (New York: Anchor Books), p. 49.
2   Shlomith Rimmon-Kenan (1989), *Narrative Fiction: Contemporary Poetics* (New York: Routledge), p. 95.
3   David Lodge (1990), *After Bakhtin: Essays on Fiction and Criticism* (London: Routledge), p. 47.
4   Sarah Waters (2002), *Fingersmith* (London: Virago), p. 7.
5   Janet Burroway (2003), *Writing Fiction: A Guide to Narrative Craft* (6th edn, New York: Longman).

6   Orson Scott Card (1999), *Characters and Viewpoint* (London: Robinson).
7   J.D. Salinger (1951), *The Catcher in the Rye* (London: Hamish Hamilton), p. 5.
8   *Ibid.*, p. 31.
9   Oakley Hall (1985), *The Art and Craft of Novel Writing* (Cincinnati: Story Press), p. 28.
10 David Lodge (1992), *The Art of Fiction* (London: Vintage), p. 27.
11 Jay McInerney (1985), *Bright Lights, Big City* (London: Jonathan Cape), p. 1.
12 Jeffrey Eugenides (1996), *The Virgin Suicides* (London: Bloomsbury), p. 8.
13 John Gardner (1991), *The Art of Fiction: Notes on Craft for Young Writers* (New York: Vintage), p. 111.
14 Collected in R.P. Blackmuir (1934), *The Art of the Novel* (New York: Charles Scribner's Sons), p. 320.
15 Jennifer Egan (2001), *A Visit from the Goon Squad* (New York: Anchor Books), p. 14.
16 Card, *Characters and Viewpoint*, p. 163.
17 David Mitchell (2004), *Cloud Atlas* (London: Hodder & Stoughton), p. 430.
18 *Ibid.*, p. 89.
19 Gardner, *The Art of Fiction*, p. 158.

14   Dialogue

1   Graham Swift (1996), *Last Orders* (London: Picador).

15   Setting

1   Graham Swift (1999), *Waterland* (London: Picador); Gerald Durrell (1969), *My Family and Other Animals* (Harmondsworth: Penguin).
2   Alan Paton (1983 [1948]), *Cry, the Beloved Country* (Harmondsworth: Penguin), p. 7.
3   E. Annie Proulx (1994), *The Shipping News* (London: Fourth Estate), p. 24.
4   *Ibid.*, p. 52.
5   William Gibson (1999), *Neuromancer* (New York: Vintage).
6   Anne Michaels (1997), *Fugitive Pieces* (London: Bloomsbury), p. 253.
7   Quoted in Larry W. Phillips (ed.) (1999), *Ernest Hemingway on Writing* (New York: Touchstone/Simon & Schuster).
8   Umberto Eco (1994), *Six Walks in the Fictional Woods* (Cambridge, MA: Harvard University Press), p. 59.
9   Quoted in Mickey Pearlman and Katherine Ushe Henderson (1990), *A Voice of One's Own: Conversations with America's Writing Women* (Boston: Houghton Mifflin).
10 Jane Campion (1993), *The Piano* (New York: Miramax Books).
11 *Ibid.*, p. 38.

12   James Frazer (1993 [1890]), *The Golden Bough: A Study in Magic and Religion* (Wordsworth Reference Series, London: Wordsworth Editions).

13   Quoted in Phillips, *Ernest Hemingway on Writing*, p. 36.

16   Plot: Your Vehicle

1   Anne Lamott (1995), *Bird by Bird – Some Instructions on Writing and Life* (New York: Anchor Books), p. 55.

2   Robert McKee (2003), *Story: Substance, Structure, Style, and the Principles of Screenwriting* (London: HarperCollins), p. 181.

3   Russell Hoban (1993), 'Telling Stories', in Duncan Minshull (ed.), *Telling Stories: Volume 2* (London: Coronet), p. 195.

4   Richard Ford (1990), *Wildlife* (London: Flamingo), p. 7.

5   Ansen Dibell (1998), *Plot* (London: Robinson), p. 21.

6   Patricia Highsmith, 'Thickening My Plots', in Clare Boylan (ed.) (1993), *The Agony And The Ego: The Art and Strategy of Fiction Writing Explored* (London: Penguin), p. 155.

7   Based on Michael Baldwin (1986), *The Way to Write Short Stories* (London: Elm Tree Books), pp. 3–4.

8   James N. Frey (1988), *How to Write a Damn Good Novel* (London: Macmillan), pp. 40–2.

9   *Ibid.*, p. 34.

10   David Lodge (1993), *The Art of Fiction* (London: Penguin), p. 10.

11   From 'McKee's Ten Commandments' in McKee, *Story* (workshop manual). The full Ten Commandments:

   1   Thou shalt not take the crisis/climax out of the protagonist's hands.

   2   Thou shalt not make life easy for the protagonist.

   3   Thou shalt not give exposition for strictly exposition's sake.

   4   Thou shalt not use false mystery or cheap surprise.

   5   Thou shalt respect your audience.

   6   Thou shalt know your world as God knows this one.

   7   Thou shalt not complicate when complexity is better.

   8   Thou shalt seek the end of the line.

   9   Thou shalt not write on the nose – put a subtext in every text.

   10   Thou shalt rewrite.

12   Quoted in George Plimpton (ed.) (1989), *The Writer's Chapbook* (London: Penguin), p. 189.

13   Quoted in *Ibid.*, p 192.

14   Annie Dillard, 'Ruining the Page', in Mark Robert Waldman (ed.) (2001), *The Spirit of Writing: Classic and Contemporary Essays Celebrating the Writing Life* (New York: Tarcher/Putnam), pp. 17–18.

15   Mike Sharples (1999), *How We Write* (London: Routledge), pp. 71–3.

16 Rob Watson (1999), *Extracts from a Work in Progress: Writing Life*, www.nawe. co.uk/forum.html.

17 Lucy Ellmann (1998), *Sweet Desserts* (London: Virago), p. 117.

18 Rose Tremain (1998), *The Way I Found Her* (London: Vintage), p. 7.

19 *Ibid.*, p. 41.

20 *Ibid.*, pp. 258–9.

21 Wayne C. Booth (1961), *The Rhetoric of Fiction* (Chicago and London: University of Chicago Press), p. 191.

22 Peter Barry (1995), *Beginning Theory: An Introduction to Literary and Cultural Theory* (Manchester: Manchester University Press), p. 84.

23 In 'Transitions and Breathing Space', in Frank A. Dickson and Sandra Smythe (eds) (1970), *The Writer's Digest Handbook of Short Story Writing* (Cincinnati: Writer's Digest Books), p. 214.

24 This analysis of traditional masculine plotting can be found in any number of texts which examine writer's craft; for example, Dibell, *Plot*; Janet Burroway (2010) *Writing Fiction* (8th edn, London: Longman) and Frey, *How to Write a Damn Good Novel*.

25 Ronald B. Tobias (1995), *20 Master Plots (and How to Build Them)* (London: Piatkus), pp. 160–7.

26 Judith Fetterley (1985), *Provisions* (Bloomington: Indiana University Press), pp. 14–15, cited in Elaine Showalter (1991), *Sister's Choice: Tradition and Change in American Women's Writing* (Oxford: Clarendon Press), p. 153.

27 *Ibid.*, p. 153.

28 *Ibid.*

29 Ibid, pp. 158–9.

30 'Elizabeth Stock's One Story', in Kate Chopin (1983), *The Awakening and Selected Stories* (London and New York: Penguin), p. 274.

17 Immediacy: It's Showtime

1 Lubbock's *The Craft of Fiction*, cited in Oakley Hall (1989), *The Art & Craft of Novel Writing* (Cincinnati: Story Press), p. 2.

2 Wayne C. Booth (1987), *The Rhetoric of Fiction* (London: Penguin), p. 21.

3 Monica Wood (1995), *Description* (Cincinnati: Writer's Digest Books), p. 55.

4 Kurt Vonnegut (2003 [1969]), *Slaughterhouse-Five* (London: Vintage), p. 1.

5 Browne and King also suggest a way to avoid one kind of telling. They say that as editors they are prone to writing 'R.U.E.' in the margin of a manuscript ('resist the urge to explain'); Renni Browne and Dave King (1991), *Self-Editing for Fiction Writers: Show and Tell* (New York: HarperCollins), pp. 48–50.

6 *Ibid.*, p. 3.

7 Anne Tyler (1992), *Dinner at the Homesick Restaurant* (London: Vintage), p. 57.

8 Robert Olen Butler (2005), *From Where You Dream: The Process of Writing Fiction* (New York: Grove Press), pp. 14–15.

9   Jhumpa Lahiri (2000), *Interpreter of Maladies* (London: Flamingo), p. 55.

10 Alice Munro (1997), 'Walker Brothers Cowboy', in *Selected Stories* (London: Random House), p. 14.

11 Cate Bailey, 'Concessions', in *Mslexia*, http://www.mslexia.co.uk/magazine/newwriting/nwstory1_49.php (accessed 30 October 2012).

12 J.D. Salinger (1951), *The Catcher in the Rye* (London: Hamish Hamilton, p. 5.

18   Style

1   Richard Ford (1995), *Independence Day* (London: Harvill), pp. 4–5.

2   Ann Beattie (1998), 'A Vintage Thunderbird', in *Park City: New and Selected Stories* (New York: Vintage), p. 218.

3   Robert Clark (2001), *The English Style Book* (Norwich: University of East Anglia).

4   Anton Chekhov (1899), letter to Maxim Gorky, 3 September, from *Anton Chekhov on Writing, Nebraska Centre for Writers*, http://mockingbird.creighton.edu/NCW/chekwrit.htm (accessed 4 May 2004).

5   Helen Garner (2009), *The Spare Room* (Edinburgh: Canongate), p. 56.

6   Thomas Pynchon (1998), *Mason & Dixon* (London: Vintage), p. 543.

7   Raymond Carver (1989), 'One More Thing', in *Where I'm Calling From* (New York: Vintage), p. 150.

8   Raymond Chandler (2013 [1939]), *The Big Sleep* (Harmondsworth: Penguin), p. 10.

9   Elmore Leonard (1988), *Freaky Deaky* (Harmondsworth: Penguin), p. 227.

10 Oakley Hall (1989), *The Art and Craft of Novel Writing* (Cincinnati: Story Press), p. 86.

19   Memoir

1   Augusten Burroughs (2004), *Running with Scissors* (London: Atlantic Books), pp 34–5.

2   Judith Barrington, 'Writing the Memoir', in Steven Earnshaw (ed.) (2007), *The Handbook of Creative Writing* (Edinburgh: Edinburgh University Press), p. 109.

3   Lee Gutkind (1997), *The Art of Creative Non-Fiction* (Chichester: Wiley), p. 118.

4   A.M. Homes (2008) *The Mistress's Daughter* (London: Granta), p. 63.

5   Dave Eggers (2000), *A Heartbreaking Work of Staggering Genius* (London: Picador), p. 3.

6   Bob Dylan (2004), *Chronicles Volume 1* (London: Simon & Schuster), pp. 203–6.

7   Andrea Ashworth (1999), *Once in a House on Fire* (London: Picador), pp. 3–5.

8   Gutkind, *The Art of Creative Non-Fiction*, p. 73.

9   Calum Kerr (2010), 'Stranger Than Faction', conference paper delivered at Great Writing Conference, University of Wales, Bangor.
10 Homes, *The Mistress's Daughter*, p. 62.

21   Scriptwriting: for the Nervous Beginner

1   Melissa Hillman, http://bittergertrude.com/2013/03/21/why-your-play-was-rejected/.
2   William Smethurst (2009), *How to Write for Television* (Oxford: How To Books).
3   Alex Epstein (2006), *Crafty TV Writing: Thinking Inside the Box* (East Peckham: Owl Books), p. 1.

22   Poetry

1   Basho (1985), trans. Lucien Stryk, *On Love and Barley: Haiku of Basho* (Harmondsworth: Penguin), p. 14.
2   *Ibid.*, p. 14.
3   *Ibid.*
4   Ezra Pound, 'Imagisme', in Peter Jones (1972), *Imagist Poetry* (Harmondsworth: Penguin), p. 129.
5   *Ibid.*, p. 130.
6   *Ibid.*
7   *Ibid.*, p. 129.
8   *Ibid.*
9   Basil Bunting, *Cut Out Every Word You Dare* (fact sheet, Basil Bunting Centre, University of Durham), p. 4.
10 Pound, 'Imagisme', p. 131.
11 William Carlos Williams (1979), *Selected Poems* (Harmondsworth: Penguin), p. 133.
12 Pound's poem may be found in Jones, *Imagist Poetry*, p. 95.
13 Pound, 'Imagisme', p. 129.
14 *Ibid.*, p. 131.
15 Charles O. Hartman (1980), *Free Verse: An Essay on Prosody* (Princeton, NJ: Princeton University Press), pp. 24–5.
16 Pound, 'Imagisme', p. 133.
17 *Ibid.*, p. 133.
18 Bunting, *Cut Out Every Word You Dare*, p. 4.
19 Pound, 'Imagisme', p. 133.
20 *Ibid.*
21 William Carlos Williams (1954), 'Author's Introduction to *The Wedge*', in *Selected Essays of William Carlos Williams* (New York: Random House), p. 256.

22 Attridge, quoted in Marjorie Perloff (1998), *Poetry On and Off the Page* (Evanston, IL: Northwestern University Press), p. 143.
23 Giorgio Agamben (1995), *The Idea of Prose* (Albany: SUNY Press), p. 40.
24 Stephen Burt (2002), 'Chicory and Daisies', *London Review of Books,* 7 March.
25 Bunting, *Cut Out Every Word You Dare,* p. 4.
26 *Ibid.*

23   Poetry for People Who Don't Like Poetry

1 Tony Harrison, in his poem, 'Them and [uz]'. See him reading it at http://bardfilm.blogspot.co.uk/2010/07/littererchewer.html (accessed July 2013).
2 These lyrics and thousands of others are available at http://www.lyricsmode.com (accessed 16 November 2012).
3 Sylvia Plath, 'You're', in *Collected Poems*. Read it at http://www.guardian.co.uk/books/2008/mar/13/poetry.sylviaplath (accessed 5 September 2012).
4 John Fuller, 'Valentine', in *Penguin Poems for Love*. Read the whole poem and a lot more at http://www.guardian.co.uk/books/2012/feb/10/love-poems-writers-favourites-valentines-day.

24   Digital Writing

1 Jay David Bolter (1991), *Writing Space* (London: Lawrence Erlbaum), .p. 2.
2 Another way, of course, is to know somebody who can give you a leg-up, an introduction, a word in somebody's ear, etc. I'd be showing up my chippy side if I implied that going to Oxbridge might give you a better chance of making it as a writer/politician/banker than if you come from Moss Side, so I'll just mention it here in the notes, which almost nobody reads. But, who knows, maybe the digital revolution will change all that?
3 Rhodri Marsden, 7 September 2012, http://www.independent.co.uk/life-style/gadgets-and-tech/news/technology-how-writers-block-fatal-distractions-8114000.html.
4 Lee Rourke, 3 November 2011, http://www.guardian.co.uk/books/2011/nov/03/creative-writing-better-pen-longhand.
5 Given the time gap between writing and reading, it occurs to me that you may be doing exactly that at this very moment. Hail to you from the old world!

25   Writing as Self-Invention

1 Alice Sebold (1999), *Lucky* (New York: Simon & Schuster); (2002) *The Lovely Bones* (London: Pan Macmillan).
2 Adam Thorpe (1998), *Ulverton* (London: Vintage).

27   Getting Published

1   *The Writers' and Artists' Yearbook 2004* (London: A&C Black); Barry Turner (ed.), *The Writers' Handbook 2004* (London: Macmillan).

29   Paragraphing and Punctuation

1   Frank L. Cioffi (2005), *The Imaginative Argument: A Practical Manifesto for Writers* (Princeton , NJ: Princeton University Press).

30   Agony Aunt

1   Richard Kelly (2001), *Donnie Darko* (Metrodome); Christopher Nolan (2000), *Memento* (Twentieth Century Fox); Tom Tykwer (1999), *Run Lola Run* (Columbia Tristar).
2   Kurt Vonnegut (2003 [1969]), *Slaughterhouse-Five* (London: Vintage); Martin Amis (2003), *Time's Arrow* (London: Vintage).

A Writer's Bookshelf

1   The mother of all books for writers? It doesn't set out to teach you much about craft, but it does teach you almost everything you need to know about understanding your writer's gifts. It has been in print most of the time from the 1930s onwards. In the UK this 1996 edition was the most recent, but is now out of print. Dorothea's day will come again (and again), but in the meantime, hunt a second-hand version of this essential text down at e-bay or on Amazon.
2   This is a reference work with teaching on craft thrown in. 'If you haven't started writing your book yet, don't do so until you have consulted *Everything You Need to Know about Creative Writing*, an A–Z of essential tools of the writer's trade.' (J.C., *Times Literary Supplement*).
3   Around 1500 pages of short stories from across time and space, with wonderful essays about each other's craft by many masters and mistresses of the form.
4   For many, this and Volume 1 are all you need to know about poetry. Volume 2 is chosen because of its more recent focus.
5   Read it online at http://www.bartleby.com/141/.
6   The book has gone through many editions in its 85-year life, but this online version is available free of charge. It was designed as a set of guidelines for Guardian journalists, but it's a very useful guide to correct usage and any writer will benefit from studying it.

Index

Index of *Try This* – Writing Exercises